JOHN STEADMAN

Days In The Sun

Other books from *The Baltimore Sun*:

Postcards of Maryland: Sports

Goal: A History of the Baltimore Blast Indoor Soccer Team

Marylanders of the Century

A Century In The Sun: Photographs Of Maryland

A Century In The Sun: Front Pages Of The Twentieth Century

A Century In The Sun: Postcards Of Maryland's Past

Gaining A Yard: The Building of Baltimore's Football Stadium,
    by Jon Morgan and Doug Kapustin

*Hometown Boy: The Hoodle Patrol And Other Curiosities Of
    Baltimore*, by Rafael Alvarez

The Wild Side Of Maryland, An Outdoor Guide, 2nd Edition

Cal Touches Home

Other books by John Steadman:

From Colts to Ravens, Tidewater Press, 1997

The Greatest Football Game Ever Played, Press Box Publishers, 1988

Baltimore Colts' Pictorial History, Jordan & Company, 1978

The Best (and Worst) of Steadman, Press Box Publishers, 1974

Miracle Men of Football, Pennington Press, 1959

Baltimore Colts Story, Press Box Publishers, 1958

This *Baltimore Sun* book was published by SunSource, the information service of *The Sun*. To order any of the above titles published by The Baltimore Sun or for information on research, reprints and information from the paper's archives, please call 410.332.6800 or visit www.sunspot.net/sunsource.

JOHN STEADMAN

Days In The Sun

THE BALTIMORE SUN

Published by
The Baltimore Sun
501 N. Calvert Street
Baltimore, MD 21278

Edited by Ray Frager
Layout and design by Jennifer Halbert
Photo research by Paul McCardell

Photo of Mr. Steadman by Jim Burger
Photo of Don Whitmire courtesy Street & Smith. Reprinted with permission.
All other photos from *The Sun's* archive

ISBN — 1-893116-16-6
Library of Congress Control Number: 00-133174

John Steadman: Days In The Sun — 2000 —
Baltimore, MD: Baltimore Sun Co.: 2000

To Mary Lee,

who read more lines of more columns than any reader we know. Now that's endurance. And a lot of love, too. Words can't convey what you have meant. Style and refinement personified, plus putting up with me, eccentricities included.

CONTENTS

Preface

Just about the most coveted accolade in this business that columnist-commentator Bob Considine once referred to as the "Daily Miracle" is to hear that you are being read — pro or con. And now, perhaps, some of you will be doing it for the second time around with the same, old Steadman. What's that they say about recycling?

A "Best (and Worst) of Steadman" was published in 1974, an assortment of columns that had appeared in the *Baltimore News-Post* and *American*, later to become the *News American*. The press run sold out.

Hopefully, this issue of later vintage will be received with similar acceptance, but, like with a batter in the box, you never know what's going to happen until he gets there and takes his stance. But he's only dangerous when he's swinging.

In retrospect, we had no idea how *The Sun* would even care about our availability when the rival paper in town shut down in 1986. But, within days, the invitation was extended to come join a different staff — *The Evening Sun*, then the Sunday *Sun*.

The publishers, editors and, of great importance, the readers have been exceptionally considerate. They put up with our good and bad days. We hope you're satisfied with the book effort, be it a second reading or for the first time. Either way, we're elated.

Thanks for helping us enjoy what we believe to be the most pleasing adventure known to mankind — working on a newspaper.

John Steadman
Stevensville, Md.
June 2000

Introduction

A colleague of his once wrote: "Steadman you know all about. He is the dean of Baltimore sportswriting, a towering, cohesive presence..."

After the better part of four decades with the staff of the *News American*, in all its incarnations, in 1986 John Steadman joined *The Evening Sun* and *The Sun*, whose pages have been all the richer since.

Collected here are some of the highlights from his time with *The Sun* — stories about superstars, fallen idols and unsung heroes, remembrances of good times and bad. Reading through these pages, one realizes what makes Steadman's writing so special — a rare gift for words combined with an understanding of the human spirit and insight into what drives an athlete to compete.

Steadman witnessed historic moments in football, baseball, golf, horse racing, boxing and more. He brings them to you here as only he could. He's been a baseball player, a PR man and an editor, but here you'll find him at his best, as a storyteller.

Chapter 1

PRIDE *of* MARYLAND

Sudlersville set for a hot time

Oct. 23, 1987

SUDLERSVILLE — So strong was Jimmie Foxx that he could take a new baseball right out of the box, twist it with his hands and loosen the cover. The frequency with which he drove them for astounding distances created a special identity. He became an American hero, admired by presidents, and befittingly was enshrined in the Hall of Fame.

Now his old hometown (population 475) will offer the ultimate tribute tomorrow. In the heart of downtown, a monument will be dedicated in his honor with family and friends coming from all over the country to revere his memory in a day-long ceremony of speeches, band music and nostalgia.

Foxx's figures with a bat in his hand read like fiction. He had a lifetime average of .325 for 22 major-league seasons, and he is the only man in history to hit 30 or more home runs 12 straight years. In three World Series, he batted .344; in seven All-Star Games, .314. He won three MVP awards in the American League in 1932, 1933 and 1938.

Although primarily a first baseman, he played every position but second base in a glorious big-league career.

Born in Sudlersville, Oct. 22, 1907, he tried at age 10 to run away and join the Army in World War I as a drummer boy. His parents admonished him for wanting to leave home and insisted it was important he stay in school.

But at age 16, he signed with the Easton Farmers of the Eastern Shore League, managed by Frank "Home Run" Baker, who, after three months, sold him to the Philadelphia Athletics. Before his 17th birthday, he batted nine times with the A's for a mark of .667. This was the prelude to astounding accomplishments.

His 1932 campaign was the pinnacle — a batting average of .364, 169 runs batted in and 58 home runs. There have been distorted reports through the decades that Foxx lost five home runs in Sportsman's Park at St. Louis and three more to a screen at League Park in Cleveland or else he would have amassed 64 homers. That's all wrong, according to respected historian Bill Jenkinson, author of "Kings of The Tape Measure," who researched every game Foxx played.

"It never happened," said Jenkinson. "Foxx was so great embellishment isn't needed. I have been a devoted fan of Babe Ruth, and I'd never try to diminish what he did. But for a right-handed hitter, Foxx had more distant fences confronting him in left field than Ruth did it in right field. The only place it was easier for a right-handed batter was Boston's Fenway Park.

"There were two balls Foxx hit in the same game in April of 1932 at Yankee Stadium that carried 450 feet. He got triples on both. You have to remember, although few people do, that Yankee Stadium was 475 feet in left field from the time it was built in 1923 until it was altered in 1937. So Ruth had more convenient targets than Foxx. Just another important factor in respecting the records of a truly brilliant performer."

A ball Foxx hit off Vernon "Lefty" Gomez came close to being the only one ever driven entirely out of Yankee Stadium. It landed in the third deck, three rows from the top, and broke the back of a seat. Had it gone 20 feet to the right, it would have carried out of the park. Gomez said it went so far he decided to visit the location the next day and it took him 20 minutes to walk up there.

Gomez holds Foxx in terrifying awe. "He could hit me with one eye closed and the lights out at midnight," he quipped. Once, when Gomez faced Foxx, he continued to shake off the signs from catcher Bill Dickey. Finally, Dickey went to the mound to ask Gomez what he wanted to do with Foxx. "I'm hoping he'll get tired and just go away," Lefty replied with a smirk.

His physical presence, 5 feet 11, 190 pounds, with arms the size of huge tree limbs, made him an imposing specimen, yet he remained a gentle man who was easily approachable.

Besides his legendary strength, he was a fast runner, holding the Maryland state 100-yard dash championship while in high school. He later became, by reputation, one of the quickest men in baseball for picking up a check at a restaurant or bar.

Drinking presented him with impossible problems and led to hard times. He also made bad investments, including building a golf course near Tampa, Fla., at the outbreak of World War II, when there were no tourists because of travel restrictions. However, if his stay in the majors had only continued for part of one more year, he would have qualified for the baseball pension system.

His late years were difficult, but Tom Yawkey, the benevolent owner of the Boston Red Sox, who had traded for him in 1936, never stopped trying to be helpful. Foxx, nicknamed the "Maryland Broad Back" and "The Beast" because of his strength, died at 59 in 1967 in Miami. Of all things, while he was having dinner at his brother's house, a piece of meat lodged in his throat. His breathing was cut off when he wasn't able to free the restriction. The sudden passing of an immense hero saddened America.

The community of Sudlersville didn't forget his achievements, which is why at Church and Main streets tomorrow the memorial will be unveiled. It'll read "Jimmy" Foxx, not "Jimmie" Foxx, which has made for continuing debate, but Mrs. Loretta Wells, a third cousin who is with the Sudlersville Betterment Club, made an intelligent decision.

"As a child and young man, he signed his name 'Jimmy,'" she explained. "It wasn't until he got to Philadelphia that he started to use 'Jimmie.' We went back and forth asking opinions, but there was a slight edge among the town folks for making the dedication material read 'Jimmy.'"

Foxx was an illustrious figure whose deeds approached those of his fellow Hall of Fame deity from Maryland, Babe Ruth, but there was no petty envy between them. Jimmie, or Jimmy, once said without offering any regret, "I guess I was just born to be broke." But his old hometown remembered in the year of his 80th birthday, and that makes his memory rich in a perpetual way.

More precious than gold

July 21, 1996

There's a style, sensitivity and substance to Theresa Andrews that sets her apart in any arena of activity. She's intelligent, articulate and caring and worthy of emulation. The two gold medals earned in the Olympics of 1984 attest to an extraordinary measure of swimming ability, and she displays exceptional manner and humility in the wake of worldwide acclaim.

What Andrews is doing "with the rest of her life" is tantamount to heeding a call to a vocation. It shouldn't be surprising that her objective no longer is directed to the tiled-wall finish line at the other end of the pool, but rather an effort to try to make a difference in the lives of others.

If this isn't part of the Olympic creed, then it should be. Our bravest and finest athletes answer the crack of the starter's gun. A measure of fame awaits the cherished few, of which Andrews was counted among the exclusive honor roll of winners. Then the tall, slender young woman lifted herself out of the water, ascended to the highest level of the awards platform and heard the national anthem in conjunction with the presentation of the gold medallion and what would be, for her, the preservation of a keepsake moment.

"What was in my thoughts?" she asked rhetorically. "It's a memory that will never leave me. I kept thinking, well here I am, just a 'summerly swimmer,' and I've come all this way. I never felt that would happen, because I figured things like this only occur to special people. I was merely a 'summerly swimmer.' That's all, a 'summerly swimmer.'"

That's typical of Andrews. And what she's doing now is more important than hearing the cheers, waving flags or having her name included in the all-time elite list of Olympic winners. She is on the staff at the University of Virginia Children's Center, where she deals with youngsters suffering from cancer and blood disorders. No two days are the same. She sees the rich and poor, the prominent and the unknown, all caught up in the same crisis — a child battling the odds against cancer and fighting, with every breath, to live.

"You can't take hope away," she says. "And I'm convinced there are some remarkable guardian angels out there. I watch children and their families dealing with tough times. They become heroes to me."

Played back in moments of reflection are a montage of faces, the anguish, the pain, the smiles, the varied personalities. Each one is different. And the parents, too, so eager to provide every chance that a child lives to see another day and somehow fulfills the potential God endowed. Not every race with cancer results in victory. Hardly. "But you can't take hope away," she comes back to saying.

Andrews, now 33, is a year older than brother Danny, who was struck by an automobile in 1982 near Annapolis while riding a bike and suffered paralysis from a spinal injury. But it didn't deter him.

It was his attitude of concentrating on the things he could do, rather than the limitations, that conveyed an inspiring message to Theresa. At the Olympics, there was Danny looking on from a wheelchair as his sister won the 100-meter backstroke and again as she contributed to the U.S. championship 400-meter relay team.

It became a precious moment for both of them. A sister swimming for her brother and, instead of adding to the pressure, feeling a strength, yet a relaxation, that motivated her beyond all expectations. Danny went on to graduate from the University of North Carolina, then went to law school and is now an assistant district attorney in Queen Anne's County. He has been married for four years and is the father of a 2-month-old daughter.

The Andrews family is the kind storybooks are written about, with chapters on each of them. Father Frank, a native of Newport, R.I., and mother Maxine, from Quincy, Ill., live in this huge house not far from the banks of the Severn River. They have raised 12 children, all with college educations. Frank is a 1942 graduate of the Naval Academy, went to the Pacific in World War II and became a captain.

There's a respect and honor among them, pulled together by this love for one another that has been so deeply ingrained. A remarkable testimonial in itself. "The Andrews family of Annapolis" is not your ordinary next-door neighbors. Theresa's becoming an Olympic champion was a time for elation, yet the emotional scale was balanced over what had happened to Danny.

The Andrewses always felt as if they were in it together. The captain and his crew put forth the total effort. Theresa attended high school at St. Mary's in Annapolis and spent her final two years at Archbishop Keough in Baltimore, so she could train under the influence and direction of coach Murray Stephens and compete for the North Baltimore Aquatic Club.

"I lived with five different families in the Baltimore area, and they treated me as if I was one of their own, not just some girl occupying a room," she recalls. "That was important because I was so family-oriented. Catholic education gave me a lot of values that were beneficial. You learn in that kind of a system that nothing is given to you, and the rewards, if you're to get them, must be earned."

Andrews graduated from the University of Florida with a bachelor's degree in therapeutic recreation and then received a master's degree in social work at Ohio State. For three years, she was on the staff of the National Rehabilitation Center in Washington, specializing in helping adults with spinal injuries.

The value of athletics isn't to be trivialized; it's an enduring part of her outlook.

"The Olympics allow you to strive to learn what you can do with your talent, to own up to mistakes when you make them and to give help to others and not expect anything back," she says. "I tell that to kids and to heads of corporations. But, you know, everything you do that's good has a way of somehow returning and adding productively to the good things in your own life."

To hear Andrews, this woman gifted with eloquent expression and intellect, speak before an audience is a moving experience. About the Olympics, she says, "It's more than having your picture on a Wheaties box or being on the Dream Team and walking away with compensation. There are probably 9,000 athletes who won't get a medal, but their drive is the same, emotionally, physically and spiritually. I don't see any losers there."

In her own case history, it was six hours a day, six days a week for six years of training in a pool. She "retired" at 21 and didn't feel she missed anything that couldn't be made up. Traveling the world to compete was beneficial in understanding other cultures and the entire human network.

Theresa Andrews has never lost the feeling of what it was like to touch the wall first in the Olympics. What she's doing now doesn't bring a gold medal, but there is a far greater reward. Nothing compares to comforting a sick child and helping, of course, to entice a smile.

Hometown celebrates Keller

Sept. 27, 1998

MIDDLETOWN — Idle boasting or engaging in empty rhetoric wasn't his style. No pretense or sham.

Charlie Keller was the genuine article. Twenty-four karat. An authentic gentleman of conservative ways, who by his presence upgraded humanity and epitomized the fundamental values: love of God, family and country, and the highest regard for those he encountered in the game of life.

The only exceptions were pitchers about to throw a baseball from 60 feet, 6 inches away.

Keller didn't need a bat in his hand to gain respect. He was strong enough to knock down a building, but more important, never lost the sincerity and honesty of purpose that underlined his quiet yet noble demeanor.

What he could do for the New York Yankees created cheers in an earlier time, but Keller, by his exemplary virtues, represented much more than could be found in the agate lines of a box score.

His old Frederick County hometown honored him posthumously as part of its annual Heritage Celebration yesterday when the AMVETS Post No. 9 unveiled a plaque in Memorial Park reading, "Middletown's Own Pride, Character and Sportsmanship."

As was the case at the funeral eight years ago, his best friend and one-time roommate, Tommy Byrne, a fellow Yankee and Marylander, came from his home in Wake Forest, N.C., to be here. Mrs. Martha Keller and her children and grandchildren were obviously elated with the festivities. Martha served as grand marshal of the parade.

It was in 1939 that Keller produced one of the most explosive performances by a rookie in a World Series. He led all players with a .438 average and three home runs as the Yankees demolished the Cincinnati Reds in four straight. When he returned to the Middletown Valley, some of his admirers intended to put on a testimonial parade and dinner.

Keller didn't want to appear arbitrary, but said he'd feel uncomfortable. With reluctance, he arrived at the dinner and, so typically, said: "I'm not much of a Keller booster. I guess I was swinging where they were throwing. My luck was good."

That's how he tried to explain away the accolades that followed his first World Series, a year in which he earlier batted .334 while another newcomer to the league, Ted Williams, checked in at .327.

Keller had been signed as a senior off the University of Maryland campus in 1937 and was assigned to the Yankees' top farm team, the talent-laden Newark Bears. Immediately, he led the International League in batting with .353. The Yankees were impressed, but not enough to take him to spring camp the next year. They merely told him to go back to Newark and do it again.

He took them literally and improved to .356. In 1939, he played in an outfield that included Joe DiMaggio and Tommy Henrich. Keller hit the ball to all fields with vicious results, but manager Joe

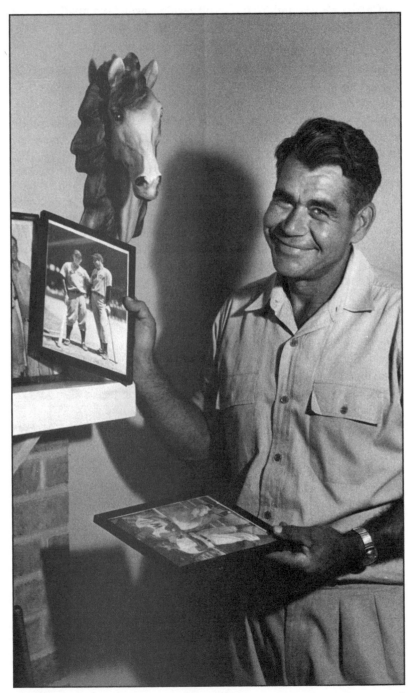

McCarthy wanted him to direct his swing toward the inviting right-field stands at Yankee Stadium.

He became a forced pull hitter rather than letting his natural swing evolve. Keller never complained (but others did) that tampering with the stroke reduced his average. He also was bothered by injuries to his spine, ankle, hips and hand.

When World War II came, he tried to enlist in every branch of service — Army, Navy, Marines and Coast Guard — but was rejected. He could have played out the war in the major leagues, but was determined to help his country as best he could.

The Merchant Marine finally accepted his enlistment despite his congenital back condition. Aboard ship, he drew the difficult North Atlantic run to Murmansk in the dead of winter, which wasn't much fun.

"As a Yankee, I roomed with Charlie," said Byrne. "If he wouldn't have had the back problem, he'd have been one of the top five Yankees of all time, with Ruth, Gehrig, DiMaggio and Mantle. The type person he was got your attention and kept it. Players admired him and sought his friendship. We had a special camaraderie, and it wasn't because we were both from Maryland. More so because we had a lot in common: our families and baseball ambitions."

The Yankees promised Keller he could have a job with them as long as he lived. He went back to coach, but eventually decided to breed and train standardbreds at his farm, which he called "Yankeeland," outside Frederick. It became a proficient producer of championship stock and, to this day, under the jurisdiction of the grandchildren, continues to dominate the sales book.

When Keller closed his career with the Yankees in 1949, management insisted on giving him a "day." He objected. Finally, they got him to relent by asking, if he didn't want the expensive car they'd ordered, then what might he like?

"You all have been good to me," he told them. "I don't want or need a single thing."

Ultimately, he decided to go through with the farewell if the money could be directed to funding two scholarships for boys who wanted to attend his alma mater, Maryland, but lacked tuition. The first selection was Jack Scarbath, a shortstop and quarterback at Baltimore Polytechnic. Scarbath's father told Jack "to go thank Mr. Keller for the scholarship." So one afternoon, after borrowing an automobile, he drove to Frederick to find where Keller lived.

Scarbath knocked on the door, and Keller was astonished that the young man had called to express his gratitude. The two were eventually to became close friends.

Little did either realize that the recipient of the Keller scholarship would become Maryland's most famous football player, a consensus All-American, a first-round draft choice of the Washington Redskins and later a member of the College Football Hall of Fame.

Keller, with enormous hands and arms, developed while working on his father's farm near Middletown, presented an imposing physical presence. Vernon "Lefty" Gomez, standout pitcher, dugout philosopher and resident entertainer, once said, "The greatest thing to happen to civilization is Charlie Keller was born good-natured." He drew physical respect, yes, but more so for the man he was.

'Lefty' Grove in class by himself

Sept. 22, 1996

LONACONING — On the steep slopes of the Alleghenies, where for generations coal miners and their sons burrowed into the rock-hard earth, lived an independent man who refused to dig for a living. His name was Robert Moses Grove, otherwise known as Lefty, who threw a baseball with extraordinary effectiveness and thus found a comfortable way to enjoy days in the sun by not having to put on a lanterned helmet and go underground.

He had incredible speed, amassed enormous strikeout totals and pitched his way into the Hall of Fame. Hitting off him was like asking to be blindfolded and then trying to swing an ax handle to hit a lump of coal in the darkness of midnight.

Winner of an even 300 games and with a record of 31-4 with the Philadelphia A's in 1931, he received the first Most Valuable Player Award presented by the Baseball Writers Association of America — a magnificent trophy, the kind of work they don't create anymore, with a pitcher depicted on top of a globe-like baseball designed by Dieges & Glust, well-known silversmiths.

Hitting off [Grove]
was like asking
to be blindfolded
and then trying
to swing
an ax handle
to hit a
lump of coal
in the darkness
of midnight...

Its value can't be estimated, which is why it's kept in a bank vault in downtown Lonaconing. A visit here to see and touch the "holy grail" of baseball was arranged by John Meyers, once a standout athlete at Frostburg State and later a high school teacher and coach for 35 years.

He's the "keeper of the flame," a caretaker of the trophy, so to speak, the overlord of what Lonaconing likes to fondly remember about its most celebrated son, something of a paradox for a man who was only truly comfortable when he was with the home folks.

Grove was considered by some teammates as difficult to get along with, someone whose temper triggered him, on occasion, to tear up the clubhouse. Such an occasion occurred in his record-setting year of 1931, when Grove, after winning 16 straight, lost 1-0 to the St. Louis Browns because a rookie outfielder, Jim Moore, playing in place of Al Simmons, who had gone home to visit in Milwaukee, misjudged a fly ball.

Grove knocked down the clubhouse door, kicked over lockers and destroyed his own uniform. "If Simmons had been here and in left field," Grove screamed, "he would have caught that ball in his back pocket."

To the day he died, in 1975 at age 75, Lefty held Simmons responsible.

"After I lost that game, I came back to win six or seven in a row. I could have had about 24 straight wins except for that 1-0 loss."

That same year, Grove toured Japan with an all-star team and the prime minister presented him with an oversized baseball glove as a memento of the trip. Crossed flags of the United States and Japan were stitched into the leather. But, 10 years later, when Pearl Harbor was bombed, which coincided with the day Grove announced his retirement, he took a penknife and cut away the rising sun.

Meyers remembers Lefty, on other occasions, at the pool hall and bowling lanes he operated, taking a cue stick and breaking it over his knee to vent anger. Another time, he went home to replace a radio he thought would offer better reception than the one he and friends were listening to, but all it offered was nonstop static. Lefty picked it up, fired it against the wall and said, "That's not as good as the one we had."

Meyers and Suter Kegg, sports editor emeritus of the *Cumberland Times*, remember Grove with affection, not disdain, simply because they understood and liked him. "I think there was a shyness to him," said Kegg.

"He felt comfortable when he was at the Lonaconing Republican Club with his friends or at 'Lefty's Place,' a pool hall and bowling lanes. Sometimes he'd drop in at the newspaper office, put his hand over my typewriter and say, 'That's enough work for one day.' Lefty liked to kid around."

"He came from strict parents," recalled Meyers, 79. "He was honest and blunt in his manner. He only went to the sixth grade in school and maybe that bothered him when he was around better-educated people."

But how did the MVP trophy come under the care of Meyers?

"In 1955, Lefty said if he gave it to the Hall of Fame at Cooperstown, none of the folks in 'Coney,' which is what we call Lonaconing, would have a chance to see it," replied Meyers. "It was on display at Valley High School for almost two decades before it was suggested it be moved for security reasons."

Whether it eventually will go on loan to Cooperstown, the Babe Ruth Museum in Baltimore or to the baseball exhibit at the Smithsonian Institution in Washington is a decision that will be made in the future. Meyers realizes in this era of memorabilia collectors the trophy would bring a heavy price if offered at auction, but that's not going to happen.

Lonaconing, a Maryland mountain town with a population of 1,122, reflects pride in its past, and Grove is the centerpiece of conversation when earlier glories are discussed, like down at Marshall's Confectionery store, where six pictures of Lefty are on the wall, or at Shorty's Service Station or Kelly's Bar. Tom Shockey, owner of Marshall's, remembers Grove for his snow-white hair and the cigar he usually was smoking.

Meyers produced a brown pay envelope dated March 2, 1918, made out to Robert Grove. He earned $11.30 for the week working at the Klotz Silk Mill. He later was employed by the J.M. Sloan & Son Glass Factory and worked for a short time in a mine. But he quit almost as soon as he started in the mine, telling his father, "I didn't put that coal there, and I'm not going to dig it out."

His reputation as a pitcher led to a tryout with Martinsburg of the Blue Ridge League, and he soon caught the eye of Jack Dunn, owner of the Baltimore Orioles. A storm had leveled the outfield fence in Martinsburg, so Dunn, to get Grove, agreed to pay the price of a new one — which meant Grove came to the Orioles for $3,000, or what it took to erect the barrier. Yes, an ill wind that blew Grove and the Orioles much good.

In slightly over four years, he won 109 games and lost 36 for the Orioles, on their way to becoming the greatest dynasty baseball has ever known, underlined by the fact the club Dunn put together won seven straight International League pennants.

The Orioles sold Grove to the A's in 1925 for a then-record sum of $100,600, and Connie Mack, Philadelphia's owner/general manager/ manager, got a high return on his investment. But in 1934, with the A's suffering from an anemic box office, he dealt him to the Boston Red Sox for $125,000.

In eight of his 17 seasons, he won more than 20 games, topped by the 31-4 mark in 1931, led the league in ERA nine times and was the strikeout king on seven occasions.

Robert Moses "Lefty" Grove. An original. The premier left-handed pitcher the American League has known in its 95-year history. In this tiny mining community of yesteryear, the pitcher who was called the "Lion of Lonaconing" is literally lionized, as if he's about to turn the corner and come walking up Main Street — if only in memories of days gone by.

Chapter 2

MASTERS *of* AUGUSTA

Golf's unforgettable moment

April 1, 1988

During every lifetime, be it that of a trash collector, oyster shucker, berry picker or sportswriter, there are implausible moments to remember. This reporter, like anyone else in the business of observation and communication, has personal memories that even now, decades after the fact, stand as indelible points of historical reference.

There was Sonny Liston refusing to come out of his corner for the seventh round because he said his shoulder hurt, continuing to remain on his stool and thereby resigning the coveted heavyweight championship of the world to Cassius Clay ... the New York Yankees losing the 1960 World Series to a Pittsburgh Pirates team that was vastly inferior ... the Baltimore Colts, favored by 16½ points, bowing to the New York Jets in Super Bowl III.

They would qualify as incredible chapters in all the pulsating, intriguing annals of boys and men playing frivolous games. But there was an occurrence 20 years ago that stands alone. It was when a veteran golfer, the gregarious, respected Roberto De Vicenzo, holder of 140 tournament titles in all parts of the world, literally signed away the right for a chance to win the Masters championship.

"I a stupid," he said in his fractured English, and all the world wanted to cry for him. It happened that De Vicenzo tied Bob Goalby at the end of four rounds of the 1968 Masters, but inadvertently his playing partner, Tommy Aaron, put a 4 on the scoreboard as they completed the 17th hole and not the birdie 3 he had clearly earned.

It was Aaron's mistake, but De Vicenzo, under the ancient and honorable rules of golf, in a way comparable to the Ten Commandments, officially notarized the result by signing his name. It became a binding, irrefutable contract. Instead of the honest 65 he had recorded, the error gave him a 66. It was a gross injustice, but life and golf bring no written guarantees of equity.

Instead of De Vicenzo's meeting Goalby in an 18-hole playoff the next day, as was the custom then with the Masters, a winner was immediately determined via the blunder of Aaron's pencil. Goalby's total at the end of four rounds came to 277; the unfortunate De Vicenzo had 278. Both men were gracious. Goalby, though, was demeaned because the true credit he earned and was entitled to never came to him. But he didn't complain. That's because Goalby, as an individual, is as strong in character as he is physically endowed.

For De Vicenzo, it was total heartbreak. "I just signed a wrong card," he explained. "The other fellow [Tommy Aaron] put down a 4. It's my fault."

The scene at the usually serene and formal Augusta National Golf Club was suddenly so traumatic you had to be there to attempt to comprehend. One minute, spectators were canceling airline reservations for the next day to avail themselves of the playoff. Then, almost in the blink of an eye, they were calling back in an attempt to restore plane departures — only to learn, in numerous instances, their seats had already been assigned to those on a standby basis.

Herbert Warren Wind, one of America's classical writers and certainly a perceptive and respected chronicler of the golf scene these last 50 years, wrote, "What had been a glorious day of golf and the climax of an extraordinarily exciting tournament had been turned to ashes by an arithmetical technicality. I know that the moment I heard the official announcement I was struck numb."

Meanwhile, Bobby Jones, the president of the host Augusta National Golf Club, was distressed by what happened. He talked with four members of the tournament committee and consulted with experts on the subject. Was there some way De Vicenzo could legally be given relief, the injustice corrected and a playoff held to decide the champion?

Jones was told there was no part of the record book that offered any such interpretation, not even what might be regarded as an area of vague or ambiguous language. "That's all I want to know," he replied. Jones would never have placed himself ahead of the rule book. So Goalby's name and numbers stayed up and De Vicenzo remained in second place, one short but long, yet painful, stroke behind, caused by the errant pencil of Aaron.

As fortune would decree, five years later, Aaron became the first native-born Georgian to win its famous tournament with a one-shot victory over J.C. Snead. But the interpretation that applied to the Goalby-De Vicenzo finish in 1968 is spelled out by the U.S. Golf Association as rule 38, Paragraph 3:

"No alteration may be made on a card after the competitor has returned it to the Committee. If the competitor returns a score for any hole lower than actually played, he shall be disqualified. A score higher than actually played must stand as returned."

So De Vicenzo was beaten by the unintentional bookkeeping mistake of a third party, Aaron, who was crestfallen over what had happened. Bob Goalby won the green coat emblematic of the Masters championship.

Amateurs dream of Masters birdies

April 6, 1990

AUGUSTA, Ga. — Atop the antebellum clubhouse at the august Augusta National Golf Club is a room of modest dimensions and unpretentious furnishings. It's not elaborate — yet comfortable and convenient. The price is right, $6 a night. But there's a limited clientele.

The abode is the temporary home for the amateur golfers playing in the Masters tournament. This is garret living at its best, a place where the golfers can dream of low scores, tumble out of bed in the morning and be right where they are supposed to be, the actual scene of the action.

For want of a better name, it's called the "Crow's Nest." There's a center room for relaxation, offering a card table and television set. Four small bedrooms — measuring about 10 feet by 6 feet, with drawstring curtains — are along two sides.

This is where Jack Nicklaus and Ben Crenshaw lived on their first trips to the Masters, before they joined the pro tour and created reputations of regal importance. Amateurs before and after Nicklaus and Crenshaw have experienced what it's like to sleep in the Crow's Nest.

Nicklaus says he remembers it well, being able to look out the window for a view of the first and 10th tees and the ninth and 18th greens. That was in 1959, and one of his roommates was Phil Rodgers.

"We could buy breakfast for a dollar, lunch for a dollar and dinner for $2 in the main dining room," Nicklaus recalled. "We would eat two and three steaks and finally one of the waiters told us they were going to have to charge us $2 every time we reordered. Now that was real fun to be here as a kid, even though I shot 76-74 and missed the cut."

But Nicklaus was to come back twice more as an amateur, 28 times as a pro and win an unprecedented six Masters championships over a course rich in history and heroes, the place he first "discovered" from his perch in the Nest.

For this Masters, only two players, Chris Patton, the national amateur champion, and Tim Hobbym, who won the U.S. Public Links, are availing themselves of the opportunity to be guests of the management.

Some amateurs in the past, no doubt members of wealthy families, passed up the Crow's Nest and stayed with their parents in more expensive surroundings. That seems a shame, because it would appear to be a delightful part of growing up in golf and seeing it from such a different perspective.

Imagine how it must be in the quiet of an evening. The pictures on the walls are of renowned performers such as Horton Smith, Henry Picard, Gene Sarazen, Craig Wood, Arnold Palmer, Claude Harmon, Sam Snead, Ben Hogan and Bobby Jones — when he was only 14.

The hallowed surroundings lend themselves to intimately contemplating the possibility of record scores and green Masters jackets and wondering what the reality of tomorrow's round is going to bring. Meanwhile, this is the place to dream.

Crenshaw win worth a good cry

April 10, 1995

AUGUSTA, Ga. — Moved by the respect and love for the man who once held his hand, taught him the game and pointed the way, Ben Crenshaw had a motivation stronger than any inherent desire to win a golf championship — even one so regal as the coveted Masters tournament.

Yesterday's scene of Crenshaw holding his head in his hands and crying his heart out after the final putt dropped in the cup will be an unforgettable tableau forever etched in the minds of those who accompanied him on this moving sentimental journey to "win one for Harvey."

It was an emotionally wrenching but immensely satisfying scene that penetrated deeply into the soul of all America. If you shed tears that denoted pride, rather than sorrow, along with Crenshaw, then tell yourself there was a full justification for emoting such feelings.

This tender, moving climax on the 18th hole will be reserved as one of the most memorable moments in all of golf. It will be a companion piece to the feeling generated in New York's Yankee Stadium when Lou Gehrig, hit by a fatal spinal disease, offered his final farewell to baseball and also to life.

Harvey Penick was Ben Crenshaw's inspiration to win his second Masters crown, which the record book tells us he previously won in 1984. Only last Wednesday, the day before the Masters was to commence, Crenshaw helped carry an "old pro" to his eternal resting place in the clay hills of Texas after funeral services were held in Austin.

Harvey Penick was the always-encouraging father figure who gave Crenshaw an inner strength on this occasion to reach into his deepest reservoir of resolve and made it happen by sheer will. It was his lasting gift to the memory of a revered tutor, a man admired for his goodwill toward all men regardless of their station in life.

Harvey was humble, modest and well-mannered. He didn't know how good he was at communicating the complex elements of what looks like a simple kind of a sport, this trying game called golf. Penick underrated himself to such a degree that he was still charging $5 for a golf lesson while contemporaries were asking and getting $50 and up.

Crenshaw and Tom Kite were two professionals of high standing whom he met when they were mere children, the sons of members at the Austin Country Club in Texas. He showed them how to hold a club, to swing it and execute the other fundamentals.

But, more than that, he explained much about life in his simple downhome way, often talking in parables that they understood and implemented. "Think of the greatest person in life you have ever heard about or known, and you have Harvey Penick," said Crenshaw in tribute.

On Wednesday, Crenshaw and Kite were pallbearers for Penick, who died at age 90 only a week ago. So contrast the feelings of Crenshaw — losing his older pal, Harvey, one Sunday and then winning the Masters in a memorial to him on the following Sunday.

Thus, this was more than a golf tournament, even if it was the grandest of them all, the Masters. It was a love affair, the 43-year-old Crenshaw paying a debt to his friend and teacher.

When Ben last visited with Harvey, then bedridden, only 10 days before his death, they had a discussion about putting. And the putter they used on that occasion was placed alongside Harvey in his coffin for the trip to the eternally green fairway where he rests in peace.

There was such a profound feeling and warmth for Crenshaw and why he so much wanted to succeed in his ambition to "win for Harvey" that the concluding round of the tournament, played intensely, was almost forgotten in the aftermath of what was a tearful but joyous triumph.

Fondly poetic was the fact his nearest challenger in the quest for the prize was Davis Love III, whose late father, a golf professional, was coached by Penick when he was a student at the University of Texas. Young Love had met Penick as a child, but didn't have the relationship with him that Crenshaw and Kite enjoyed.

Still, Love was prepared to attend his funeral when Crenshaw told him that it wasn't necessary and felt Harvey would have wanted him to remain in Augusta and practice.

Love threw the best round of the day, 66, at the closely contested field and finished one stroke behind Crenshaw, who had a closing 68. This gave him a total of 274, the right to ownership of a second green jacket, emblematic of the Masters, and a first-place check worth $396,000.

Love, as gracious in defeat as any man has ever been, said it all so appropriately when he remarked, "There couldn't be a better end to Harvey Penick's life than to have Ben win the Masters the Sunday after he passed away."

The kind and wise Crenshaw, at age 43 the second-oldest ever to win here, said he didn't know if he would ever score a repeat in the Masters. "I just have to believe in fate," he added. "Yes, fate decided another championship here as it does so many times."

He couldn't adequately describe how the shots fell his way, but something else, assistance from the great beyond, was working in Ben's behalf. "He [meaning Penick] was with me the whole way. I told some people I had a 15th club in my bag and it was Harvey. He put his hand on my shoulder."

Penick, of course, only a year ago allowed author Bud Shrake to print his teaching notes that he had accumulated for more than 70 years into what was titled the "Little Red Book," which quickly became the best-selling sports book in all publishing history.

The royalties allowed Harvey to pay his medical bills and, as he said, to go into a restaurant with his wife and order a meal without having to check the right side of the menu to see how much it was going to cost.

The spirit of Penick carried into the soul and fiber of Crenshaw, who extended himself to the limit in an effort to please the man who most influenced his life and career.

"Harvey had his hand on my shoulder," insisted Crenshaw. There was no willingness by anyone to dispute such a claim. The Masters record book, therefore, should read co-winners of the 1995 championship. Their names were almost synonymous on this gorgeous day of sunshine while a light breeze caressed the tall pines.

Harvey Penick and Ben Crenshaw, playing as partners, won it together. Let the celebration begin.

--- --- --- --- --- --- --- --- ---

Tiger Woods better than fiction

April 14, 1997

AUGUSTA, Ga. — On the same hallowed ground where golf's sainted heroes of the past gained their own immortality, walked a slender, smiling young man with skin the shade of brown sugar and a swing just as sweet. The coronation of Tiger Woods defies reality, approaches the make-believe of pulp fiction and tests every element of credibility — yet it's all so authentic.

This is not a grand hoax, like those pranksters of yore who once unearthed the Cardiff Giant. Yes, Tiger Woods, by dint of his deeds, recorded one of the most astonishing achievements in the vast concept of modern sports.

The scene of triumph was beneath the sprawling magnolias and towering loblolly pines, near the impressive antebellum clubhouse — a so typical old Southern plantation setting, where a black player had never performed until 1975 in the Masters.

Now comes a champion of exceptional merit who covered himself with a distinction that is a credit to perseverance and diligent pursuit of precise objectives. A minority member attained a major goal.

Yes, dreams do come true. Ambitions can still be realized. Youth

knows no limitations. Tiger Woods has touched the stars. No matter his age, 21; lack of practical experience as a professional, eight months; or social circumstance, there is always the chance to succeed, as proven with such emphatic finality and genuine grace by Woods, who accepted the roaring cheers of the crowd by either tipping his cap, raising his hand or offering a smile and a nod.

Nothing surpasses natural ability in any calling and Woods, by his unprecedented accomplishment in the Masters, has proven that, yes, the impossible is always possible, that barriers can be hurdled and ambitions, no matter how seemingly remote, are within grasp.

None of this would have happened without the well-disciplined presence of his father, Earl, a retired lieutenant colonel in the Army, who put a golf club in the hands of his child and showed him the way. He's a product of impeccable training by parents who cared so deeply about him, emphasizing his academic standing in school and sensing he had the aptitude to solve the mystery of learning to strike a golf ball — a test that's mental as well as physical.

It can be said, without fear of contradiction, that he learned his lessons well. "I wanted him as a young boy to find that swinging a golf club was as natural as throwing a ball," explained the elder Woods in what reveals the simplistic clue to how his son became the golfer he is.

Right there is the secret of a swing that has the consistency of pure honey. So look no further to find out why. This is what separated the 21-year-old Woods from the rest of the Masters' field. He toyed with the opposition as if they were mere sparring partners.

His victory was complete. Overwhelming. He beat a group of 85 classic contenders, including the best from 13 foreign lands. The nearest competitor, Tom Kite, in second place, was 12 strokes back, which put him in the next county.

He wiped 'em out, shattering seven Masters' records and preparing a definitive place for himself, this spectacular shooting star, on the worldwide golf stage.

Earl Woods didn't fill his son's head with all kinds of technical verbiage or convoluted theories that might hamper his development. He let Tiger be himself by doing nothing more than letting him practice a smooth, natural swing.

To find Woods entering the Tom Butler Cabin (named to honor a prominent Maryland citizen and a onetime Masters' member), on the Augusta National property, for the awarding of the symbolic green jacket was a historic moment — especially for a black. It had never happened before, although Lee Elder, Jim Thorpe and Calvin Peete had qualified for earlier Masters appearances.

Elder, now living in Pompano Beach, Fla., and a member of the PGA Senior Tour, pioneered the way in 1975. He put it in perspective by saying, "This is a happy and glorious day for all blacks, not just for me, because everyone has hoped and prayed this would happen."

Twenty-two years ago, when Elder made the breakthrough, he admits to being nervous but said he had a great time, even though he missed the cut by five shots. Signifying the Woods domination, he continued on: "It's magnificent. I'm so proud and so happy to see something of this nature come about. Tiger is the bridge to the future and the past. He's a bridge to the past for me and the bridge to the future for him."

At the final turn, Woods had established a nine-stroke margin. Had it been any other Sunday afternoon match, say at a country club or on a public course, there would have been an adjustment of strokes just to make things interesting on the back nine.

But this is the Masters, where the competition is at the highest level. Still the comments by the trailing players before yesterday's round virtually conceded the outcome. It was going to be Woods all the way.

When Jack Nicklaus came out of the amateur ranks and quickly dominated golf, it was Bobby Jones, builder of the Augusta National club, who said, "He plays the kind of game I'm not familiar with." Nicklaus now wonders what Jones would be saying about Woods if he had lived to see this phenomenal performance. Tiger turned the otherwise demanding 6,925-yard course into a drive, a pitch and a putt.

Nicklaus was 22 when he joined the pro tour in 1962 and won the Masters the next year. He went on to win six in all, plus the PGA five times, four U.S. Opens and the British Open on three occasions.

So Woods, admittedly, still has a way to go. Yet his ability is so immense there's no way to minimize his chances — not after what he demonstrated in his first try at a major.

It's interesting to measure the score differential he posted in the four rounds against the rivals he was paired with. He bested England's Nick Faldo, defending champion, by five shots; fellow American Paul Azinger by seven; Scotland's Colin Montgomerie by nine; and Italy's Constantino Rocca by six.

It translates to a total annihilation. Tiger Woods was the youngest to ever win at Augusta; shot the lowest score for victory, a four-round total of 270; and the margin of triumph, 12 shots, had never been so commanding.

He plays as if he rode in on a meteorite to demonstrate for all of us something that has never before been witnessed on planet Earth. Shake your head in disbelief, doubt if you must, but Tiger Woods is mystical.

Chapter 3

STAR-CROSSED ATHLETES

Fall from racing glory

May 19, 1996

From the throats of the multitudes come the special sound effects identified with the massive and roaring crowd that gathers for Maryland's greatest horse race and the sprawling lawn party that goes with it. Yes, the Preakness. Historic and momentous. A celebration.

But for Ron Franklin, it's all about memories and deep personal regrets, highlighted by the fact he won this classic event in 1979, with Spectacular Bid carrying him on a joy ride to the victory circle. Yesterday, he wasn't allowed to be there — not even permitted inside the gates to merely watch. It's the peak of the racing season, the festival-like Preakness, but Franklin was on the outside looking in — excluded.

A sad and troubling circumstance . . . but necessary.

It's what every jockey dreads to hear, the harsh posted notification that he has been suspended indefinitely. Disbarred. Persona non grata. Franklin doesn't try to cop a plea or make excuses. He points to himself and says, in a tone of dreary, downcast resignation, "I'm to blame." The poison that comes with using cocaine has resulted in his being ruled off the tracks on two occasions, first in 1992 and now, a similar sentence six weeks ago by the Maryland Racing Commission. Franklin is candid about his situation because he has come to terms with being truthful to himself. It's likely that this self-revealing honesty is the only chance he has to make it back — if not to the racetrack, then to a productive life in some other occupation.

Right now, through the graciousness of a brother-in-law, Danny Kaminkow, he's working part time for a family business, Dundalk

Aluminum Specialties.

He helps put siding on buildings.

A jolting contrast when compared with his situation of being in the starting lineup for the Triple Crown — with its gold and glory, attention and prestige.

Spectacular Bid and Franklin were a twosome, winning the Preakness, Kentucky Derby, Flamingo, Florida Derby, Blue Grass and so many other elite events on the racetracks of America. "Riding him and then some other horse was about the difference in driving a Rolls-Royce as compared to a cheap truck," he says. "The Bid, which is my name for him, was like being on two horses at once."

All that's in the past, a time when the saga of Franklin even surpassed the tall tales of fanciful fiction or the intriguing stories that happen every day in the vagaries of racing, a sport that mirrors the destinies of life like no other.

Franklin knew the heights.

Success came in a hurry; something he couldn't predict.

Nor could he forecast the circumstance that led to his fall, worse than any he ever took from a horse.

Now, he's retrospective and contrite. Also honest. But as his widowed mother, Marion Franklin, who has been tried to the limit and still believes, says, 'Nobody can help him but himself."

And Ronnie, who has to wage the fight against this insidious addiction, agrees. If not, then any chance he has of getting clean is unrealistic. The horse, in a manner of speaking, is on his back.

Addressing the problem head-on, Franklin talks openly of what he has done to himself. "I never planned to do it this way," he said. "Taking cocaine is a disease that you make your friend. Nobody tied me down and made me do it.

"I paid the price, and I'm keeping on paying the price. With drugs, you get so low you can't go any lower, except living on the streets. I don't want to wind up in some alley."

Franklin, now 36 and weighing 116 pounds, is trying to turn around a shattered career but, more importantly, his life. He got immense help from a counselor at the racetrack; from a trainer, Kimberly Godwin, who employed him as an exercise rider at Sagamore Farm during his previous suspension and offers constant encouragement; and Larry DeAngelis, who has reached out to him and sees that he's in a recovery house, where the tuition is $80 per week and the program he follows is fittingly called Courage to Change.

"I do have a choice," he self-consciously said. "I can stay on it or get off. I was a practicing addict, and a lying drug user is the greatest manipulator in the world. I got to pick my head up and stay clean.

"In the recovery house, there are seven of us, from all lines of work — jewelers, salesmen and other things. We all have jobs to do, like cleaning the hall or taking a turn cooking once a week or mopping floors. We each keep our bedrooms in an orderly fashion. Then I get on the bus and head for work."

Franklin, who left Patapsco High School as a junior, has no trouble expressing or explaining himself. He takes a listener behind the curtain of mystery that is associated with drugs and, when asked, offers an in-depth description of what it was like to venture there and become trapped.

His most compelling comments come when he describes what the habit does to the mind. "It puts you in a world of grandeur. You think you can master anything. Then it escalates into a horrendous mountain. It's all a big lie.

"Recovering addicts will tell you all values go out the window. It's like a storm coming up in your life. I'm content where I am today, thinking of God and thanking God."

To get to cocaine, he first smoked cigarettes, tasted beer while under age and then sampled marijuana. He insists he was introduced to cocaine by the "wrong crowd," but never rode a race while under the influence. "I was out of control because the disease controlled me," he said.

Now, he's in a 12-step program for rehabilitation. "I let down my mother, my brother and sisters, even people who didn't know me. Thank God, it didn't take my life. I believe God wants me here. I'd love to ride again. My counselor thinks I have one more chance if I comply. And I plan to do just that."

How Franklin became a rider is one of the most astonishing of long shots. He was "discovered" while wrestling with other boys on the lawn of a neighbor, Henry "Hank" Tiburzi, who was reading a *Daily Racing Form* before going to Pimlico.

"Hey, you little — come here, I want to talk to you," hollered Tiburzi. He asked Ronnie if he had ever thought of becoming a jockey. He had the weight, 101 pounds, and was strong in his hands and arms.

They left at 4:30 a.m. two days later for Pimlico, and Franklin waited at the stable gate while it was announced that a kid looking for work was standing by. The call was answered by Bryan Delp, a nephew of trainer Grover "Buddy" Delp. That's how Franklin was hired as a hot walker, and this evolved into exercising horses, then to becoming an apprentice jockey.

Fourteen months later, he touched the stars. Franklin won the

Derby. Was he in any way feeling the pressure as he took Spectacular Bid to the post? "Yeah, I was nervous. My knees were shaking. The rider in the No. 4 hole said, 'Just settle down, jock. When the gates open, you'll know what to do.' And the Bid did win. You know, horses will run for me. I think I have a talent for it."

After the Derby and Preakness, the Bid went to the Belmont Stakes, where, with a quarter of a mile to go, he was on top by three lengths. It was learned later that, on the morning of the race, the colt had gotten a safety pin embedded in his left front foot, apparently in the barn area after a wrapping had come loose, or else it had been dropped there accidentally by one of the attendants.

Franklin takes full blame for the Belmont loss and how he handled the horse. "I got a little antsy," he recalled. "I went too soon. I never let him go that early before. I certainly didn't ride him to perfection.

"Most good riders know when they give a bad ride. I had two bad ones, in the Florida Derby and the Belmont. But I won the greatest race in the world, the Kentucky Derby, when I was 19, and then the Preakness, in my hometown. Great thrills.

"Now, I'm concentrating on being another kind of winner. I'm content where I am. If I get a craving for it, I take a deep breath and say a prayer. Some miraculous things happen in this program. I have to stay relaxed, not be in a hurry and pray. I have peace of mind. I don't need money."

It's his strong intent to beat cocaine to the finish line. Ronnie Franklin most emphatically doesn't want to be an also-ran in the race for life.

— — — — — — — — — — — — — —

Dalkowski threw away career

Aug. 11, 1996

NEW BRITAIN, Conn. — Now it's a world that he sees as a nonstop blur, out of register, much the way a photo looks when the camera won't focus. Steve Dalkowski, the most phenomenal talent the Orioles ever had, stands there staring into space, unsure of what's going on around him and not offering a word of protest. Benign. Childlike.

He was never the complaining type, nor did he cause trouble for others — only himself. Dalkowski was — and is — regarded by those who saw him as the fastest-throwing pitcher in baseball history, which covers the sacrosanct territory of Walter Johnson to Nolan Ryan and all the others in between, such as Bob Gibson, Tom Seaver and Bob Feller. Yet he never made the major leagues.

Dalkowski was a tragedy unto himself. In baseball and life. A paradox of pain and frustration. He never scratched the surface of the vast potential he brought with him. Though he failed to touch the stars, his reputation has endured. He had to be seen to be believed, the awesome force he could generate in throwing baseball with his modest physical build (5 feet 11, 170 pounds) and a somewhat unorthodox delivery.

Instead of his deeds being documented in the record books, they are now recounted only by former teammates, ex-managers and sportswriters who saw him. Cal Ripken Sr., who coached and managed the Orioles, said from the perspective of having caught him in the minor leagues and comparisons with all the other pitchers he's seen, that Dalkowski stands alone.

"He threw harder than anyone," said Ripken, a man not given to exaggeration. "I saw Nolan Ryan from the coaching box, and I know you might think I'm stretching the point, but Ryan didn't compare with Steve. I believe if Steve had pitched in the big leagues, he was capable of striking out 21 batters a game."

Now, Dalkowski is at an age, 57, where legendary status befits him, only there's not much that he remembers. The saturation of alcohol, from his early teen-age years and through adulthood, has damaged his brain. When he makes his way through the halls of the Walnut Hill Nursing Home, where he has been a resident for the past 15 months, he is passive from the medication that's administered daily, and seems at peace with himself.

The best thing he has going for him is a sister, Patti, who cares for his needs. They were separated for practically 25 years, and she had no idea where he was — except for an occasional story that told of him in the fields of California's San Joaquin Valley, where he picked grapes, oranges and lemons, dug potatoes and chopped cotton.

Then he'd take his pay, usually $15, and begin to drink it all up when the sun went down. The next morning, he was on the flatbed truck with the migrant workers for another day under the scorching sun. He'd carry his wine bottles with him, place them in alternate rows so he'd have an incentive to pick faster. When he moved along, he'd

*He never
scratched the
surface of the
vast potential
he brought
with him.
Though he failed
to touch
the stars,
his reputation
has endured.*

reward himself with another drink of the grape.

The Association of Professional Baseball Players and the Baseball Assistance Team (BAT) have come to his aid in the past, paying for extensive counseling and rehabilitation in hospitals and clinics. "He'd often just walk away," said Patti, "and the organizations trying to help him would have no idea where he was.

"From Aug. 1, 1992, until Dec. 24, he was on the streets of Los Angeles. You wonder how he got along. I just believe the indigent look out for each other. He was found sitting in a laundromat in Los Angeles on Christmas Eve by a wonderful Spanish family, who took him home and eventually found out who he was."

Two of his former teammates, Ray Youngdahl and Frank Zuppo, extended themselves to the limit in efforts to help Dalkowski. "I guess we just hit if off," Dalkowski said. "Both would do anything for you. Tell Boog Powell, John Miller, Lou Sleater and Barry Shetrone I said hi. Also Earl [Weaver] and Pat Gillick."

His drinking is something Dalkowski, in his limited recall, doesn't blame on baseball. He said it started as a kid when he and other boys would go to a neighbor's wine cellar and drink until they got drunk. "I guess I was 12 or 13. It's hard to explain why I drank so much."

Patti remembers growing up in a family in which their father was a heavy drinker, usually inebriated from Friday evening until Sunday afternoon, when he knew he had to sober up for work on Monday. "But after all, we were ethnic, and drinking is almost a way of life," she said. Patti, five years younger than Steve, is everything he isn't — articulate, smart, organized and a woman of style.

"It makes me content to be with my brother again. I'm so happy when he has a visitor. Often, old friends promise to come, but they forget and he feels let down. I have the peace of mind that he is getting good supervision and nutrition. The state of Connecticut takes care of him, because I don't know how else we could afford it."

The Dalkowski pitching stories abound. He once hit a batter and tore off part of his ear in the Appalachian League. Another time, a pitch struck the umpire in the mask and sent him to the hospital with a concussion. In Elmira, N.Y., to win a $20 bet, from either Andy Etchebarren or Youngdahl, he can't remember whom, he threw a ball through a wooden outfield fence.

At Aberdeen Proving Ground, arrangements were made in 1958 to check his speed with ballistic equipment — not intended to clock a baseball. He had pitched the day before and threw off flat ground, not a raised mound, and got a reading of 93.5 mph.

"I think I might have thrown up to 110, but I don't know," he said.

"That seems to be about what's in my mind."

Harry Dalton, former general manager of the Orioles, Angels and Brewers, said neither Ryan nor Sandy Koufax threw as hard as Dalkowski. "I saw Ryan clocked at 100.6, but when Steve was pitching, they didn't have the radar gun," Dalton said.

Dalkowski was so wild, he usually walked as many as he struck out. In 1960, at Stockton in the California League, he fanned 262 and walked the same number in 170 innings. As a rookie at Kingsport, Tenn., he once struck out 24, walked 18 and pitched a no-hitter — which he lost, 8-4.

The 1963 season found Dalkowski in the Orioles' camp, and he had made the final roster. That evening he was measured for his uniform, but two hours later, going against the Yankees in an exhibition, he heard "something go pop" in his arm when making a pitch to Bobby Richardson. He was never the same after that. Cruel destiny had knocked him down again.

Steve Dalkowski doesn't ask for pity. All his days are the same. The routine never changes. A man who drank himself into "another world" has finally found sobriety, even if he's not sure where he is or how long he's been there.

A career and life that might have been.

Chapter 4

Baltimore's
BEST

Mary Dobkin's way of life

Aug. 24, 1987

When a crisis developed, like when a bill to be paid for a set of uniforms, there was little patience demonstrated by Mary Dobkin. Her inherent tenacity refused the luxury of backing off if a cause required attention — and this always involved the needs of children.

If it took tears or a slight exaggeration of the facts to dramatize the situation, Mary was capable of playing the role. The Mary Dobkin A.C. sponsored football, basketball, baseball and softball teams in Baltimore, and remarkable success came about because, in heart and spirit, she was an unspoiled child herself.

Born in Russia and abandoned as an infant, she suffered from deformities in both legs which called for, at her last count, 117 operations. Mary died on Saturday at the reported age of 84, but, actually, she didn't know how old she was. But that didn't matter.

From humble beginnings and discouraging setbacks, which included living on welfare and enduring physical disabilities, Mary refused to accept explanations over why something couldn't be done if kids were concerned. But never for herself — only those she wanted to help. Charging into the mayor's office, or making an in-person call to the sports department of the *News American*, while on crutches, became a frequent calling. There were documented occasions when the police department, a judge in juvenile court or a Johns Hopkins Hospital psychiatrist turned a case over to Mary, meaning she had another kid to look after who might be helped by her special kind of supervision.

Although she functioned in predominantly white neighborhoods, black youngsters who wanted to join her teams were, of course, extended the same opportunity. Every kid got a fair shake from Mary.

She once showed up in the newspaper office with a would-be left-handed catcher, a Lumbee Indian, who was crossed-eyed, which qualified him in three ways as a member of a minority. All she wanted was to have it explained, for practical baseball purposes, why maybe he should find another position as he grew older.

Jay Mazzone, a child who had lost part of both arms in a backyard gasoline explosion, knocked on her door with one of the hooks he had for a hand and asked to try out for the team. He was welcomed, too, playing right field and, ultimately, becoming a batboy for the Orioles, where he drew national attention with his capabilities despite the handicap. Now, Jay Mazzone no longer handles bats but drives heavy-duty construction equipment.

There were times, but only rarely, when a con man would spell out "pie in the sky" and she became a believer until nothing happened or the faker was exposed. We're reminded of a middle-aged man, with a 16-year-old wife, who said he was ready to "build her a Boys Town in Glen Burnie," where kids would be taken by bus to what he described as a land of enchantment.

He promised facilities for all sports, indoor and outdoor swimming pools, horses to ride and a huge dining room. The man showed up and, unfortunately, wasn't the Santa Claus he made himself out to be. In a matter of one conversation, he went from being the "angel" who was going to construct this huge "dream-like" complex to literally and fiscally a total zero.

Asked if he would buy Mary a new station wagon, he shook his head. Lou Grasmick, one of her benefactors, offered to pay half if the pseudo-millionaire would do likewise. Still "no." It eventually evolved he wouldn't so much as give $5 to the cause. Exit a phony out the door.

William Donald Schaefer, then mayor, and Doug Tawney, former director of Parks and Recreation, approved a field be named in her honor, which made Mary happy, but it got little use by teams. It has fallen into decline and is overgrown with weeds, plus ruts and sinkholes that would prevent any kind of a game from being played there.

The Orioles, Colts, Bullets and Skipjacks opened the gates whenever she brought children to games. An opportunist who said he once played on one of her teams paid $100 for her life story and shopped it around Hollywood until he found a buyer. But two friends refused to let her give away the biography for a mere $100 and shamed the entrepreneur into seeing she at least receive a new station wagon and a donation to the Dobkin Children's Fund.

An earlier network television show, "End of the Rainbow," had featured the Dobkin story. In return, it made promises of gifts, mostly ath-

letic equipment, but few materialized. Mary's team was later so broke it didn't have $1.25 to pay for a baseball to put into a sandlot game, and it couldn't afford to provide an equal share of the umpiring fees.

But that was subsequently alleviated, and an obligation was assumed to help get her on more solid financial footing. The late Benny Trotta, a boxing promoter, got his friend Rocky Marciano to appear at a fund-raising banquet. Brooks Robinson and John Unitas participated without a fee, too, just because they recognized this was an unusual woman who dealt with kids of the street in need of help.

Comedian Henny Youngman performed at the request of Jack "Mace" Sober, who was intent on making her lot an easier one. Grasmick prevailed on Eddy Arnold to perform in concert at Painter's Mill to raise money. Likewise "Country" Charlie Pride. They all came to Baltimore in behalf of Mary Dobkin. The result was Mary's monetary problem eased, which meant she could concentrate on directing the informal program and appoint her assistant coaches.

Not one penny raised was ever used to pay for an executive director, postage or an office. When Mary retired from active duty and entered Levindale home, $14,000 remained in the treasury, and this was divided, per her suggestion, to the Police Youth Clubs and Red Shield Boys Club. So, until the end, Mary Dobkin thought of children first and relegated herself to second place.

The full worth she accomplished can never be written in words. It was a life that presumably was pleasing to her maker because it contained only a profound desire to do good for others.

--- --- --- --- --- --- --- --- --- --- ---

How to hit and run away

Sept. 30, 1988

On the morning after becoming the bantamweight boxing champion of the world, a glorious achievement, a weary but excited Harry Jeffra hurried out of his New York hotel room and took a "tube" ride to Jersey City. There he asked directions of a street car conductor as to how he might reach a certain parochial school.

He rode, transferred to another line and walked six blocks. He found the building, entered, traversed the hallways and systematically peered in the glass of each classroom door, searching for a familiar face. He was, specifically, looking for a teacher.

Finally, he found her, a nun who had befriended him when he was a child attending St. Ambrose School in Baltimore. As he entered, the students immediately came to their feet, almost on cue. "Boys and girls," said Sister Mary Josephine, "I want you to meet the new boxing champion of the world."

It's a story from out of the past that gives sensitive insight into Harry Jeffra, a boxer who confused opponents with speed, acceleration and flawless footwork. He was a Fred Astaire of the boxing ring who went on from there to win another world title when he moved up to the featherweight division.

Jeffra died at age 73 earlier this week after creating a reputation as one of Baltimore's most decorated boxers in history: a two-time champion, member of the Boxing Hall of Fame and a walking public relations man for the human race.

"He might have had the greatest set of legs in the history of the sport," insisted Julius Weiner, a onetime boxer. "Harry could 'dance' all night."

Jeffra won the featherweight crown from Sixto Escobar by taking a 15-round decision as part of the "Carnival of Champions," a 1937 presentation of master promoter Mike Jacobs that offered four title bouts. It was always said it took Harry "two days" to beat Escobar. The match started close to midnight and lasted into the next morning, a delay brought on by the fact three of the encounters carried the 15-round limit and found Fred Apostoli stopping Marcel Thil in the 10th round.

A year later, Escobar decisioned Jeffra in Puerto Rico. Jeffra's jaw was broken in the fifth round, but he didn't quit, going the 15-round distance. Doctors there told him after the fight he had an infected tooth. But, almost a week later, after returning by ship from San Juan, specialists in Baltimore informed him his jaw had been broken.

In five meetings with Escobar, the victory went to Jeffra four times. Then, in 1940, he moved up to the featherweight class and beat Joey Archibald, making him Baltimore's first and only world champion in two different divisions. Buddy Ey, respected boxing historian, says Jeffra was once regarded as a respected puncher, but, after breaking his hand in a preliminary against Leroy Dugan, became more of a tactician.

"He always had a good overhand right," recalls Ey. "Harry was a first-rate boxer and a respected gentleman. His top purse, even though he had well over 100 bouts, was $3,000. He never made much money from the sport, but was mighty rich when it came to making friends."

The Jeffra record reads 97 wins, 19 defeats, 7 draws. Stop to consider he was considered a poor amateur boxer. He lost 27 straight before scoring a knockout in Richmond, Va., for his first victory. The win brought such instant pleasure he turned professional, and Harry Jeffra, who had his hand raised only once as an amateur, went on to earn two world titles.

After retiring, he worked as stable manger at the Pimlico Race Course and decided, in retrospect, that if he had a philosophy as a fighter, it could be simply explained. To wit: "He who hits and runs away lives to fight another day."

In 1982, this reporter introduced Jeffra for his enshrinement in the Boxing Hall of Fame at ceremonies in New York. Harry looked around at the huge hotel ballroom and remarked, "I must be dreaming. If I am, please don't wake me up."

On that occasion, he also opened the collar of his shirt and showed the audience a religious medal he wore on a chain. He explained Sister Mary Josephine had given it to him when he was in sixth grade. When he's buried tomorrow, the same medal will go with him to his grave.

Harry Jeffra. Slow to anger. Fast on his feet. And a two-time champion who celebrated his first boxing championship by sharing it with his favorite teacher and a classroom filled with children.

Triple play only part of Neun legacy

March 29, 1990

Turn the pages to review the extraordinary life of Johnny Neun, a gem of a gentleman who attained exceptional accomplishment. And there's his profound love for family, friends and, by all means, baseball.

Neun was considered one of the cornerstones of the illustrious New York Yankees farm system that paid off with 23 American League pennants during the time he managed, coached and schooled their exceptional fund of minor-league players. But Neun touched all the bases in a career that found him identified with professional baseball from 1929 until he died yesterday at age 89.

He remembered dollar-a-day meal money, bus rides, skinned infields, Ty Cobb batting with his hands apart, Babe Ruth lofting cloud-high home runs, the Yankees training at Atlantic City during World War II and seeing Mickey Mantle at age 19 when he emerged as a phenomenal prospect in a pre-training camp at Phoenix in 1951.

Yes, Neun was a part of all that and much more, including an unassisted triple play in the major leagues, the only one that ever ended a game. And for 69 straight years, without interruption, he went to spring training as a player, manager or coach in either the majors or the minors.

Neun, as incongruous as it seems, was almost forced into a professional baseball career. It happened by dint of circumstance. He was attending Baltimore City College and officiating amateur soccer games, for which he was paid a grand fee of 50 cents. But because he had accepted money, he was ruled a professional and declared ineligible for all high school sports.

"So I went to my professors, and they gave me permission to leave school early to join the Martinsburg team of the Blue Ridge League," he explained. "When the season was over, I came back and finished my studies."

It was May 31, 1927, that he was responsible for the triple play. That morning, he was fascinated to read a newspaper story relating how Jimmy Cooney of the Chicago Cubs had recorded a triple play. "I remarked to a couple of my teammates on the Detroit Tigers that it would probably be 50 years before that occurred again. But that exact afternoon it happened to me against the Cleveland Indians."

It took a span of 41 years for it to occur again, only the eighth in major-league history, when Ron Hansen of the Washington Senators made a solitary triple play, also against the Indians. For documentation, here's how Neun scored three outs on one batted ball.

Homer Suma lined to Neun at first base. He touched Charley Jamieson in the base line and continued to run to second base, where he tagged the bag Glenn Myatt had vacated. A fiction postscript was added when Neun supposedly said, "I'm not going to throw the ball because I want to run into the Hall of Fame."

That never happened. But the triple play was much a part of Johnny Neun. He liked to tell of when he managed the Cincinnati Reds in 1947 and 1948. "I would be coaching third base and this fan with a good sense of humor and a strong voice would always holler, 'Hey, Triple-Play Neun. What the hell else can you do?' "

Milwaukee Brewers general manager Harry Dalton, who hired

Neun in his late years as a scout and instructor of first base play, said, "He was one of the finest living men I have known. He took exceptional care of himself, which is why he was coaching in our minor-league camp last year at 88. He never drank or smoked and wouldn't allow himself to put on weight."

Dalton said John's approachable manner built confidence, and drew young players to him. Having him around was like being able to call on Frank Lloyd Wright to demonstrate or lecture young architects.

Thirty of Neun's 69 years in baseball were spent with the Yankees. He was such an exceptional organizer that he coordinated training camps under managers Casey Stengel and Ralph Houk. But he would step into the background, like a good soldier, and quietly make sure the proper time was being allocated to each drill.

"Seeing Mantle was something special," he once related. "He was just a kid, coming to us a shortstop after only two years at Independence, Kan., and Joplin, Mo., in our farm system. When Stengel saw him run, he said, 'Mickey is so fast, it looks as if he runs on the tops of the blades of grass.'"

With all his admiration of Mantle, he believed Joe DiMaggio was the best outfielder and all-around player he ever saw, Mark Belanger the leading infielder and the almost-forgotten Harry Davis, who was briefly with the St. Louis Browns, the most proficient first baseman.

"Just remember," he told us one time, "accept greatness in an athlete for what it is. Don't try to separate it, because it can't be done."

For 24 years, during the off-season, his byline was a part of these sports pages. Yes, a reporter, writer and analyst along with officiating high school and college basketball, and then he'd go off to training camp. It happened every spring ... 69 years worth.

Johnny Neun was wise, but not a braggart; strong in conviction but never a despot. Truly a joy to know, respect and, yes, even revere.

Greatest coaching job

Dec. 13, 1991

More than the players he helped shape for the major leagues, the amateur championships that were achieved and his profound passion for baseball, Sterling "Sheriff" Fowble was a momentous force for good. His presence epitomized all that's worthwhile about a game, its fiber and the boys and men who identify with it.

The reason Fowble had such an impact on Baltimore is this is where he coached sandlot teams for 46 years, never taking advantage of a youngster and being a part of their lives during the critical period of early adolescence. Saturday morning practices were at 8 or 9, and his introductory remarks at the start of every season were consistently the same:

"All of you want to be professional baseball players, or you wouldn't be here. Only a few of you are going to be able to do that. But what you can all do, without exception, is grow up to be a real person and make your families proud."

So, along with being a sound teacher of fundamentals, which enhanced individual play and, in turn, team victories, Fowble realized he was involved with something far more precious — influencing and helping to direct young lives.

"A great tribute to him is the way he took such an immense interest in each and every kid," said Ron Bradley, who was his assistant coach for 10 years and thought so much of Fowble he encouraged his own two sons to come play for him. "The substitutes on the team knew he wanted them to do as well as the so-called stars.

"He insisted the players be in uniform and ready to practice 50 minutes before a game. It was his idea that neatness in how they dressed, on and off the field, was important. He'd say, 'We can't look like a rag-tag outfit because that would be an embarrassment to me, to our sponsor, who is paying the bills, and to your mothers and fathers.'"

From the opposite side of the field comes the perspective of Pat O'Malley, who managed teams that challenged Fowble and, for a six-year period, dominated the 14- to 16-year-old age bracket. "We had a bitter rivalry," remembers O'Malley. "He wouldn't tolerate laziness and, for some special reason, had a magnificent way of helping hitters. That was a true talent."

O'Malley, temporarily, puts all that aside. Then he remembers something else about the manager and the man. "As tough as we fought to win, when it was over we'd always meet at home plate and shake hands. In 1971, our Brooklyn Optimist Boys' Club beat one of his best teams. Moose Haas pitched for him, and we won, 6-1. As we shook hands, I looked into his eyes, and they were filled with tears. That's when I really knew how much he wanted to win."

Some of the players he helped shape on the sandlots, such as Haas, made it to the majors. One, Al Kaline, was voted to the Hall of Fame, and Fowble and his wife, Virginia, were present to witness the induction. Kaline never reflected on his Baltimore baseball background without mentioning the role his early manager had played in the ultimate success he enjoyed.

But there were others, too, such as Jim Spencer, Phil Linz, Ken Biscoe, Dave Boswell, Denny Neagle, Tim Nordbrook, Rusty Gerhardt, Ron Swoboda, Carroll Moulden, Bucky Guth, Dave Hollifield, Greg Smith, Chuck Porter, Danny Welsh, Rick Senger, George Kazmarek and Haas. From 1946, when he had a team backed by High's Ice Cream Co., until last year, when it was Harbor Federal Savings & Loan, he was the dominant force in Baltimore's junior baseball program.

His wife, Virginia, who had met "Sheriff" when they were attending Western Maryland College, was attached to every team he coached. She was there as scorekeeper and statistician and caring for the young players with the same kindness and understanding as the manager — her husband of 51 years.

In 1980, 1981 and 1984, his city championship teams went on to the National Amateur Baseball Federation tournament and won the Junior World Series. But "Sheriff" Fowble (so nicknamed because his father was a Carroll County sheriff) was more than just the manager of a team that had a collection of title-winning seasons.

More importantly, he was a man who was vocal and not afraid to speak for the things he believed. Loyalty to old friends was another

Fowble characteristic. A memorial service is to be held tomorrow at Grace Methodist Church, when this citizen of stature is given a fond farewell. The crowd may want to applaud for the grand opportunity of having known him.

— —— —— —— —— —— —— —— —— ——

Burman looked Louis in eye

Feb. 20, 1991

Merely the thought of facing Joe Louis was known to induce panic. Leaving the dressing room at Madison Square Garden to travel the long aisle leading to the ring, amid the din and clamor of an impatient crowd, could tighten the emotional knot. With each step, the intimidation factor fueled an infamous case of muscular paralysis.

Louis, the "Brown Bomber," carried dynamite in his fists and had the quickness of a cat. Fifty years ago, Clarence "Red" Burman made that ominous walk and, to his everlasting credit, unlike so many other boxers before and after, couldn't wait to get there.

There was no trauma in his eyes or fright in his heart as he became the first and only Baltimore challenger to contend for the world heavyweight boxing championship. Burman was there to make a fight, not to fall over in quick surrender. "I wanted the title," he said. "That was my only thought. I trained hard, got in great shape and was there to give it my best shot because it was a once-in-a-lifetime opportunity."

Burman stayed around until 2:49 of the fifth round with Louis and never retreated. "I answered the opening bell and tried to bust him up," he said. "I think I ripped his eye. I never lost confidence. I wasn't nervous. I trained for 60 days at Madam Bay's Camp in Chatham, N.J. Road work, sparring, proper rest, watching fight movies and talking boxing all the time."

Trainers Eddie Ross and Harry "Heine" Blaustein had Burman, a pronounced slow starter, shadow-box at a rapid pace for 30 minutes in the locker room. Red was ready. As a 10-to-1 underdog, he quickly got the attention of the 18,061 spectators who recognized how intent he was to engage the champion. Not a power hitter, but a wearing, relentless workman, Burman had his strategy defined by co-managers Jack Dempsey and Max Waxman.

"Dempsey told me to make the fight, to stay right on top of him and never let up. That's exactly what I did." Louis, at 202½, had a 14 1/2-pound advantage over the Baltimore-born battler. In the third round, Louis went down and the roar was deafening. Referee Art Donovan, however, ruled it a slip, but Red insisted he had dropped him with a left to the chin.

Burman earned compliments from the press and public for a courageous effort, even if he got counted out in the fifth round. Gayle Talbot, of the Associated Press, wrote: "The big crowd saw Burman light into Louis like he never had heard of him, and continued to fight with everything he had until a final sickening right under the heart sent him down.

"That was about the round that generally had been picked for the Redhead's exit, but no one had foreseen the excitement he was to generate. He went across to throw himself at Louis before the sound of the opening bell died away and never took a backward step."

Sports editor Paul Menton, of *The Evening Sun*, offered this ringside opinion: "Let it be said that Burman made a gallant stand as long as he was able. He didn't quit as did Max Baer. He didn't run away as did Bob Pastor. He didn't attempt to hold off the champion and box as did Tommy Farr. He didn't go down with one punch as did so many of Louis' opponents."

Rodger Pippen, sports editor of the *Baltimore News-Post*, observed: "The criticism was made that Red didn't throw all his efforts into one desperate gamble early, before he had taken so many blows. Red did try, but Louis never fought a better defensive fight. He blocked at least 50 of Red's shots."

Jack Cuddy, of United Press International, described Burman as "entirely fearless, pursuing the champion — bobbing and weaving in Jack Dempsey style, the style the Old Manassa Mauler taught him."

Burman, a half-century ago, was the world's third-ranked contender behind Max Baer and Arturo Godoy. Louis, always generous, praised the game loser. "I hit him the hardest I ever hit a man. He fought with all he had. That's all you can ask a man to do, ain't it?"

Burman, now 74, hasn't been feeling his best, but isn't one to complain. He says the bout with Louis brought a measure of fame and, for that, he's eternally grateful . . . even if the champion put him down and out. "You know, there's not a night in my life I don't say a prayer for Joe. Boxing for the title, even though I lost to one of the greatest, meant a lot to me."

Clarence "Red" Burman looked the champion in the eye, never blinked, flinched or clinched. He made it a fight and created a lasting identity. It was an honorable defeat.

— · — · — · — · — · — · — · — · — · — · — · —

Young let others enjoy glory

June 3, 1991

Much about the man is measured by the profound consideration he shows for others. George Young helped create an auspicious success story for himself and the football team he represents — the New York Giants. So on this first Sunday afternoon in June, there was a party at the Baltimore Country Club that was extraordinary in its social intent.

George and his wife, the former Lovey Reddington, modestly called it a "gathering of old friends," but it was more than that. The fact the Giants won the Super Bowl was never mentioned. There wasn't any self-aggrandizement of "I did this and I did that." That's not Young. He was back in his hometown as host, reveling in the present but mostly in the past.

There were guests he had played football with in college and others he had met from his association as a high school coach, including the mayor of Baltimore, one Kurt L. Schmoke, who had once been his quarterback. And also in the reception room were scouts, agents, a team doctor, another general manager and players he once scouted for the Baltimore Colts, plus a member of the Pro Football Hall of Fame.

It was all so fitting. Young and football became synonymous. He was voted the National Football League's leading executive of 1990. But, again, that wasn't important to him because it didn't enter into the reason for being there. This was a reunion, a huddle with the past.

Young doesn't put old friends on waivers or trade them in for new ones. Included in the gathering were classmates and teammates from Calvert Hall, namely the most Rev. William Newman, bishop of Baltimore; George Thomas, Carlo Crispino, Tom Sweeney, Lou and

Joe Cerrato. They were contemporaries in high school, and their mutual fondness has perpetuated itself.

George wanted them there. On a personal note, his mother and brother were present and also close relatives, along with men he has been associated with in all facets of his life, as an athlete, teacher, coach and now general manager of the reigning champions of pro football.

It was particularly relevant that he remembered Bishop Newman, Thomas, Crispino, Sweeney and the Cerratos twin brothers, because they can't forget him. "When George was student manager of our basketball team," said the bishop, "he was such a student of the game, even though he didn't play [after all, he approached 300 pounds], he'd go out on his own to scout upcoming opponents. Imagine that from a student manager during the late 1940s in high school."

And there was Thomas, signed the night he graduated from Calvert Hall by the Philadelphia Phillies, as one of the finest pitching prospects the city ever produced. "Before games, when catchers would be warming me up," recalled Thomas, "it was helpful to have a batter stand alongside the plate. George volunteered. He had bad eyes and wore thick glasses, but wasn't afraid. I hit him once with my best fastball, and he never even went down."

Crispino thought back to when Young, a preponderant size for a pitcher, gave up a single to the leadoff man, Jack Lay of Poly, and never allowed another hit. "George had twin loves back then, baseball and, get this, wrestling. We'd go to the old Coliseum together. He liked Ali Babi and Nanjo Singh, who had the cobra hold. They were wonderful times for all of us."

The Cerratos had stories, too. "In football practice," said Lou, "I was a 135-pound guard who hated to run a play called '65 left' because I had to pull out and block the tackle, who was George. I never budged him. I was like a rubber ball hitting a wall." Brother Joe said Young had an intimidating presence. "He weighed about 298 or maybe a little over 300."

Sweeney, another ex-teammate, a retired United Air Lines pilot, brought up how George would draw plays in the classroom. "I'll never forget the Christian brother who taught us. He would look down and say, 'Never give a peasant a book.' I still don't know what that means."

But Young was oriented to education, even more than football. He has been able to keep a perspective on life. He continually reminds those trying to make more out of his career than he does, Super Bowl and all, "that football isn't essential to the overall scope of things."

Instead of throwing a party to signal his own achievements, George reversed the game plan. He merely wanted them to know how much they meant to him, as indicated by his schoolboy pals dating back more than 40 years. George Young is not the emotional or effusive type, but doesn't try to hide the impression that old friends, to him, are a precious priority.

—·—·—·—·—·—·—·—·—·—·—·—·—·—

Waibel's wins only part of success

Feb. 15, 1998

Almost 40 years of pep rallies, touchdowns and games won and lost, fulfilling the all-encompassing role of teacher, tactician, surrogate father, counselor, disciplinarian and cheerleader. August Waibel has been all of that. There were those repetitive practices into the darkness of evening and, if need be, taking a moment, while on the way to the locker room, to patiently explain to an ambitious father why his son was still running with the second team.

A pure package of sensitivity and sincerity. Kindness. Decency. Devoted to what he was doing and not inclined to embarrass a rival coach and players on the other side of the field — only to beat them, without aspiring to huge numbers on the scoreboard to satisfy an out-of-control ego. Meanwhile, he became the most successful coach in the history of Baltimore high school football with a record of 280 wins and 75 defeats.

He has retired from the football fires, and on Friday night at Marriott's Hunt Valley Inn he will be extended a commanding salute by friends, associates, former players and coaching rivals with a dinner that will attempt to portray how much he has meant to those he has met along the way. Waibel truly represents what a coach means to a boy, such virtuous qualities as trust, understanding, interest in his welfare and cooperation.

His unpretentious manner has made him easy to know and admire. For the last 31 years, he has brought pride to Baltimore Polytechnic Institute and, before that, at Edmondson High School for four seasons and, during a junior-varsity apprenticeship, at Southern High School, where he had earlier been an athlete. It was

at Southern where he was able to play for coaches Leon Horowitz, Sid Lipsch, Al Malone and Bill Anderson. He regards them as his boyhood heroes.

"They were sincere, wondered about the welfare of we kids, never put out a lot of baloney and seemed to be having fun," he said. "It was obvious they were enjoying what they were doing. I hoped when I got out of school I could do the same thing. They told us what the players could expect from them and what they expected from us. I remember Mr. Anderson saw me smoking a cigarette. I was about 15 years old. He said, 'If I see you doing that again, I'm collecting your equipment.' "

Waibel, whose father was an expediter for General Electric and for 30 years commuted to Philadelphia from their home on West Ostend Street, was recruited by the University of Maryland to play football and lacrosse. He was a member of the national championship football team in 1953 under coach Jim Tatum and made two trips to the Orange Bowl — losing to Oklahoma on both occasions. His contemporaries on those teams included the likes of Bernie Faloney, Dick Bielski, Bob Pellegrini, Frank Tamburello, Dick Nolan and Ron Waller.

What were Tatum's strengths? "His wonderful rapport with players and the way he stressed fundamentals," Waibel said. "At Maryland, he had the center call the snap count. I carried that same idea to Poly. It minimizes bad exchanges, gives a center responsibility and allows the quarterback to concentrate on calling the plays."

After Maryland, he spent 14 months with the Army in Regensburg, West Germany, and played football for the 11th Armored Cavalry, comprised, for the most part, of other college players. One day, while walking through a PX line, a woman attendant noticed his name badge and said, "With a name like August, it means you're a leader." But he brought laughter to the soldiers around him when he replied, "If that's true, then why am I still a private first class?"

Waibel, with college and the military behind him, headed toward the coaching opportunity he wanted and never looked back. He had opportunities to move to higher levels, but said: "I knew how precarious it could be to join a college coaching staff. I was married, had three children and a house mortgage. Besides, Poly was a great place for me. In college, when you don't win, even though it may not be the fault of the coaches, you get fired."

So he remained in the Baltimore public school system and never regretted the decision. Four of his players turned out to be exceptional performers in college and at the professional level, Charlie

Pittman (Penn State, St. Louis Cardinals), Greg Schaum (Michigan State, Dallas Cowboys, New England Patriots), Mike Pitts (Alabama, Atlanta Falcons, Philadelphia Eagles, Patriots) and Antonio Freeman (Virginia Tech, Green Bay Packers). But he also remembers fondly Vladimir Washington, a sturdy guard and linebacker who went to Michigan State not to play football but to excel in academics and is now a federal judge in Michigan.

"He came to Baltimore for a vacation with his family and was staying at the Cross Keys hotel, and I had a chance to tell him how proud I was for his success," Waibel said. "Football at Poly meant so much to him that a couple years ago he spent his vacation time in his hometown, watching our preseason, two-a-day practices."

One of Waibel's student managers, Keith Lai, had a 4.0 average in four years while taking Poly's demanding "A" course, and his brother, who succeeded him in the position, went on to the Massachusetts Institute of Technology. Lai never missed a practice and is now a doctor and teacher at Johns Hopkins Hospital, involved in the organ transplant program and other life-saving procedures.

Waibel succeeded Bob Lumsden, another perennial winner, in 1967 and remembers being told by him: "There are 2,500 boys at Poly, and with that many to pick from, you should win. But if you don't win, you'll hear it's your fault." Waibel carried on the tradition Lumsden created; even improved on it. Then the enrollment dropped to 1,000 and Poly became coed — almost equally divided between boys and girls. Still, his teams, with fewer to choose from, continued to win.

For most of his coaching career, he has had George "Bucky" Kimmett as an assistant. "An excellent coach who never played football," he describes him in an appreciative voice. "We were together at Edmondson High and then at Poly. He comes from a basketball and baseball background. But he knows how to devise and explain pass defenses. He's one of the finest."

Waibel believes the best team he ever faced was Brockton, Mass., which invited Poly to play there in 1988 when it had an open date. "Brockton had 5,000 students in the school, was considered a national champion at the time. We lost to them, 19-7, but were told it was a creditable showing."

For the most part, Waibel never tried to play anything but a basic offense, virtually notifying the defense that "here we come" and running straight ahead. He believes football is better today, mostly because of the things defensive linemen can do, especially the way they rush and rip their way to create penetration.

Waibel, never much for trick slogans or gimmickry, always stressed a singular message to his team: "Poly First, Me Second." He more than fulfilled his own words as a coach, exemplifying what football is all about in its purest perspective.

Chapter 5

A STORY to TELL

Twist of fate created an admiral

Dec. 4, 1986

ANNANDALE, Va. — From a posted picture of Don Whitmire in a football magazine there evolved an astonishing chain of events, signifying again how fate plays the role of a silent quarterback in every man's life.

The history of the U.S. Navy is replete with legend and lore, but it never recorded a more implausible success story than what happened to Whitmire, who went from an All-American tackle to an even greater All-American achievement — a rear admiral decorated for heroic action and leadership in behalf of his country.

Whitmire was invested with the responsibility of calling signals in the mercy evacuation of Saigon, the largest such operation ever undertaken by the United States in war or peace. And, yes, it never would have involved him had it not been for the published photograph, which is where a distinguished career had its humble origins.

To start with, it is a personal scenario, without precedent, that brought Whitmire to the attention of the Naval Academy and, ultimately, the glorious career that followed. He had been an All-American at Alabama on teams that won the 1941 Cotton Bowl and the 1942 Orange Bowl.

World War II was raging, and the Navy, besides its massive involvement, also became interested in recruiting football talent.

Standout college players who could pass the physical and academic requirements were coveted — and welcomed — by the Naval Academy.

It was also an attractive arrangement for the athletes. But almost the minute the war was over, most of those same "name" performers wanted to ease out of the obligation. And they did, conveniently returning to Notre Dame, Penn, Indiana, Arkansas, Texas and other places.

An exception to this mass defection was midshipman Donald Boone Whitmire. How he arrived at the academy came via a flash of pure luck, a dazzling smile from the goddess of destiny. It was 1943 and the annual *Street & Smith Football Yearbook* was on the stand. In an office at Annapolis, Edgar "Rip" Miller, who was in charge of locating talented players interested in becoming Naval officers, and head coach John Whelchel were discussing the upcoming season.

They were interested in the content of the magazine and stopped to view a picture of a lineman in a three-point stance who looked mean enough to play. The caption identified him as Whitmire of Alabama. At that precise instant, Miller looked up to see Bobby Tom Jenkins, a former Alabama halfback, walking past their open door. Miller yelled for Jenkins to join them.

With book in hand, Miller asked Jenkins, "Do you happen to know this fellow?" They showed him the picture. Jenkins said he not only knew Whitmire as an Alabama teammate, but he had also been his roommate until the war separated them. Jenkins related that Whitmire had entered a Marine Corps program and was assigned to the University of North Carolina.

Miller and Whelchel suggested Jenkins try to reach Whitmire, something of a long shot. "What happened was the most incredible coincidence in my life," explained the retired admiral. "There were about 200 of us Marines in a dormitory, and I got a late start this particular morning. As I went to go out the door, I knew I had to hurry. A wall telephone was ringing. I didn't know whether to answer it or not. We can all relate to something like that."

But Whitmire picked up the phone and heard the voice of Jenkins inquire if Private Whitmire was around. They had a quick long-distance reunion, and Jenkins asked if he would be interested in joining him at the Naval Academy.

The answer was in the affirmative, and, within 24 hours, after processing, Whitmire was on a train to Washington and on a bus to Annapolis, where he waited at an academy gate to be cleared for admittance. "I didn't like the Naval Academy at first," he frankly admits. "Being a plebe is rough. I thought I'd stay two years, get a degree and then tell the Navy to jam it."

But it didn't work that way, and America can be grateful for the service and dedication that followed. Whitmire was the officer appointed to direct the evacuation of Saigon in 1975, at the end of the Vietnam War, in which 82,200 men, women and children escaped to freedom. He remembers that U.S. Ambassador Graham Martin was one of the last to leave.

Over 7,000 Vietnamese came out by helicopter, the largest airlift of humanity that ever occurred. Whitmire, commanding the attack transport USS Navarro, devised ways to feed the evacuees and transport them to the Philippines and Guam, where they were dispatched to the United States.

His earlier days at the academy had prepared him well. The perception of an admiral is stereotyped. Pompous, cold and demanding ... but he's different. Whitmire remembers the first game he played for Navy. It was against Cornell in Baltimore, and he helped in a second-half onslaught that produced a 46-7 victory.

"At Navy, during the war, there was so much ability the coaches took the veteran players, who had been elsewhere, and put us on what they called the 'fifth team.' I'm sure it was difficult for them to let us come in and dominate.

"So the week after Cornell, they put us, the so-called 'fifth string,' on the 5-yard line and let the other four teams take turns running at us. We scrimmaged from 3:15 until 6:20. They never once put the ball in the end zone. None of us had ever been subjected to anything like that, but we proved to the coaches just how good we were."

Needless to say, the "fifth team" became the first team, and Whitmire went on to become a Navy All-American, winner of the Rockne Award as the best lineman in the nation. Later, he was elected to the College Football Hall of Fame.

After graduation, he was besieged by offers from the Green Bay Packers, Chicago Bears, Los Angeles Rams and Los Angeles Dons. "Curley Lambeau of the Packers and George Halas of the Bears insisted they could get me out of the service, but I decided to stay," he said.

What changed his attitude about the Navy, from negative to positive? "Well, it's quite simple and somewhat personal. But when I went back home to Decatur, Ala., to visit I found I was held in high esteem by the town folks," he said. "My parents and four brothers and sisters were proud seeing me in uniform. It made me realize there was more to life than football."

But he also agrees it's a game that does much for the making of a man. "When it's tough out there, you suck it up, reach back and do more," he said. "Of course, like with any game, the camaraderie is a pure joy." In a way, he captained a ship as though he were a coach. He says most disciplinary problems are caused by only 2 percent of the complement.

Under Whitmire, men without high-school diplomas were given a half-hour off, but had to provide the same amount of their own free time to go to the ship's library for regular study and tutoring. Then they took the equivalency exam and 12 passed.

Rules for liberty pertained to officers as well as enlisted members. He made it a policy that when a man had a birthday he be given a steak dinner and a cake, with photographs taken of friends to mark the occasion. Every month, he sent letters to wives and parents to enlighten them about what was happening aboard ship.

Christmas was an auspicious occasion. A committee of six enlisted men and two officers was delegated to buy presents out of the welfare and recreation fund. "Like if a kid was interested in photography, we'd get him packages of film," he said. "Another fellow might like to read, so they would get him a book. All the gifts were wrapped and tagged with individual names."

Just because the men were out to sea or in port was no reason to ignore holidays. "I remember once we were short of Christmas candy and put out a call," he said. "A carrier replied it was sending a helicopter with just what we needed.

"A Coast Guard ship came alongside and said its galley ovens weren't large enough to cook turkeys. So we cooked for them. We couldn't resist a bad pun — messaging how much we loved giving the Coast Guard the bird."

While engaged in Vietnam patrols, the Navarro picked up a distress call. The Habib Marikar, a merchant ship, with a Chinese and Indian crew, was floundering on a reef near the Paracel Islands. The Navarro itself was trying to avoid the fury of an approaching typhoon.

"But when the SOS came, we had to respond and head into those counterclockwise winds that accompany a typhoon," he said. "Somebody wondered, 'What if it's a communist ship?' But in a sea rescue, you don't worry about that. Lives are on the line. So you help if you can."

The Navarro turned into the front of the typhoon and, in laborious seas, located the distressed vessel. A Greek ship had arrived, but couldn't manage a rescue attempt because of the weather conditions.

"We put over two boats, called LCM6s, and officers volunteered to go along with the youngest and strongest enlisted men we had," he said. "The freighter was caught on a reef. Water was sweeping its masts.

"When we got near it, the problem was making sure our men didn't get thrown against the side of the troubled vessel. They would have been crushed. How they managed the rescue, under such conditions, was one of the most extraordinary things I have ever witnessed.

"Forty-three men were brought to safety. Only one was lost, who had fallen overboard and slipped out of his life jacket. It made me realize again what I already knew — that when an American sailor is asked to turn to and get a job done, there is no man who can surpass him."

Whitmire, from the time of graduation, served on 10 ships, including command of the Navarro and the submarines Redfish and Salmon. He also was instrumental in helping to refine and advance submarine training, which brought forth numerous commendations.

At age 64, and retired since 1977, he lives here with his wife, the former Jean Corcoran of Southport, England. They have two sons, one a Naval flyer stationed at Jacksonville, Fla., and another in the investment business in Dallas. One youngster went to the Naval Academy, the other to Alabama — which is personally fitting because they represent his civilian and military alma maters.

As to his philosophy of running a ship or a team, he says, "It's important to be fair and firm. First, you have to know what you're doing. Make men know what's expected and then let them do it. It's that basic.

"I learned from every man I ever talked with. We had a boatswain mate on the Navarro who was exceptional. I can't remember his name right now, but when he talked, I listened because I realized realized he knew his job.

"One time I found men putting some kind of lacquer on deck fittings. We stopped that. The only thing I told the crew is that everything on this ship that will shine must shine."

In studying the promotions Whitmire received, it is evident he was a highly effective and respected officer, in the finest of traditions. But had the Naval Academy not happened upon his picture in a magazine, a pure accident, the country would have missed the value he would provide later.

It led to the making of an admiral, a narrative that stands alone in the annals of sports ... and the sea.

— - — - — - — - — - — - — - — - — - —

Surviving Castro's dungeon

April 24, 1991

When Joe Prado's world came crashing down, after Fidel Castro robbed him and his family of all their possessions, he knew only one reaction: to fight oppression all the way to the finish line, even if it ended in death.

Prado was to spend nine years in Cuban prisons before getting to the United States by way of Guatemala. Now Joe is to be in Baltimore tonight for a momentous occasion. He'll be presented an award he should have received 45 years ago, when he was voted Mount St. Joseph High School's finest senior athlete, class of 1946.

His friends are excited about seeing him again. And it's that way with Joe, too. The dinner is the occasion of the school's athletic hall of fame, of which Prado will become a member. "All I got out of Cuba with was the shoes on my feet, the pants I was wearing and my high school yearbook."

Prado has all the important dates etched into his mind. It was Oct. 9, 1960, when Castro, a Communist dictator, devoured the country. "My father had immigrated to Cuba from Spain and worked, worked, worked. He saved penny-by-penny and probably had a half-million dollars. Castro took it all."

Joe, at the time, was in a sales position with the Colgate Palmolive Co., and his future was promising. Suddenly, with Castro, the dictator, Cuba was in turmoil and tears. Prado said, "I could only try to conspire against the system. I fought every way possible. I never spent two days in the same place.

"I was on the run, fighting and hiding out. Then back on the run again. I was up in the hills Jan. 21, 1961, living off anything we could find to eat, when our group was surrounded by Castro's soldiers and I was taken prisoner."

He was imprisoned on the Isle of Pines, south of Cuba, and then sent to a dungeon in Havana. Prado laughed scornfully when asked about a trial. "I was in prison three years before they had a hearing. We went to an auditorium, 804 of us. Then they picked out 21 and shot them."

Prado remembers four different hunger strikes — lasting eight, 12, 18 and 36 days. "The guards tortured us with bad beatings. It was living hell. At a time like that you evaluate yourself. You learn the honest realities of life."

He said the dark days in the dungeon had him reviewing his happy years at Mount St. Joe, where his father sent him as a boarding student in 1943. He played baseball and basketball, but it was in soccer that he excelled, leading the varsity in scoring three years and making the All-Maryland team.

The "Brother Eugene Award" was emblematic of being the best athlete in the school, but Joe graduated in an accelerated course and wasn't there for the presentation. Now, 45 years later, cheers will greet the mention of his name and friendly faces, older but sensitive to what their onetime classmate and teammate endured, will beam forth in profound respect.

Prado is now living in Miami and celebrated when he became an American citizen. His son is a pitcher at the University of Miami, where he is one of the most sought-after prospects in the country and was offered $328,000 to sign with the San Francisco Giants.

"But I don't like to brag about him," says his father. "Talk to Bernie Walter, who coached him on the U.S. Junior Olympic team. His mother and I are proud he wants to stay in college and concentrate on studies. Our house is only five minutes from the campus in Coral Gables."

Now 63, Prado is involved in a different line of work, representing an international seafood company. His mother, 93, lives in Tampa with two of his sisters. A brother, Juan, is a vice president of Bacardi International.

Joe recalls his friends at Mount St. Joe, almost as if he has never been away, and mentions coach John Plevyak, schoolmates Jack Skelly, Bucky Ward, Leo Delcher, Lou Reich, John Allen Herbert, Jim Kirchner, John Geppi, Tony Lipton, Tom Lind, Tom Healy, George Eikenberg and Lou Sleater. "Oh, the left-handed pitcher, Sleater, he became a big-leaguer. That was so wonderful."

What does being in America mean to him? With profound eloquence, he answers: "Our country is the biggest boarding house in the world. It does so much for so many. Freedom means America. Life here is so wonderful."

Joe Prado has known physical and mental torment. Bad beatings and personal indignities. But he smiles, almost as if it never happened, and savors the next breath of life.

Visiting in Baltimore with high school companions takes him back to another time — when every day was for dreaming, chasing some kind of a ball, enjoying youth to the ultimate and, fortunately, not knowing what was coming later.

From Civil War to the NFL

May 31, 1998

Because Mike Donovan died in 1918, there's no earthly way he can attend his induction into the Boxing Hall of Fame. Grandson Arthur, the first Baltimore Colt to enter the Pro Football Hall of Fame, will be his living substitute. The Donovan between them, Arthur Sr., already is in the Boxing Hall of Fame, located in Canastota, N.Y. A grand family honor. Unprecedented.

Three generations, spanning well over a century, have now achieved Hall of Fame status. All hail the Donovans. More than an accident. They're achievers, making all the rest of us believers. The genes asserted themselves.

The Donovans, endowed with amiable ways, have evidenced strong allegiance to their country, willing to stand up and fight for it, a fact thoroughly documented. Grandfather Mike enlisted in the Union Army at age 14, an orphan, and fought throughout the Civil War; Arthur Sr. was in the Mexican War and World War I in France with an Army field artillery unit, then was commissioned by the Merchant Marine (at age 51) in World War II; son Art was with the Third Marine Division in the Pacific during the same war.

Art, the Donovan who was to make his reputation in football and wasn't interested in boxing, still holds the massive silver championship belt presented to grandfather Mike by his admirers in San Francisco in 1878 when he was the middleweight titleholder.

Also, the two medals awarded his grandfather for service in the Civil War, in which he was in heavy combat and a member of Gen. William Tecumseh Sherman's army during the "march to the sea."

Asked to discuss his impressive lineage, Art said: "The reason I never talked much about my grandfather is I didn't want to sound as though I was bragging or spreading lies. But, my hand to God, he had to be a tremendous man. Now tell me how in hell did he ever get to Cheyenne, Wyo., in 1868 to fight a bout refereed by Wyatt Earp. You could say he didn't drink much, or nothing at all, which I guess makes him different from my father and me."

Grandfather Mike's Civil War experience typified the Irish immigrants' love for their adopted country, because more than 170,000 of them fought as volunteers for the federal cause. They didn't want to see their new country split.

Mike instructed both John L. Sullivan and Gentleman Jim Corbett at various points in their boxing careers. He was a second in the corner of Jake Kilrain when Kilrain opposed Sullivan in Richburg, Miss., in 1889, last of the bare-knuckle fights. Kilrain lost in the 75th round when, taking a brutal beating, Donovan threw in the sponge to end the mauling.

After the war — we're still talking Civil War — Donovan made his boxing debut in 1866 in St. Louis against Billy Crowley. The bout lasted 92 rounds, or 3 hours, 15 minutes, before Mike lost on a foul.

A clever mover, feinter and counterpuncher, he was known as "Mike the Master." Although outweighed by 30 pounds, he twice met Sullivan. One bout was called an exhibition, the other a draw. But Donovan used skill against power, finesse against muscle.

Donovan was close with President Theodore Roosevelt. He instructed Roosevelt in boxing when he was police commissioner of New York, then governor and, finally, president. Art has the original copies of White House invitations from Roosevelt to his grandfather.

The night before his inauguration in 1904, the president-to-be said he needed a workout and sparred with Donovan for 10 rounds. When, the next day, Roosevelt was having difficulty getting into his tuxedo for the ceremony, it was Donovan who came to his rescue and provided assistance.

The president, talking about Donovan, was quoted as saying: "I got to know him well, both when I was governor and while I was president, and many a time he came and boxed with me. Mike is a devoted temperance man and can be relied upon for every movement in the interest of good citizenship."

Indeed, Roosevelt thought so much of Donovan he had him teach boxing to his sons. Later, Donovan wrote his second book, which ran 234 pages, titled, "The Roosevelt That I Know."

Sixteen years before, his first book, "The Science of Boxing," was hailed the world over as the best technical explanation the game had yet been given. George Siler, sporting editor of the *Chicago Globe*, wrote: "I say, without any reserve, it is the best book ever published on the science of the manly art. The descriptions of blows, guards, feints, ducks, are complete, accurate, and yet so brief as to be easily remembered."

The grandfather, then known as Professor Mike Donovan, served 35 years as boxing instructor at the New York Athletic Club, a preserve for dignitaries and the swells of society. The sport then carried a special dignity. Rich men, including members of famous Wall Street firms, were more inclined to box than play golf or tennis.

When Donovan No. 1 retired, he turned the athletic club position over to his son, Arthur, who remained there for 50 years. Meanwhile, Arthur enjoyed a reputation as perhaps the most respected referee in history.

He officiated more than 30 championship fights, 12 involving Joe Louis, and was called by Joe Williams, sports editor of the *New York World Telegram*, "the best and most honest man in the business." Donovan, reviewing the duties of a referee, said: "He must know the rules by instinct. And when the rules don't apply, he must be fair above all else."

Donovan was strong in the ring, moving fighters around and breaking clinches, staying in total control. He was in exceptional physical shape, due to the fact that he was in the gym every day boxing with students, the same as his father before him.

To young Arthur, there was no interest in the game, "but a lot of times on Saturdays I'd accompany my father when he would go to the homes of wealthy men in Westchester County or out on Long Island to teach them and their sons how to box.

"When I was a Marine, at Parris Island, I was picked to fight at a Friday night boxing show. The captain said I had to represent our regiment. I took on 'Big Stoop,' who had a reputation as being one of the toughest men at Parris Island. He was from Minnesota. I was so scared, I wet my pants before the bell rang.

"Here comes 'Big Stoop,' and I couldn't believe it. He held up his hands like a girl. I busted him a couple and he went down. The Marines were screaming. I got carried away and went over and gave him a good kick. They screamed some more. The Marines had me brainwashed. They said one Marine was the equal of three soldiers. I tried that once and just about got killed."

The Donovans, capped by Mike, have made a lasting impression on American sports. Three generations and one from each time period gathering Hall of Fame acclaim. A glorious past.

Chapter 6

Unbowed
SPIRITS

'Judy' Johnson: 4 games and a day

Sept. 26, 1986

WILMINGTON, Del. — Playing a triple-header, or even four games in one day, became an occupational demand that William "Judy" Johnson, member of the Baseball Hall of Fame, accepted without complaint because, realistically, he couldn't change the mood of the world.

Johnson, a consummate third baseman in the pioneering period of black professional baseball, endured the second-class treatment that went with the social circumstances of those demanding and demeaning years. He remains Maryland's only black native to qualify for the Hall of Fame but, more importantly, stands as a splendid citizen in all ways a man can be measured.

Much of what Judy, now 86, uses for a working philosophy can be found inscribed on a decorative plaque displayed inside the entrance to his house. It reads: "A Wishbone Ain't As Likely To Get Ye Someplace As A Backhoe."

Born in 1899 in Snow Hill, in Worcester County, he moved to Wilmington, Del., because his father shipped out of the port as a seaman on a freighter. Young Judy's innate and maturing ability as a baseball player later found him playing for such leading teams as Hilldale (maybe the only club in the Negro leagues not to have a nickname), the Homestead Grays and Pittsburgh Crawfords.

The competition was often so cruel and intense that sliding base runners deliberately cut infielders with their spikes. That's when John Henry "Pop" Lloyd, a manager of high esteem, advised Johnson to wear a pair of catcher's shinguards to protect his legs while covering the bag on plays at third base.

Johnson had the distinction of participating in the first Negro World

Series, a nine-game marathon, in 1923 between Hilldale of Philadelphia and the Kansas City Monarchs.

Being a player in the struggling Negro leagues was a life of constant turmoil and travel, much like that of an itinerant worker. It meant accepting the racial indignities that mirrored the travail of the times. There was little remuneration. Johnson and his colleagues realized there was no reason to protest because baseball, for them, wasn't going to get any easier, so they made the best of the conditions that prevailed.

Judy was a teammate of such talented performers as Leroy "Satchel" Paige, Josh Gibson, Oscar Charleston and James Thomas Bell, the celebrated "Cool Papa" who was said to be so fast he could turn off a light switch and be in bed before the room went dark. They are among the leading characters from a rather primitive past that represents misery and pain but a measuring of redeeming fun, too.

They arranged games anywhere a date could be booked and, in winter, went to Cuba and Mexico to play. It was migratory existence, compounded with low pay and horrendous living conditions. Frequently, they would play a morning game in one city, a double-header in the afternoon somewhere else and then at night be in an entirely different community — and never change uniforms.

"The only places we could usually find to stay on the road would be private homes," says Johnson. "Some were clean, but too many were filthy. I remember if you tried to sleep, the bedbugs ate you alive. You could hear them coming up the walls. Otto Briggs, my roommate, finally found a way to keep them out of bed. Sleep on newspapers. It worked."

Travel was difficult because of the problems encountered in the South. Restaurants and hotels made it clear they were closed to blacks. So were some of the service stations, where they couldn't even buy a tank of gas.

"Yeah, I remember riding from Pittsburgh to Hot Springs, Ark., without sleeping in a bed," says Johnson. "We had two Cadillacs with nine players in a car, and all our equipment tied on the sides and overhead on the roof.

"You couldn't use restrooms or go into decent eating places. We went into a filling station to get gas for the car. There were three pumps, but the employees just looked at each other and laughed. Then they ignored us."

He remembers a time when they broke down alongside a country road. There was a corn crop in a nearby field, so Johnson and some of his companions picked a few ears and started to roast them over a fire while they tried to repair the car's mechanical problem. What happened next?

"Well, this farmer who owned the land shows up with a shotgun and trains it on us. We figured he'd start firing. The only thing that saved us was he was a Masonic member and we had three Masons on our team."

Paige was the leading box-office draw. He had superb ability and was a natural showman. "Easily the best I ever saw," says Judy. "He carried two or three fishing rods on top of his car. If he went by a stream, he would stop to see if the fish were jumping.

"He didn't always make it to the game on time. You could go to bed at night, but you never knew where he was going to be by morning. That 'hesitation' pitch he later threw in the American League was a balk, but he got away with it in the Negro leagues."

It remained for Jackie Robinson to be the first American Negro to break the stiff barriers of major-league prejudice in 1947 when he joined the Brooklyn Dodgers. Earlier attempts had been made to give Negroes fictitious Indian names in schemes to have them admitted to the white leagues but the clandestine efforts failed.

"There were several ballplayers with more natural skills who could have been chosen ahead of Robinson," says Johnson, "but Jackie had been a college boy. He knew what to do and say. I never dreamed the white leagues would ever open up."

Johnson comments that his most memorable moments came in postseason exhibitions when the best of the Negro leagues faced similarly recruited players from the prestigious white establishment ... Rogers Hornsby, Jimmie Foxx, Babe Ruth and Dizzy Dean. They weren't official all-star confrontations, but it was at least an informal chance for the blacks to test their skills against their more celebrated baseball brethren.

"Playing against the best white players and beating them more often than not was a thrill," says Johnson. "It was the only way to tell if we were better or they were better. They liked playing us because the games drew crowds, usually after the World Series, and we all made good money."

A contemporary Hall of Famer, the inimitable "Cool Papa" Bell, talks of Johnson in the fondest of terms: "Judy could adapt to any situation and did whatever was best for the team. He was a great hitter, a smooth third baseman and smart as a whip. When you become manager of the finest team in the Negro leagues, the Homestead Grays, at age 29, then you're doing something special, and Judy did that. He always got the job done."

Johnson, living not far from Philadelphia, developed a friendship

*...those who followed
received equal
opportunity in a
sport where
horizons have broadened
and the only
measure of failure
is to be found
in the
black-and-white
truth of the box score...*

with Connie Mack, the owner of the A's, before they defected to Kansas City and on to Oakland. He scouted for the A's and later the Phils, when Bob Carpenter owned the team.

"Mr. Mack liked me for some reason. He was a wonderful gentleman," remembers Judy. "We had lunch together many times. When I was playing, he told me, 'Judy, if you were white, you'd be on my team.' "

That was an era when blacks, even as paying spectators, weren't welcome in some parks and frequently had to watch from a pavilion marked "Colored Only." It is a sad, regrettable chapter in the history of the national pastime.

Johnson also gave Carpenter, former owner of the Phillies, rich respect. "The Carpenters, Bob and son Ruly, were great to me. I liked working for them. If you were a pitcher and could throw hard, then you could play for Bob. After the Carpenters sold the club, I never got notified by the new owners. They just let me go by not even writing or calling me."

Lining the walls of Johnson's enclosed sitting room in his home located in a quiet neighborhood outside Willmington is a gallery of pictures that highlight his career: Judy with the Homestead Grays; Judy with the Pittsburgh Crawfords; Judy being honored at banquets; Judy on the honoree's platform at the Hall of Fame; Judy visiting President Reagan at the White House.

The only single portrait — significantly — in the personal collage is of a white man, John Ogden, once a pitcher and general manager of the Baltimore Orioles of the International League. Ogden scouted for the Phils, and Johnson was usually his associate and travelling companion.

"John was the best friend I ever had," says Johnson. "He exploded when something displeased him, but I could calm him down. I'd say, 'Now, John, don't say those things.' And he'd settle back and fill up. Then, when he looked at me, a tear might be in his eye."

It was the double-team scouting effectiveness of Ogden and Johnson that got Dick Allen's name on a Phils contract. "The night he graduated from high school, I took him out the back door of the auditorium while the other scouts, from every club in the majors, were waiting in the lobby," Johnson recalls.

"How I talked to that boy. I went crazy lecturing him — day and night. His mother was wonderful. A dream. I told him to stay away from the wrong kind of people, and he would answer, 'Yes, Mr. Johnson,' but go right out with the same no-gooders I told him to stay away from.

"He was great, but he could have been even better. I never saw a player with more natural ability. He would snap his wrists and the ball would come off the bat like it was a cannon shot."

Johnson managed the Pittsburgh Crawfords when Josh Gibson, endowed with awesome batting power, joined them. He was recruited out of the grandstand, according to Judy, when the team needed a catcher.

"He was the best hitter, white or black, that I ever saw," Johnson says now. "When you say Josh, you've said it all. There is no comparison to anybody, including Ruth, Foxx and Henry Aaron."

How about Ty Cobb? "Well, you got to remember Cobb wouldn't play against any of us blacks." An obvious case of bias, but there wasn't anything Johnson and the rest could do about it. Back to Josh Gibson ...

"I made Josh a catcher. He wasn't too good, just adequate, but mighty strong. I took him out of the stands and had our other catcher go to the locker room and give his suit to Josh. I always felt he ought to be an outfielder to protect him from getting hurt."

Three times during this reporter's visit, Johnson was asked to recall his top salary in Negro baseball. He ignored the question almost as if he didn't hear it. Perhaps it would have been embarrassing to answer.

From other sources of research, however, it is learned Judy played for the Bacharach Giants for $5 a game in 1918. He then served two seasons with the Madison Stars of Philadelphia before being sold to the Hilldale club for $100. His contract called for $150 a month, but later, by the then-prevailing baseball standards, of $500 per month.

That the Hall of Fame in Cooperstown named him the sixth performer from the Negro leagues to be enshrined is testimony to his talents. It's unfortunate that the deeds of the Negro athletes are poorly documented. Record-keeping, so vital to baseball, was, at best in those days, slipshod.

The Negro National League and the Negro American League rarely played more than 70-game schedules, but were involved in what seemed to be endless barnstorming trips about the country — meeting each other on occasion but often matching up against "local yokels."

When it came to enroll the likes of Gibson, Paige, Bell, Johnson and others in the Hall of Fame, their reputations, rather than records, which were grossly incomplete, had to be relied upon as an important element for acceptance.

Johnson is deeply thankful and believes most of the deserving standouts from the Negro leagues have been included. But, among those still outside looking in, there is a player he does think belongs — one Ray Dandridge. "This boy Dandridge, an infielder, is deserving," says Johnson. "And one more is Chino Smith, who played for the

Brooklyn Royals. He could mash the ball."

Johnson's closest neighbor today is a white man, Albert Langshore, who lives next door. "If he was my own son, he couldn't treat me any better," lauds Judy. "I've had two heart attacks, and the doctor won't even let me cut the grass. But my friend looks out for me all the time."

Judy and his late wife moved to the residence in 1933. Their only daughter, Loretta, married Bill Bruton, former major-league out-fielder, and lives in Detroit. Johnson has no close family nearby.

He's perturbed by the attitude of modern athletes. "Women and liquor, now drugs, get the best of them," he says. "White players do the same. Pitchers can't pitch nine innings to save themselves. It used to be if a pitcher got three day's rest he was lucky. And the platoon plan is a lot of hooey."

Johnson has seen extensive growth in the game he played so exceptionally well for a mere pittance. He's growing old, but has a vibrancy that is infectious. It takes a cloudy day, a succession of them, for him to complain or alter his spirit and outlook.

It's just that he remembers when baseball for the black player was a series of one-night stands, sometimes three and four games on a Sunday or holiday. Little recognition. Minute paychecks. Poor lights. Bad fields.

Yet he's not bitter. To the contrary, he remains forever grateful over the changes, because it means those who followed received equal opportunity in a sport where horizons have broadened and the only measure of failure is to be found in the black-and-white truth of the box score.

Pete Gray beat his handicap

Oct. 1, 1995

NANTICOKE, Pa. — That a one-armed man could play in base-ball's major leagues stands as one of the most astonishing achieve-ments in all the history of sports. It was a half-century ago, with World War II coming to an end, that Pete Gray played for the St. Louis

Browns and, since then, has preferred to fade into the background, resisting most attempts to talk about the experience.

He's reclusive and gives the impression that even the smallest interest in him must be based on some kind of one-man "freak show" curiosity. His days are almost all the same, visiting a restaurant for morning coffee, sitting a spell in Patriot's Square, stopping by the Town Tavern operated by a cousin, Bertha Vedor, and picking up his mail.

Pete is 80 but doesn't look it. He's as slender as a fungo bat. Walks with a fast-paced, almost nervous stride, as if at all times he's in a hurry to get some place for an important appointment. He never married, lives in the same house where he was born and doesn't have a telephone.

When sportswriters call friends to intercede for interviews, he says, "Tell them I'm out of town." Or he might explain he isn't available in summer or during the winter, depending upon the season of the year. It's all an excuse.

Obviously, celebrity status has made him uncomfortable. He protects his privacy by being elusive. No doubt, he has been wounded by previous meetings with reporters, so, as personal policy, prefers to reject all requests.

We sat on a bench in Patriot's Square with Gray and Mayor Wasil Kobella and, once Gray began to reminisce, the stories of his boyhood and entrance into professional baseball came with a rapidity that belied an earlier reluctance to talk about himself. Nanticoke, with close proximity to Wilkes-Barre, had a population of 38,000 in the mid-1930s, when Pete was growing into manhood.

Now, with the coal mines, cigar factory and silk mill all memories of the past, Nanticoke has lost many of its once basic employment opportunities. The last census showed a total of 12,267 residents, predominantly Ukrainian and Russian, according to the mayor, and the community is 70 percent Catholic. Gray is of Lithuanian ancestry; his real name is Peter Wyshner.

The city has a cleanliness and order to it that makes it immediately attractive. It was here that Pete Gray grew up in the rolling greenery of Luzerne County, where men going underground to work in the mines always faced the inherent danger of losing their lives.

Nanticoke is where at age 6 he jumped off the running board of a vegetable truck, owned by a huckster who was allowing Pete to make deliveries for pocket change, and an accident occurred that changed his life.

When he fell to the ground, his right arm was caught in the spokes of the wheel and almost torn from his body. Amputation was necessary. "I don't remember," he said, "but my brother Tony always said I was a natural right-hander, that I held a pencil and fork that way. So I had to become a left-handed ballplayer."

This makes what Pete was to achieve later even more remarkable. By necessity, he changed over to bat and throw with his left hand, the only one he had. With one arm he had to devise a system to play the outfield.

He caught the ball in his glove, pushed the glove under the stump of his right arm, let the ball roll across his body, grasped it in his bare hand and made the throw — all in a split-second motion.

The glove, now on display at the Baseball Hall of Fame in Cooperstown, N.Y., was given to him by an undertaker who lived in nearby Hanover. "I took out all the padding," he explained. "I went to a shoemaker who put a piece of stiff leather on one side of the glove that gave it firmness. When the ball hit the glove, it kind of closed."

At the plate, he batted from the left side and held the bat in his left hand. His reputation as a young player became established in the Wilkes-Barre area and led to his joining Three-Rivers of the Canadian-American League in 1942, where he batted .381 in 42 games. The surprised owner didn't know he was getting a one-armed player but, because Pete had made the trip, decided to give him a chance.

"You could hear a pin drop when I came up the first time," recalls Gray. "They announced my name in French and English. The bases were loaded in the ninth inning, a tied game. I hit a line drive on a 1-1 count and we won, 2-1. The fans took up a collection. They gave me $850."

He once had what he thought was an opportunity to go to Philadelphia for a tryout with the A's. He entered the club office at then-Shibe Park but, while waiting to see owner-manager Connie Mack, met his son, Roy.

"Where's the kid we are supposed to look at?" asked Roy. He was stunned to learn that the prospect was standing there in front of him, a one-armed man. "I was told then that Connie was busy and couldn't waste his time seeing me," remembers Gray.

Mack was quoted as saying he had enough trouble finding capable players with two arms and didn't see any future for a one-armed candidate. In 1944, Mack finally met Gray when the Philadelphia Sportswriters Association honored him as the "most courageous athlete of the year."

Mack, talking to Gray, said, "There was a one-armed fellow one time who wanted a tryout. Are you the same boy?" Gray, of course, answered in the affirmative. The next year, Gray particularly enjoyed dominating a series when the Browns beat the A's in St.

Louis and Connie, the rival manager, was there to watch him do it.

Another similar incident happened in Miami, where the other Philadelphia team, the Phillies, was in training camp in 1940: "All I wanted was for manager Doc Prothro to look at me. I went down to the field and asked him to let me work out. He said, 'Get off the field, Wingy, or I'll have the police come get you.'"

That scenario had a similar postscript, too. In 1944, he played for the same Prothro when they were together at Memphis in the Southern Association, where this one-armed marvel batted .333 and led in stolen bases with 68.

He won the league's most valuable player award, and his contract was sold to the St. Louis Browns.

Gray, by his performance, made Prothro revise his opinion. The Memphis manager, after seeing what he could do, said, "The majors are in for a big surprise. They'll be amazed to find out a fellow with just a left arm can do things better than a lot of two-armed guys around. I'm sure he'll stick." Remember, a war was on and baseball rosters had been depleted.

Gray batted only .218 with the Browns in 1945. The most impressive thing was that in 234 at-bats he struck out only 11 times. "Fastball pitchers never bothered me," he said. "I was weaker on change-ups."

The reason is that once he began to offer at a pitch he couldn't "stop the bat" because he didn't have two hands to use as a brake. With only one hand, off-speed deliveries had him out in front and vulnerable with little to hit with.

The 1945 Browns were defending champions and had a chance to win again. Some teammates were critical, saying that rival clubs were taking an extra base on balls hit to Gray in center field.

"That's the way I remember it," said Irv Hall, who played for the A's. "But let me tell you, it was amazing what he could do. Infielders knew they couldn't make a mistake on any ball he hit, because we all found out how fast he could run."

Another surprising thing is that Pete used a 36-ounce bat, heavier than most players were swinging then and now. He was doing it all with one hand. About the only thing he couldn't do was tie his baseball shoes, so a coach or another player had to assist him.

His reputation was of a tough hombre, who could fight effectively with one arm if he had to, and that he was distant in personal relationships. We once asked a Browns coach, Zack Taylor, if it was true that Pete was a "mean SOB."

Taylor answered, "Let me put it this way. To play in the big leagues with one arm, you better had be a mean SOB."

Bob Feller, Hall of Fame pitcher, says Gray provided "an enormous emotional lift for wounded veterans coming home from World War II who saw what honest-to-God determination could do."

Gray made $5,500 with the Browns, but remembers that Bill DeWitt, a team official, gave him a bonus of $1,500.

The saga of Pete Gray, 50 years from his emergence in the majors, is intriguing and exciting. He's an everlasting credit to the human spirit, a man who sits on a park bench with his memories and only rarely shares them with others.

Chapter 7

HISTORY MAKERS

Earl Banks joins coaching elite

Jan. 17, 1992

Dealing in honesty, never deception, Earl Banks has chosen to live the way he played and coached football. Direct. Head on. No hypocrisy or trickery. Fair and equitable. Every man, black, white or polka dot, got the same treatment.

The College Football Hall of Fame, aware of his extraordinary abilities and citizenship, reviewed the record, examined personal achievements and voted to elevate him to a place among the all-time coaching elite.

So Banks is to be included in the same regal assemblage that lists among its honor roll the names of Knute Rockne, Amos Alonzo Stagg, Frank Leahy, Bob Zuppke, Jim Tatum, Dick Harlow, Earl "Red" Blaik, Dr. Eddie Anderson (his coach in college) and 106 others dating back to the inception of football more than a century ago. Or, to put it another way, they are with him.

In this momentous moment of elation, Banks was thinking of two men — both white and Jewish — who shaped his future and, without them, isn't sure he would have found his way in life. There was Leonard Sachs, coach of Wendell Phillips High School in Chicago; and the owner of a drug store, Jack Luvin, in Iowa City, Iowa. Both were there when he needed them in an important bygone era, and the impressions they made are still with him.

"What Leonard Sachs did for me led to how I coached," he said. "He was white and coaching an all-black school. But he taught us respect. He told us about hurdles in life and you had to get over them. Nothing worthwhile is easy. It's not the offense or defense but the work a team puts into it. I always told my Morgan squads not to expect any magic plays from me."

Yes, but what else did Sachs do and what made him the coach he was? "He had played for the Chicago Cardinals in the National Football League in the 1920s. An unusual thing, he coached us in football and then in basketball season coached Loyola University," Banks recalled. "But he taught us discipline and good conduct. If he saw a kid with a cap on in the hallway at school, he'd knock it off his head. And to do that to a black guy usually meant war, but not with Coach Sachs. We knew he was teaching us to respect ourselves and other people, too."

And then there was Jack Luvin, who had a drug store near the Iowa campus, where Banks enrolled in 1946 after service in the Army. Earl was the only black on the team and decided it wasn't the place to be. "I used to go in this drugstore for a soda and stand around reading the newspapers and magazines for free and then put them back in the rack.

"At Iowa in practice they told us to pair off in blocking drills. But I was left alone. None of the players were interested. I figured I can't handle this. So I told Jack when I went in the store I was packing to go home. He told me, 'Well, they've been playing football at Iowa for almost 100 years and what'll be said about you is you couldn't take it.' So I went back and stayed and earned my way on the varsity."

Banks grew up in Chicago with his high school classmate and team-mate, the late Claude "Buddy" Young, who preceded him into the College Football Hall of Fame in 1968 as a player after an extraordinary career at Illinois. They were inseparable. "Growing up, Earl lived in what could be called the 'High Ghetto,' and I was in the 'Low Ghetto,'" Young used to say.

In fact, it was Young, who interceded and went calling on Dr. Martin Jenkins, then the president of Morgan State University, and told him that Banks, who was an assistant at Maryland State College, was available and would make an ideal successor to the retiring Ed Hurt. That was the way it evolved, as Banks proceeded to earn distinction for himself and Morgan over the next 14 years — showing a winning record in each of those seasons.

As a poetic and personal twist, Banks and Young were picked on the 1943 Illinois All-State High School team by Pat Harmon, sports editor of the *Champaign* (Ill.) *News Gazette*. Now Harmon is curator of the College Football Hall of Fame, in Kings Island, Ohio, and yesterday was the man who announced Banks had received the highest honor that can come to a college coach.

But how did Banks get from Chicago to Maryland State, in Princess Anne, Md., where he was a line coach? "That happened because Dr. John T. Williams, the school president, had been at Kentucky State and had tried to recruit me. When I got to Princess Anne, I couldn't believe it. A lot of students camped out. Buildings were old. The dining room had a pot-bellied stove. I had never seen anything like it. This was 1950 and segregation was a problem, but you had to hurdle it. You know, I learned to love Maryland State. I cried when I left there."

At Morgan, he put up a career mark of 96-31-2, had a 31-game winning streak, won the Orange Blossom Classic in 1965 and the Tangerine Bowl in 1966. Thirty-six of his players at Maryland State and Morgan went into pro football, and one of them, Willie Lanier, is in the Pro Football Hall of Fame and at least one other, Leroy Kelly, will eventually get there, too.

Banks is only the second black coach (Jake Gaither of Florida A&M was the first) to make the College Football Hall of Fame. It's necessary to be retired from the game before a candidate can be elected. In retrospect, what has football done for Earl Banks?

"I like to think it made me a better man," he answered. So a tough sport has a walking, talking, animated billboard proclaiming, with a touch of tenderness, its virtues by a coach who gave players lessons on the field that led to working toward whatever goal line they wanted to reach.

Integration too late for Leon Day

Feb. 3, 1992

Now the mood is sympathetic, generally followed with words of remorse, to Leon Day and the legion of black baseball players who had the ponderous doors of prejudice slammed in their faces before R&R (Rickey and Robinson). Branch Rickey, owner of the Brooklyn Dodgers and the game's emancipator, signed Jackie Robinson as the first black to a major-league contract.

In tandem, they, in 1945, changed an all-white establishment to a sport where it wasn't the color of a man's skin that was important but how well he got around on the fastball or fought off a sliding runner.

Leon Day, now 75 and living in Baltimore, doesn't look back too often and, when he does, it's not accompanied by regret. That's left for his friends. Besides, a man can't change the past — certainly not the social structure of a half-century ago — so why try? But he admits there are moments when he wonders how it might have been if he could have pitched against Babe Ruth, Jimmie Foxx, Hack Wilson and all the rest of the pre-eminent white standouts.

It's Day's belief, measuring ability, that Josh Gibson, a fair catcher who he says might have hit 100 home runs in a season if he had had the opportunity, or infielder John Beckwith could have presumably preceded Robinson in breaking the color line.

"I never saw Jackie with the Kansas City Monarchs," says Day, but he respects Robinson for his achievements, along with fighting the demeaning racial abuse that accompanied his role as a pioneer.

Day's days in the Negro National League were bracketed between the years 1934 and 1949 with the Baltimore Black Sox, Newark Eagles and Baltimore Elite Giants. In 1947, he went off to pitch in Mexico, where he made his highest salary, $5,000. It was a time when major-league "jumpers" Danny Gardella, Sal Maglie, Mickey Owen, Freddie Martin and others, all white, bolted their teams because they, too, decided more money could be made outside the country.

An effort to substantiate Day's record by historians has led to frustration and inadequate totals, but the mission continues. In only 11 of the 22 years he pitched, his mark is 63-26, a winning percentage of .708, 667 innings, 442 hits, 256 strikeouts and 142 bases on balls. Day knows that's not right, and researchers readily agree it's incomplete.

"I couldn't tell you," he says, "but I think I won around 300." That's because Negro teams played league schedules that rarely exceeded 60 games a season, but barnstormed the country, playing semi-pro competition or independent town teams. Just anywhere they might draw a crowd and, most of the time, the results never made the sports pages of metropolitan newspapers.

Traveling conditions were abysmal. Often, they changed to their uniforms in an old bus that had long seen its best days and got back on, after nine innings, to hit the highway for another game later that day or night.

"A lot of times, we didn't have a hotel or a rooming house, so we just slept on the bus," Day recalled. "I started out getting 75 cents a day meal money, then $1 and the highest was $2 when I was with the Newark Eagles."

In 1944 and 1945, Day was in the Army, attached to an amphibious unit that landed at Normandy (D-Day, plus six) and carried supplies to the forces. "I was scared as hell," he comments. "I'll never forget June 12. I lost a lot of good friends."

When World War II was over in Europe, Day pitched for the Third

Army team and twice beat Ewell Blackwell, the whiplike Cincinnati Reds right-hander, 2-1, in Nuremberg, and 8-0, at Marseille, before a combined audience of 150,000 servicemen and women.

Both Monte Irvin, a Hall of Fame member, and Larry Doby, the first black to play in the American League, put Day in a special category. Both compare him favorably to Bob Gibson, a powerful winner with the St. Louis Cardinals.

"Leon was fantastic," says Irvin.

Doby adds, "I didn't see anybody in the major leagues better than Leon Day."

Todd Bolton, a ranger at Harpers Ferry National Historical Park, who is a member of the Society of American Baseball Research, says, "My guess is Leon won 300 games or close to it, because only about a third of the box scores of all the games he played in have been located."

To see that Day be given proper attention during Black History Month, it was significant that Mayor Kurt L. Schmoke honored him with a special proclamation. Dr. Bob Hieronimus and wife Zoh gathered friends together to add luster to the occasion and to present Day with a copy of the baseball shirt he wore when he was pitching for the Newark Eagles.

Day holds the distinction of playing in more Negro league all-star games than any other player, seven, and establishing a strikeout record of 14. He had a single-game strikeout high of 19 in the Puerto Rican Winter League and once he struck out 18 Baltimore Elite Giants, including Roy Campanella three times.

In 1942 and '43, the *Pittsburgh Courier* ranked him ahead of Leroy "Satchel" Paige as the best pitcher in the Negro leagues.

When Day came home from the Army, his first effort produced a no-hitter against the Philadelphia Stars but, unfortunately, he injured his arm when he slipped after fielding a swinging bunt and made an off-balance throw. He pitched in the summer in the United States and, come winter, usually went to Cuba, Puerto Rico, Mexico or Venezuela.

That was the lot of the black baseball player, to endeavor to play 12 months of the year. Day didn't sign with organized baseball until 1951 when, at age 35, he went with the Toronto Maple Leafs of the International League and posted a 1.58 ERA in 40 innings. He stayed around four more years, pitching for Scranton in the Eastern League, Edmonton in the Western League and Winnipeg and Brandon in the Canadian League.

"I remember going to Puerto Rico, and Satchel Paige was happy with himself over having a bat 38 inches long," recalls Leon. "He had it especially made. Satch was going to use it to hit wide breaking curveballs. But, wouldn't you know, the first time he used it, he broke it."

Leon Day doesn't grumble over opportunities lost because he was born black and couldn't, in a bygone era, measure his abilities on the field of fair play against those of the white baseball player. It's a career that when measured from any perspective deserves accreditation and applause.

— —— —— —— —— —— —— —— ——

Jeannette paid dues and more

Feb. 9, 1994

He came to professional basketball when it was primitive, played in dance halls, skating rinks, auditoriums and smoked-filled arenas not much larger than oversized cigar boxes.

Harry "Buddy" Jeannette hoped to be a high school history teacher when he came out of Washington & Jefferson College, but the lure of the bouncing ball and the promise of being able to make $25 a game offered what to him was an irresistible opportunity.

Jeannette never again saw the inside of a classroom. The job he sought was filled by another applicant in Claysville, Pa., so basketball became his professional calling. The imprint he made and the sterling accomplishments led to his selection yesterday to the Basketball Hall of Fame, where he'll be enshrined in formal ceremonies May 9 at the Springfield (Mass.) Civic Center.

His name was first suggested to the committee in 1976 by Seymour Smith, the widely respected basketball historian and now-retired assistant sports editor of *The Sun*. It's a sport that's crowded with talent at every level of play, making it difficult for nominees to gain attention and sufficient support in the ballot box.

The wait for Jeannette, as it has been for others, is merely a belated affirmation of exceptional ability that made him respected by teammates and adversaries. Jeannette was called "Mr. Basketball" in Baltimore.

He played and coached the Baltimore Bullets to their first title in 1946 when his team won the American Basketball League and then, the following season, repeated in the Basketball Association of

America, forerunner to the present National Basketball Association. Jeannette, now 76, was an inspirational leader who wanted the ball when the game was in the balance. He had an accurate set shot and was a clever driver, one who could penetrate to the inside and, when he did, maneuver underneath either to score the field goal or draw a foul.

He came up in the game when the style was "give and go," pick and pass, hit the pivot man and drive off his hip, either getting the ball back or setting up to battle for the rebound. Jeannette was smart, smooth, a stylish playmaker who handled the ball with precision, dictated the pace of the game and rarely took a bad shot.

"Buddy was the guy who could beat you when the game counted," said Red Holzman, who preceded Jeannette in the Hall of Fame by eight years. "I know all about his ability. I had to play against him."

Jeannette, working out of the backcourt, made few mistakes. He won four Most Valuable Player awards, three in the National Basketball League and another in the American Basketball League. In what used to be called the World Championship in Chicago, involving such powerful contenders as the Harlem Globetrotters (when they played straight), New York Rens, Fort Wayne Pistons and Sheboygan Redskins, the outstanding player award twice went to Jeannette.

After being notified by the Hall of Fame yesterday, the first person Buddy called was Smith, who had trumpeted the Jeannette cause for 18 years. It was as much a pleasure for Smith as it was for Jeannette. Now all seems right with the world.

"Buddy used to say it didn't make much difference if he ever made the Hall of Fame," said Smith. "He never campaigned for it. But when he got the news, he was ecstatic. Four of his contemporaries — Lou Boudreau, the baseball Hall of Famer who also was a standout basketball player; Al Cervi, Bob Davies and Red Holzman — continued to tell the selection committee by letter and personal testimony how capable he was."

Overall, Jeannette played 10 years with the pros and was on five title teams, in Detroit, Sheboygan, Fort Wayne and Baltimore. After retiring in 1950, he coached Georgetown University for four seasons and then returned as coach and general manager of the Bullets until 1967.

His Hall of Fame recognition comes 56 years after he began playing professionally for Warren, Pa., a time when he got paid by the game, not by the season, and frequent exhibitions were staged in "tank towns" in the Northeast and Midwest.

"I remember a time in the coal region when some fans watching the games had just come right out of the mines," he said. And, if disgruntled, they would pelt the teams with two-penny nails they would heat with their mining lamps before throwing them at the players on the floor.

Harry "Buddy" Jeannette more than paid his dues for the highest of all rewards, the Hall of Fame.

--·--·--·--·--·--·--·--·--·--·--·--

Baltimore tough on Jackie

April 28, 1996

Until Jackie Robinson, anointed by a deeply religious man, Branch Rickey, was to walk across the hot coals of the infield and into baseball's blazing bastion of all-white segregation, there was a distinct color line that offered a painful message: Blacks need not apply.

It was 50 years ago that it happened, Robinson becoming the first of his race to prove that he had the capabilities — physically and mentally — to break down the barriers that then confronted all African-Americans. What occurred to him in Montreal was more important than what transpired in Brooklyn, where he ultimately was to earn his way to the Baseball Hall of Fame.

Had there not been the 1946 season he spent with the Montreal Royals of the International League, it's likely Robinson wouldn't have been the man, a year later, to be the first to integrate the major leagues.

Failure in the minors, from the standpoint of on-the-field performance or an ability to handle the pressure of being the first black in organized professional baseball, would have doomed him to a lesser role and projected another black player, at some later date, to be the designated pioneer.

Robinson, though, wouldn't allow his name to become a mere footnote in history. What he achieved in Montreal was directly correlated to what followed. He dealt with the competition between the foul lines, the brutal verbal abuse from opposing dugouts and what emanated from the stands. In the end, Robinson prevailed.

It was not an easy transition from the Kansas City Monarchs of the Negro National League to Montreal, where he was picked to take on a challenge no man ever faced before. On his way to spring training, Robinson and his wife, Rachel, devoted to him for all his days, were bounced off two commercial airplanes, en route to Daytona Beach, Fla., for the vaguest of reasons.

Later, in DeLand, Fla., an afternoon exhibition game was canceled because it was announced the park lights were out of order. A sheriff in Sanford, Fla., interrupted an exhibition against the Indianapolis Indians and said Robinson would have to leave then and there because the law said no interracial athletic contests could be conducted.

In Jacksonville, Fla., a similar exhibition with the Jersey City Giants wasn't played because authorities insisted it violated a city ordinance. A month later, when he played his first official International League game in Jersey City, N.J., Robinson broke in with four hits, including a home run, and two stolen bases.

It was a smashing debut that foretold what would happen as Robinson went on to lead the league with a .349 average and election to the all-star team. The Most Valuable Player vote went to a Robinson of a different color, first name Eddie, the Baltimore Orioles' silk-smooth first baseman, who batted .318, hit 34 home runs and accounted for 123 RBIs.

Baltimore, considered a Southern city, was difficult for Robinson. He wasn't allowed to check in with teammates at a hotel, so he stayed with friends. Rachel, at what was then Municipal Stadium, heard two fans seated behind her use racial epithets in reference to her husband.

"It was almost impossible for her to keep her temper, but her dignity was more important to her than descending to the level of those ignorant bigots," Robinson explained in his autobiography.

It was 50 years ago last night that Robinson integrated baseball in Baltimore. In 1941, the first black to play in a major college football game in Baltimore was a Cornell halfback, Sam Pierce, who faced Navy, in the same stadium where Robinson played. Later, Pierce was named to President Reagan's cabinet as secretary of Housing and Urban Development.

Robinson went 5-for-13 during his first weekend visit to Baltimore with the Montreal club, and his appearance in a Sunday doubleheader drew a crowd of 25,306. As a kid sportswriter, we witnessed the game and years later would tell Robinson that our first impression was he wouldn't make the grade. The comment interested him because, for the most part, he was hearing from others, after the fact, that they were sure he had the talent to play in the majors.

He was entirely focused on what we were about to tell him. The thought was advanced that he had a less-than-strong throwing arm and appeared to be tied up in his shoulders. "You're right," he said. "I hurt my arm in the Army, but there was no way I was going to be intimidated out of it."

We told him that having seen Roy Campanella catching for the Baltimore Elite Giants, it appeared he was more talented as a catcher than Robinson was as an infielder, an observation that others in both black and white baseball probably believed. On that same occasion, we asked Robinson if he could write his own epitaph, what would it be? Again, he answered, "That's something I've never been asked and I welcome it." He paused, if only to clear his throat, and quickly replied. "Put it like this: 'He said strongly the things he believed.'"

Certainly, from that exchange, Robinson knew himself. When his rookie season in baseball was over, after Montreal won the pennant, playoffs and Little World Series in 1946, he talked with Sam Lacy, sports editor of the Baltimore *Afro-American*, on what had transpired, including the bitterness and gutter talk he encountered along the way.

The crowds in Louisville, Ky., during the Little World Series hadn't been at all compassionate. Two rivals, Fred Walters and Frank Shofner, had, in Lacy's opinion, tried to spike him. So Lacy wanted to know his reaction and, in retrospect, this is what Robinson told him:

"Baltimore was worse. The nasty things Baltimore people threw at me hardened me to the point that this was rather easy to take. Then, too, while it was bad enough, I guess I expected a lot more than I got. I knew I was coming into the South and I suppose I was preparing for just about anything. But that Baltimore, holy gee . . .

"In Syracuse, the players held up a black cat and yelled, 'Here's a black mate for you!' I had to laugh. I thought it was pretty good. Syracuse dished out everything they could to get my goat."

So Robinson, a fierce competitor, never lost his sense of focus or humor, even when he was being demeaned.

Branch Rickey, president of the Brooklyn Dodgers, explained to members of the Montreal club in a talk during spring camp why he signed Robinson and another black, pitcher Johnny Wright. "I acted on the recommendation of my scouts and not because I sought to appease any pressure groups. If I thought an elephant could play center field better than the fellow we had out there, I'd do what I could to sign the elephant."

Jackie Robinson became more than a baseball player. His presence was a symbol that social justice no longer could be denied. The conscience of the nation had to be awakened. With something as rudimentary as a glove and bat, plus the ravenous intensity of the man, he changed the thought process of America for evermore.

The Don of coaches

Nov. 15, 1993

PHILADELPHIA — From where no National Football League coach has been before, at a rarefied height that may never again be reached, stands Donald Francis Shula, who climbed his own Mount Everest and chiseled an imposing inscription of achievement.

Shula has surpassed legendary George Halas, an equally intense and vocal rival he once faced as both a player and coach. The Shula record in 31 years shows an all-time mark of 325 wins as a result of his Miami Dolphins beating the Philadelphia Eagles, 19-14, yesterday in a history-making event that may signify an unattainable mark of excellence.

The ever-resourceful Shula lost quarterback Scott Mitchell with a shoulder separation against the Eagles. Earlier in the schedule, he was deprived of Dan Marino, who tore his Achilles' tendon, so against the Eagles he finished up with a third-stringer, Doug Pederson, at the controls.

In his career, Shula, who defies adversity when it strikes and then seems to be even more determined to succeed, has had to use backup quarterbacks in 37 games and has won 29 of them. What a remarkable footnote.

Shula's longevity in a precarious pursuit — coaching football — allowed him to overtake Halas, but first he had to be a winner. And the demanding personality of the man — on himself and those he leads — was all the motivation needed to fuel the furious fire that burned within.

Now at the top of the coaching ladder, Shula replaces Halas, an old competitor who helped organize the NFL as a founder and charter member in 1920.

Shula actually remembers the first dialogue he had with Halas. It was when Shula, a cornerback for the Baltimore Colts, heard Halas uttering some descriptive language during the pre-game drill (yes, Papa Bear was warming up his vocabulary even before the kickoff).

"Hey, coach," Shula hollered, "do you think that's the proper way to talk for a man I saw in church this morning?" Halas dropped his head and turned away. Silence reigned . . . temporarily.

Still later, Halas looked at Shula from in front of the Bears' bench and, typically, tried to get the rival player's mind off what he was doing. Harlon Hill, a wide receiver for the Bears, was flanked to the left. "Kid, this guy is getting ready to fly right past you," Halas screamed.

The fact Halas often asserted himself with a litany of strong words and Shula was known to do the same certainly takes nothing away from either as football leaders. Battlefield generals have never been known to address the troops as if they are talking to Little Lord Fauntleroys. Players, the same as an army in combat, understand one thing — assertive discipline.

Halas was a God-fearing man, Shula the same. "I always respected him," Shula said. "When I came in the league, the best organizations were the Bears and Cleveland Browns. Halas and coach Paul Brown of the Browns were opposites, but highly professional."

Now Shula has gone past Halas, who was around for 40 seasons. Had Halas not retired twice and also spent three years in World War II, the chase would still be on, because the Bears, in the midst of the extensive Halas era, were perennial contenders. That would have added considerably to Halas' numbers.

If there was an embarrassing moment for Shula as a player in Baltimore, it was the start of the 1954 season. He had the coverage on Volney "Skeets" Quinlan of the Los Angeles Rams, who appeared to leave the field after the opening kickoff.

But Quinlan, on a pre-arranged plan, let himself be a "sleeper," near the Rams' sidelines, and Norm Van Brocklin passed 80 yards for an immediate score in what became a 48-0 rout in Weeb Ewbank's first game as a head coach.

The league would later tighten the rules so it never could happen again. "I still remember," Shula said. "I was wondering why Van Brocklin was throwing the ball so far downfield. I found out."

As a player, Shula often coached the coaches. "I remember some teammates telling me to pay attention to what I was doing and leave them alone," he said. "But I was intense. I studied defenses and understood what had to be done."

It was obvious Shula knew what he was talking about. After playing for the Colts four years and coaching as an assistant at the University of Virginia and for the Detroit Lions, he returned to Baltimore in 1963. That came after players Gino Marchetti and Bill Pellington told owner Carroll Rosenbloom if he was ready to fire Ewbank that Shula would be the perfect replacement.

That's exactly how it worked. Shula remained in Baltimore seven years and, when it appeared he was about to be released, got permission from Steve Rosenbloom, Carroll's son, to negotiate with Miami.

Dolphins owner Joe Robbie wanted Paul "Bear" Bryant, who rejected his offer. It was then that Bill Braucher, a sportswriter for the *Miami Herald*, who had played football with Shula at John Carroll University, became the intermediary and found Shula eager to pull out of Baltimore before Rosenbloom gave him the boot.

Because Shula was the Colts coach in Super Bowl III, the upset by the New York Jets annoyed the egotistical Rosenbloom to a point he said it left him with the legacy of being the first NFL owner to have a team lose to the AFL. Tut-tut.

Shula's exit amounted to perfect timing, because he quickly lifted the Dolphins to respectability, then dominance. Rosenbloom was to eventually trade the entire Colts franchise for the Los Angeles Rams and then, in 1984, Baltimore was left without a team.

"I owe much to Baltimore," Shula said. "I didn't like being let go as a player in 1957. To come back as a coach was fulfilling. Baltimore was a big city with a small-town atmosphere. Hard-working people spent their entertainment dollars watching the Colts."

Now, he would like to see a team back there — the place where Shula played and then coached en route to his relentless ascent to the head of the coaching class.

31-year-old bad call

Nov. 3, 1996

What showed on the scoreboard was three more hard-earned — yet highly debatable — points for the Green Bay Packers. A tie at 10-10.

Then came overtime, sudden death and ultimately the most devastating defeat the Baltimore Colts ever absorbed. A title was to be decided because of the questionable validity of a field goal. Was it in or out? Good or bad?

It became, without a doubt, the most talked-about incident in Baltimore sports history, setting off repercussions that resulted in the National Football League's changing the rules, an admission of guilt, and unfortunately, depriving the Colts of at least an otherwise well-deserved championship opportunity.

When the play is discussed, even now, more than 30 years later, it's still referred to as "The Kick." And, in truth, the clouds of controversy never lifted — until now.

Instead of the Packers' playing (and beating) the Cleveland Browns for the 1965 championship, it would have been the Colts, and rightly so, providing the challenge. Don Chandler, the man who kicked the ball, a true Southern gentleman from Oklahoma, always well-regarded by teammates and rivals, is willing to set the record straight from the basis of his perspective.

It's an unbiased report. And it's not as if snap judgment is involved or he hasn't had time to reflect. It happened 31 years ago, the day after Christmas, in Green Bay at Lambeau Field before God and 50,484 witnesses. "When I looked up," said Chandler, "the ball was definitely outside the post."

So the key witness, for the opposition, is in accord with how the Colts' players viewed the kick that sailed high and wide and kept the Packers in the game, with only 1:58 to go, and provided them the chance to play in the cold and mud of Cleveland Stadium a week later — when Chandler helped beat the Browns with three field goals, none of which was even remotely questionable.

Against the Colts, the Packers were the beneficiaries of a call, dubious at best, that influenced the outcome of a game and qualified the winner for what was then known as the world championship — which is what the NFL's grand finale was called until the euphemistic tag of Super Bowl came along.

The Colts were wronged, unintentionally, of course, by one of the most competent officials the league ever employed, Jim Tunney. But for three decades the controversy has ensued, and now Chandler, in an interview from his home in Tulsa, believes the Packers got all the best of the decision.

What added to the emotional charge of the Colts-Packers playoff for the Western Division championship, after both teams had ended the league's regular schedule with identical records of 10 wins, three losses and a tie, was the way America's football audience rallied to the plight of the Colts.

This was a team that had lost not one quarterback but had the entire position depleted. First it was John Unitas because of a leg injury; then Gary Cuozzo with a shoulder separation. It meant that coach Don Shula had to scramble for some kind of a replacement. He realized Tom Matte, a spirited halfback, had once handled the split-T at Ohio State, and that offered a remote alternative.

Matte, with only three days to practice for the role and wearing a wristband with a ready list of plays attached, had given a remarkable performance against the Los Angeles Rams to clinch a tie for the Colts with the Packers. It was an afternoon when he rationed his passes and concentrated on holding the ball. Matte ran 16 times for 99 yards and, on one occasion, was hit so hard the face mask was torn from his helmet.

Now, a week later, it's in Green Bay, still with Matte quarterbacking, and the Colts are leading 10-7 with less than two minutes on the clock. Chandler lines up to kick from the 22-yard line, endeavoring to gain a tie and force overtime.

Bart Starr, who had been injured early in the game, was still able to hold for field-goal attempts and extra points. Chandler swung his right leg. The ball was high — and slicing.

Underneath the goal post, Tunney raised his arms. It was 10-10. But Lou Michaels and Fred Miller, on the field-goal defending unit, were livid. They led the debate, screaming the kick had gone wide of the 10-foot-high upright. But it also was above the top of the post, meaning Tunney had to visualize an imaginary vertical line extending upward. A difficult call.

Chandler, as he followed through, saw the ball carry wide of the target. Instantly, he twisted his head in obvious disappointment, much the way a golfer looks when he misses a short putt. The reaction conveyed the impression the kicker knew he had failed. But the official, standing under the middle of the crossbar, ruled it was good. Charge human error. Twice.

When Chandler returned to the bench, coach Vince Lombardi quickly confronted him, saying his actions alone questioned the legitimacy of Tunney's call. "Vince really got into me," recalled Chandler. "He was the reason I was in Green Bay. I had started in 1956 with Vince at New York when I was a running back and he was my backfield coach.

"I didn't hit the ball real square on the field-goal kick, and I was surprised it was called good. It was definitely outside the post when I picked up the flight. Bart Starr, the holder, always said it was inside and then curved away, but it was higher than the pipe."

Starr, commenting on the kick, said: "I saw it as being good. Just my opinion. I know the general reaction was otherwise. My biggest personal regret is it had to come against Baltimore, a team we respected. The Packers and Colts had so much in common. You know how close I am to John Unitas and what I think of the Colts and also of Baltimore as a city. I still wish it would have worked out that I could have headed a franchise there."

The NFL knew it had a controversy on its hands in Green Bay. At 13: 39 of overtime, Chandler drilled the winning field goal from 25 yards for a 13-10 victory. But a Baltimore newspaper, the *News American*, gained access to a movie version of "The Kick" and published a series of pictures that clearly showed the ball was wide of the upright. More furor.

"Until my dying day, I'll insist that kick shouldn't have counted," proclaimed Michaels, figuring the call cost each member of the Colts as much as $10,000 in championship pay.

The league, endeavoring to find a way to prevent a recurrence, took immediate action. It placed two officials under the goal post and added 10 feet to each upright. The new uprights were facetiously called the "Baltimore extensions."

Chandler had a career comprising 12 seasons and, in nine of those years, was in a title game with either the Giants or Packers. In Super Bowl II, he recorded four field goals. But a controversial kick he was credited with against Baltimore never happened. It doesn't change the result, but it's satisfying to know that the eyes of so many dissenters didn't betray them.

Chapter 8

ICONOCLASTS

The Hawk will put it in writing

June 10, 1986

Most of Alex Hawkins' activities spin a web of bizarre behavior. He once blew curfew with the Baltimore Colts by coming down the side of the Clift Hotel. Practically anything goes in San Francisco, but this was an extraordinary event — a human fly at work while startled spectators viewed the descent under the glow of street lights.

Hawkins once uttered a paradoxical line that put his career in fitting focus. "I ain't good enough to play for a bad team, but I'm bad enough to play for a good team," he said. That explained why the Atlanta Falcons, an expansion team, handed him a release and the Colts, a contender, quickly signed him.

The irreverent Hawkins, who believes that life is a touring stage show, always deals in incongruity. Like when his wife wanted to know where he spent the previous night, but he didn't want to blow the cover on an after-hours club. "Why, I slept out in the backyard in the hammock," he answered. But then she told him the hammock was taken down six months before.

"Yeah, well, I'm still sticking with my story," he replied.

Hawkins is visiting here with a writer friend, Frank Hyland of the *Atlanta Journal*, who is helping him author a book about the laughs, antics and escapades he has helped create — either by orchestration or merely doing what comes naturally. Living in Atlanta has been enjoyable for The Hawk, but he insists Baltimore is his own capital for fun.

Soon to celebrate his 49th birthday, he was asked if he ever planned to grow up. "Now if that happened, it would spoil everything," he said. "I came up this way to attend my high school reunion in South Charleston, W.Va., but something went wrong. I was a day late."

Hawkins' after-football involvements have been diverse. His first business was to collect commercial refuse. The company slogan, on letterheads and the sides of trucks, was, "We'll Talk Trash With You." He sold out at a profit and turned to acting.

He played in a movie called "Gator." Hawkins complained the film failed because he was miscast as a policeman and, indeed, it's a valid point. "I think ol' Burt [last name Reynolds] was afraid I might steal the show, so that's why I haven't been asked back. But, on reflection, maybe I was to the movie world what Tom Matte was to football."

Matte could sue Hawkins for slander, but he won't. "Yeah, I like Matte," confessed Hawkins, "but he's the only halfback who ever made an end run and drew a delay-of-game penalty. He had an innate talent for running slow."

During a network football telecast, The Hawk announced that Jake Scott of the Miami Dolphins had two broken hands in casts and couldn't play in the Pro Bowl. Alex added that "when Scott goes to the men's room, he finds out who his real friends are."

It was a remark that brought on Hawkins' firing. Another time, he mentioned Sen. Ted Kennedy was to be a halftime guest. "But I don't know if he's going to make it; he's driving." There are few subjects Hawkins wouldn't tackle even though he gambled with propriety.

While playing for the Colts, he was the special teams captain. When he walked to the center of the field for the pre-game instructions, an official inquired, "Captain Who?" So thereafter, he was to be known as the infamous Captain Who?

As a kid in South Charleston, Hawkins gained a reputation as a bat boy for an American Legion baseball team. After practices, he would ask the players to pool their coins to see him run billy goat fashion against a tin fence. Then he would take the dare and collect the money. Did that really happen? "Sure, dollars were hard to come by in West Virginia."

Alex Hawkins is still accepting challenges. The blond hair lags across his forehead, a mischievous glint flashes from his eyes. He says the one thing he always wanted to do in Baltimore was ride a horse from the city line on York Road to Belvedere Avenue — naked.

That, he promises, will await his next visit to Baltimore, all the while insisting if Lady Godiva was able to do it, he can, too.

Veeck enlivens Hall of Fame

July 22, 1991

Now that Bill Veeck, or plain "Ole Will," as he called himself, has been memorialized in bronze and put on the wall in the Baseball Hall of Fame, there's a certain welcome irreverence introduced to this hallowed sanctuary that was created for the purpose of highlighting the heroes of the game's historic past.

Had he been alive, Veeck would have "set up" the house, as when he ventured into saloons and told the bartenders (his favorite kind of people, along with barbers and taxi drivers) to give everyone "not one but two of what they're drinking on me" — be it straight ginger ale or a stinger on the rocks. That was his favorite calling card.

Veeck enjoyed taverns, he said, because of the chance to associate with the so-called common man. He abhorred formality and thrilled for the chance to always be on a convenient conversational level with the public. When he rode in a cab, as he often did from near Easton, Md., where he once lived, to downtown Baltimore (a distance of 64 miles), he would be an up-front passenger, because he didn't want the driver to feel in any way subservient.

He used the knee hinge on his wooden leg as a walking-around receptacle for the ashes on his cigarette. Veeck owned teams in Milwaukee (then in the American Association), Cleveland, Chicago and St. Louis. The one he wanted with a passion — and never got — was Washington.

"Imagine what you could do in our nation's capital," he said. "With all those government workers, you could salute a different state every game and have special entertainment." When in Milwaukee during World War II, he scheduled some games at 10 o'clock to accommodate

the midnight-to-8 a.m. shift of plant workers, who were served breakfast. A visit to a park when Veeck, who liked to watch from the bleachers, was in charge became an exciting experience.

Look under your seat and, if a lucky number was taped there, you might be the winner of a thousand ice cream bars, a Mexican burro, a ton of salt, a barrel of pickles, a truck load of fertilizer, 50,000 nuts and bolts, baby-sitting service for all night games or a new car.

There was the time he honored Al Smith, outfielder of the White Sox, and to make the party complete invited anyone named Smith to be his guest at Comiskey Park. On another occasion, he engaged the waiters of Chicago's celebrated Pump Room to serve such delicacies in the stands as fried caterpillar, eel, seaweed, smoked sparrow and barbecued snake.

The restrooms were fitted with blackboards, because Veeck said so many visitors had a compulsion for writing on the walls, he'd make it easier for them, even providing the chalk. In 1951, with the Browns and visiting Detroit Tigers out of the pennant race, he sent up 3-foot-7 Eddie Gaedel, a circus midget, to pinch-hit for Frank Saucier.

It was a stunt that infuriated some purists, but if you admire imagination and genius, there was no way not to respect Veeck. He could never be prejudiced, and the black athletes he hired, such as Larry Doby and Leroy "Satchel" Paige, knew of his sincere love of all mankind.

In fact, in 1943, he wanted to buy the Philadelphia Phils from owner Gerry Nugent and stock the roster with players from the American and National Negro leagues. But Judge Kenesaw Mountain Landis, the commissioner, told Nugent to find another owner, and he did — Bill Cox, who was later banished from baseball for gambling.

Veeck once had pitcher Early Wynn, disguised as the Lone Ranger, ride in on horseback and execute rope tricks at Comiskey. And he summoned second baseman Nelson Fox to home plate, where he was presented a string of hot dogs that stretched 400 feet to the center-field fence. If the giveaways were perishable, Veeck encouraged they be presented to orphan homes.

If you wanted to reach Veeck, his name was in the telephone book. In the early 1950s, he was in a remote part of Arizona, where he went to a general store once a week to take calls. We were charged with offering him the Baltimore Colts' franchise for nothing. "I wouldn't take them as a gift," he said, which he admitted later was a deal he shouldn't have refused.

Every day was revelry for Veeck and those around him. There have been imitators, but none to compare — regardless of whether the team was winning a pennant (Cleveland 1948, Chicago 1959) or confined to last place (St. Louis 1952) before being shipped off to Baltimore to become the Orioles. Bill Veeck's individuality never allowed him to put a price on laughter.

Charley Eckman, one of a kind

April 19, 1995

Being confined to the house weighs heavily on Charley Eckman, who, to use one of his most inimitable phrases, would rather be "romping and stomping." Cancer is a difficult foe, as he knew it would be, but he keeps dealing with the problem and won't back down.

"They don't give you a gold medal when you get it," was the way he relayed the news to friends after the doctor informed him of the diagnosis two years ago.

Always looking for a laugh, in any and all situations, he said, "Maybe I'll kill it off with Scotch whiskey before the Scotch whiskey kills me."

Now, Eckman is tough, both mentally and physically. But none of us realized the true depth of his courage, the tenacity that burns deep within, until the current crisis. To quit isn't any part of the Eckman persona. In these trying times, he keeps pushing onward and never complains.

"My knees are weak," is perhaps his only negative report.

"Other than that, I'd meet you for lunch at the Club 4100 in beautiful downtown Brooklyn, which is located right next to beautiful downtown Brooklyn Park," Eckman said. "Manny and his brother are right guys. Tell them they make the best Greek salad I've ever eaten."

Loyal friends keep calling and wife Wilma, three daughters and a son cater to his every desire. Roland Hemond, the Orioles general manager, checks in several times a week from spring training.

"He has a lot to do, but keeps in touch," Eckman says. "Roland is a winner. When I was refereeing in the old National Basketball Association and worked in Providence, he was one of my ball boys.

"Pete Angelos would have made a serious blunder if he had fired Roland and put in either one of the stiffs they were talking about.

Roland doesn't romance the press, which means he's not a phony. He's built for the long haul. Sincere, honest, a right guy. You only need to know the most respected people in baseball to find out what they think of Roland.

"Believe me, the Orioles never had a better general manager, and I go all the way back to when George Weiss was GM of the Orioles."

Jim Lacy, whose games Eckman often officiated at Loyola College, insists basketball never had a more colorful referee. "I guess Pat Kennedy was the first of the showmen, but Charley was right with him as a crowd-pleaser and, I believe, more on top of the play," Lacy said. "Charley could really run, as fast as any of the players in the game. He covered the court."

The Rt. Rev. Monsignor Martin Schwalenberg has been a companion and confidant. Although not of the Catholic religion, Eckman goes so far as to say, " 'Schwaly,' which is what I call him, is what a priest should be. He has been my friend for about 100 years.

"If you need help, call in Schwaly. Black, white, Protestant, Catholic or Jew. He helps everybody. He was once a military chaplain; he knows the score. I remember him before he went to the seminary. He played a lot of soccer in Patterson Park and was so mean, I think he'd kick his mother to get the ball."

Eckman has made frequent trips to the hospital for treatment. One Saturday afternoon, when he wasn't feeling his best, an entourage showed up from WJZ, including Richard Sher, Michael Olesker, Ron Matz and Marty Bass. Almost as if on cue, Eckman was back at the top of his game. It was as if he was hosting the show.

The room was vibrant, as Charley talked of basketball, baseball, soccer and horse racing, then about bookmakers, cab drivers, policemen, betting horses, being a bat boy for the Albany Senators, lifting a loaf of bread out of Bond Bakery and, get this, the time he almost joined the Boy Scouts.

"I lived on East North Avenue in those days, not far from old Bond Bakery, and some troop leader got me to go to a Scout meeting way out West North Avenue," Eckman recalled.

"He talked about camping in the woods and sleeping under the stars and getting merit badges. Then he said a scout uniform would cost $10.95. But I only heard him say the '95' part. I could come up with the '95', but $10 was something my widowed mother couldn't afford. Times were tough back then."

So Charley and the Boy Scouts quickly parted company until this past January, when he lent his name and presence to a fund-raiser in Anne Arundel County.

Charley Eckman, third from left

Eckman made his reputation in basketball and, later, as a sportscaster who shot from the hip, or, more appropriately, right from off the top of his head, because he didn't need a script.

"I'm pleased at all the Jewish prayers, all the Catholic prayers and all the Protestant prayers that are being said for me," he said from his Glen Burnie home. "I know they've had to help. The proof of that is I'm still here.

"John Mooney, the general manager at Pimlico, prays for me, too, besides keeping me informed about the horses. Joe DeFrancis, the Pimlico owner, is a decent person. I just wish he'd give Mooney more authority, because Mooney knows everything there is to know about running a racetrack and he's a right guy, too."

Charley Eckman, one of a kind (the world could hardly cope with a duplicate copy), shows more courage with the heat on than any one man is supposed to have. His family idolizes him; friends revere him and he knows it. The battle he's fighting has been long and precarious, but Eckman isn't about to bow out since he was always ready to make the tough call.

He fits his own version of the best compliment he knows how to give: a right guy.

Chapter 9

The ALL-TIMERS

Hank Greenberg: hero

Sept. 5, 1986

Twilight was overtaking Griffith Stadium. Shadows had caressed the infield. The end of another game and the visiting Detroit Tigers, winners again, were heading for the exit — disappearing through the first-base dugout and into infinity. They were seeking the privacy of their locker room, a sanctuary from the maddening crowd.

Meanwhile, a kid in short pants, who wanted to be a baseball player but grew up to be a sportswriter, was in personal pursuit. Would he be able to reach his hero, Hank Greenberg, the first baseman of the Tigers? Framed in the darkness of the tunnel was a rearview glimpse of Greenberg, gray uniform with a blue No. 5 on back, who was moving out of shouting distance. But the plea, child-like in tenor, offered the plaintive cry of "Hank ... Hank ... Hank." Maybe he recognized the desperate tone the immature voice conveyed.

Right then he stopped, looked back over his shoulder and saw the boy with an autograph book in hand. He came back, almost on cue, to sign his name. We still have it as a priceless keepsake. If you ever want to see it, all you need to do is ask.

What, though, would have happened if Hank had not heard his name or preferred to keep walking? He didn't owe anything to a youthful baseball fan from Baltimore who was visiting Washington with his father to see Greenberg play. But the historical fact remains he made himself available.

There's a bit of a tear in our eye this moment. Maybe you can detect it. Greenberg is dead at age 75. But heroes never grow old, and they don't ever die. They can't. No, not Greenberg, a giant of a man and one of the most celebrated of all Detroit Tigers.

He later found out, 25 years later, how much his gracious act meant because we had the chance to tell him. As coincidence would have it, while attending a luncheon in Chicago, put on by that famed sporting entrepreneur, the late Abe Saperstein, the luck of the seating draw put us next to Greenberg. After the normal handshake introduction, or re-introduction, we took him back in time and related the incident.

Of course, he didn't remember. He couldn't have been expected to recall what to him was an obliging gesture, one that is repeated innumerable times during a season for every player. Too many more important things, personally and professionally, had transpired for him, with a world war and two World Series in between.

But Hank was visibly impressed as the story was recounted. "You don't know how important it is to me that you bring it up," he said. "Gee, I'm glad I heard your call that day in Washington. I'm happy you didn't go home disappointed."

To offer authenticity to Greenberg's name being in the autograph album is the fact his brother's signature is right alongside of the more famous member of the family. Joe Greenberg, you see, was a third baseman, briefly, with the Baltimore Orioles of the International League, and he was elated to know we wanted to meet him, too, but only because he was Hank's brother.

For Hank, it was a career that took him to the Hall of Fame. He went from a private to a captain in the Army and, upon discharge in 1945, even though he had been away from baseball for three years, returned to the game and rallied the Tigers to the American League pennant.

On the last day of the season, with a tired body and legs that had lost their resiliency, he hit a grand slam to win it all for Detroit. Then in the World Series, won by Detroit in seven games over Chicago, he hammered two home runs and three doubles.

Henry Benjamin Greenberg was a stupendous first baseman and power hitter, elected to the Hall of Fame in 1956. More importantly, he literally went out of his way to evidence a kindness we've always cherished and will take to our grave.

We only hope your hero from out of the past was similarly considerate of you.

The best Preakness ever

May 22, 1989

When old men gather their thoughts in moments of fond reverie, either beside the fire on a cold winter's night or under the spreading arms of an old oak tree during some enchanted summer evening, they will look down at children not yet born on this day and tell them of the greatest horse race they ever witnessed. There will be no need to exaggerate or embellish the personalized report.

It was Sunday Silence and Easy Goer, fighting toward a frantic finish that became a dream race born of championship reality on an excitement-charged, breeze-filled May afternoon in Maryland. The Preakness of 1989 became a genuine epic, an absolute keepsake that will live for all ages. This, indeed, was the most momentous of them all.

As they raced their way down the stretch, presenting a pounding, unrelenting challenge to each other, the ground vibrated from the expanding rush of explosive horsepower and the roar of 90,145 enthralled spectators.

In the previous 113 runnings of the Preakness, there had never been a moment like it at Old Pimlico, a place where fortunes are made and hopes have often been known to fade into oblivion via the mere trick of a clock.

No historian can deny it. The records of races past delve back to Preakness antiquity, the year 1873, a time when Ulysses S. Grant was president of the United States. Those records provide evidence that what transpired when Sunday Silence and Easy Goer put the rest of the field behind them will set itself apart as the most classic confrontation in all the lore of an event that has been around for more than a century.

The driving encounter began as they made the final turn home.

There was Easy Goer trying to prove why he didn't win the Kentucky Derby and Sunday Silence attempting to demonstrate full credibility when called upon in the moment of truth.

It's casually convenient — but dead wrong — to arbitrarily dismiss the past when attempting to assess the quality and value of a current performance. But the Preakness record book clearly defines there was never a "Battle of Baltimore" to compare to this one, excepting in 1814 when the British forces were bombarding the city in a losing effort to reclaim control of the colonies.

This was a horse race in the grand style of pulp fiction. Easy Goer went to the lead after three-quarters, running down the pace-setting Houston. Maybe the commitment was a fraction premature. But Sunday Silence, ridden by Patrick Valenzuela, quickly recognized the Easy Goer bid and accepted the offer to come after him before he vanished in front of his calculating eyes.

They were almost running as one in the now-straightened-out chase for home. Pat Day, the jockey on Easy Goer, might give an inch but not any more than that. He rallied a second startling surge from Easy Goer and temporarily regained command. Yes, Easy Goer was back in the lead, yet ever so precariously in the stretch.

Both riders asked their mounts for whatever extra stamina and speed they had to give. Sunday Silence wouldn't quit. The same for Easy Goer. The fight was on, as the black and cherry colors of Easy Goer and the gray and yellow of Sunday Silence continued on as if this were some kind of imaginative storybook tandem that had come to life.

Neither would surrender. It was fire all guns, hold nothing back, drain the engine, make the ultimate charge. That's what evolved in the concluding jumps as Sunday Silence came on again, edged ahead and stayed there to win by a nose, surviving a foul claim lodged by Day, who later admitted he didn't have much of a case.

"I was never more proud of a horse," said Arthur Hancock III, owner of Stone Farm, where Sunday Silence resides. "He was heart. I told the Phipps' family, owner of Easy Goer, that it's a shame either had to lose."

Such a feeling was unanimous.

Lending substantiation to the bold but irrefutable claim that this was the most unforgettable of all Preakness contests is the realization that only five of the previous 113 races had been decided by a nose. This was spellbinding drama in the afternoon.

No, there has never been a Preakness like this one. In agreement is Joseph B. Kelly, a retired Baltimore and Washington newspaperman who produces the annual Pimlico information manual.

Sunday Silence, left, with Pat Valenzuela aboard and Easy Goer with his jockey Pat Day at the finish of the 114th Preakness.

"I am in accord with any hypothesis or comparison that makes this out to be the most incredible Preakness ever run," he said. "The Affirmed and Alydar meeting in 1978 was exceptional, but the difference was a neck, not a nose. Greek Money beating Ridan was close in comparison, but I don't believe it offered the all-out spectacular aspect or the thrill."

The premier Preakness challengers of 1989 carried their running argument to a suspense-filled conclusion. They were almost superimposed on the photo-finish film, which should be protected in a time capsule so generations to come will be aware of its unprecedented impact.

Rozelle had lasting impact

March 23, 1989

No man in the history of professional sports and the awesome pressures commensurate with a commissionership ever acquitted himself more admirably or effectively than Pete Rozelle, who combined integrity, decency and fairness while being profoundly in love with a game that made him a household name.

He was a master of diplomacy, style and grace — a true gentleman. From a tall, gangling kid whose first job was clipping newspaper stories for the Los Angeles Rams and keeping a team scrapbook, he went on to become their publicity director, their general manger and finally, commissioner of the National Football League.

The Rozelle star ascended to the heights of prominence and remained there as a constant in the passing parade of personalities, amid controversy and a myriad of problems that accompanied the sport's booming popularity and affluence.

Rozelle walked a straight line, even though the same could hardly be said about some of the owners, coaches and players he supervised. They didn't have his character.

Rozelle and this reporter had an extraordinary relationship. It was a friendship that dates back 36 years to when we were mere boys and working in the league.

The wake-up call he always remembers came after he was elected commissioner. It was at 5:30 a.m. on Jan. 27, 1960, the morning after he was voted to the position. He had earlier told his friends his personal choice for the job was a sportswriter he knew in Baltimore. After he became the NFL leader, he attempted to hire this individual as his first assistant.

Two years ago at the Super Bowl, he leaned over and whispered to the wife of the same reporter, "See all the headaches he missed in not coming with me."

Rozelle was so adept at making a deal, in bringing about accord where there was distrust and havoc, that we felt at the time, and still do, he could have settled the Vietnam War earlier had he been on the negotiating team.

There were times when there were disagreements between the commissioner and his old friend in Baltimore regarding a threatened libel suit instituted by an official of the Washington Redskins, one Edward Bennett Williams, the ethics of enforced exhibition games on the public and the credibility of certain owners.

But, again from a personal basis, there was a respect that endured. The job responsibilities he filled when Bert Bell, his predecessor, died at a game in Philadelphia's Franklin Field in late 1959 changed dramatically. In truth, it went from a "mom and pop" operation to a highly visible entity, bought about by his adroit abilities to merchandise the product.

Rozelle understood the advertising business because he had worked for the P.K. Macker Corp. in San Francisco during a two-year period when he was away from the Rams. And he knew public relations and football. It was Rozelle, no one else, who looked at a raw Marine at Camp Pendleton, Calif., one Eugene "Big Daddy" Lipscomb, and signed him to a Rams contract.

The emergence of television as a catalyst for encouraging and enhancing the popularity of pro football became the ideal vehicle for Rozelle. They grew up together, TV and Pete, and the lean lad from South Gate, Calif., whose late father helped design sets in the movie studios, extracted all the potential the medium offered.

He made decisions, not in haste but after cool and calculating deliberation. When the late Carroll Rosenbloom, owner of the Colts, was accused of betting on games, he wanted Rozelle to clear him overnight of the charges. Rozelle wouldn't do it. A congressional committee was investigating the same allegations, and it would have made the office of the commissioner appear incompetent if he came out absolving him and then the federal probe turned up incriminating evidence.

Another time, Rosenbloom, after he had been accused of tampering with receiver Ron Jesse, was trying to bring about an impeachment that never gathered momentum. At a league meeting, much the same as the one Rozelle used yesterday in Palm Desert, Calif., to announce his resignation as commissioner, Rosenbloom got to his feet and enunciated a long defamation of the NFL leader. It went on for the better part of an hour, as Rozelle heard himself being chastised before the other owners. All eyes were on Rozelle. Would he reply in kind? Rosenbloom awaited a reaction. Rozelle merely looked about the room, checked his watch and announced: "We will now take a 90-minute recess for lunch."

Rozelle first became attuned to sports when he went to Compton (Calif.) High School and the baseball team had a talented player named Duke Snider. It was Rozelle who took it upon himself to tell the waiting world all about the schoolboy phenom. He made trips to the newspapers in Los Angeles to extol Duke and asked that they publicize his name and exploits.

And on the afternoon in 1980 when Snider entered the Baseball Hall of Fame in Cooperstown, N.Y., there was his boyhood chum, Rozelle, in the first row of the audience. On that occasion, we sat and talked with the commissioner about troubles in Baltimore, where owner Bob Irsay was running the franchise into the ground. We told him about a potential buyer, one Ralph DeChario, who once had been a minority owner of the Cleveland Browns and had the wealth, stability and desire to own a team.

"See what you can do about it," he said. But the effort died in the press box at Shea Stadium later that football season when we talked to Irsay and told him DeChario was interested in purchasing the team. Irsay, preoccupied with getting a drink and a hot dog, merely turned both thumbs down.

Ultimately, the Colts went to Indianapolis, following the lead of the Raiders, who had jumped from Oakland to Los Angeles, without any sanction from Rozelle or the league. It was a sad and troubled moment for him, losing two franchises he wanted to see remain in position.

The NFL Rozelle assumed control of in 1960 was far different from what he's leaving. It was more of a fraternity, with few lawyers present to monitor the machinations. The commissioner enjoyed an autonomy that the courts eroded when he wasn't able to stand in the way of the Oakland defection. From mere numbers, 12 teams in 1960 to 28 today, the problems increased commensurately with the progress.

There were moments of deep regret, such as having to suspend Paul Hornung of the Green Bay Packers and Alex Karras of the Detroit Lions for betting on games. And being forced to fine George Halas, owner of the Chicago Bears, for insubordination, a point Halas was later to say was justified after he examined the record. The same with disciplining Paul Brown, owner of the Cincinnati Bengals, for comments he made about Art Modell, owner of the Cleveland Browns.

But through it all, the highs and the lows, the frustration, the tough in-fighting and the politics, Rozelle carried himself in a manner that befitted the high office he held. He had a longevity that exceeded every commissioner before him, be it football, baseball, ice hockey or basketball, plus a sense of fair play and an intrinsic, intimate understanding of the game he helped elevate.

He wasn't a fake or phony. He wasn't brash or boring. Instead, he was reserved, refined and resilient. His contributions during the last 30 years will be lasting. The mere name Pete Rozelle is an enduring monument to the sport he commanded. He polished it, shaped it and sold it like no individual in the history of a game, football, that has roots in the country that are more than a century old.

There has been a comforting permanency to Pete Rozelle. Football indeed has become better because of his presence and the intellect and integrity he brought with him.

DiMaggio a graceful enigma

March 9, 1999

Always a distinctive and majestic model of grace, style and consistency. With glove or bat in hand, he was a baseball symphony. A rare gift of exquisite talent that flowed with classic movement. It all looked so easy. A Rembrandt in flannels.

Yet personally, Joseph Paul DiMaggio was far more complex. Stoic. Introverted. Secretive. Arbitrary. Even rude. The public tried to make him a prisoner of adulation. And he fought against it all the way, even to his dying day.

Joe DiMaggio was a private person, who, in a kind of paradoxical twist, absolutely craved attention even though his persona was often perceived of as being modest and withdrawing.

If a master of ceremonies at a banquet didn't provide him with a classic introduction, he went away unhappy. And, similarly, at old-timers' games, it was understood he had to be the last one brought from the dugout so the crescendo of applause would accompany the mere mention of his name.

Yet the DiMaggio who reveled in the cheers gave a false impression that glory wasn't all that important to him. He preferred to be regarded as shy, although at the same time, revered. A celebrity who held off the crowd yet enjoyed hero worship but only when he wanted it.

The first time we met DiMaggio, 1949, he had his right leg extended in traction at Johns Hopkins Hospital. He was there for removal of a bone spur on his heel, a procedure successfully performed by the noted orthopedic surgeon, Dr. George E. Bennett.

A small cage was attached to the area near the wound, and maggots, then in use for certain medical treatments, were used to cleanse the infected area. DiMaggio's presence in Baltimore meant the city's Italian restaurants were fighting over which one would have the honor of serving Joe his next meal. So many floral decorations arrived that the walls were barely visible, almost as if it were a funeral home instead of a hospital. It was the Italian-American community paying homage to one of its own, perhaps the first genuine sports hero of Italian parentage in America.

A young reporter looked up at DiMaggio, resplendent in silk pajamas, and showed his naivete when he asked, "Mr. DiMaggio, I guess the reason you're here is that when Dr. Sidney Gaynor, the Yankee physician, treated your heel last year it was a failure." Joe seemed stunned but recovered to answer, "Yes, son, but we don't say that."

Dr. Bennett repaired the heel, and when DiMaggio rejoined the New York Yankees in June, he produced an overwhelming one-man show against the Boston Red Sox. Missing spring training and 65 regular-season games because of the injury, he had the benefit of only eight workouts, yet demolished the Red Sox at Fenway Park, hitting five home runs and driving in nine runs in a three-game sweep.

Once, playing golf at Marco Island, Fla., DiMaggio shied away from the gallery, signing a few autographs but continuing to look over his shoulder and tell spectators he had to hurry or he might get hit with a ball. Yet the nearest golfer was more than 400 yards away. It was his way of providing himself a fast exit from the crowd, just as those in his chosen entourage would seek methods to extract him from banquet halls, usually through the door to the kitchen, then to the parking lot and an awaiting car to avoid the clamor of the crowd. He was gone before they realized he had left.

We saw a man on a Hall of Fame weekend at Cooperstown show DiMaggio an old picture of himself, hoping he'd sign it. But Joe examined the photo, let it drop through his fingers to the floor, turned abruptly and left without offering a word.

In his native San Francisco, when he visited from New York, he could be seen walking alone on the streets of North Beach. A stranger in his hometown, but, in short order, he would be on the move again, traveling to places where the paid invitations took him. It's estimated by a once-close friend that his estate will exceed $40 million.

Our last extensive visit with Joe was six years ago when he came to Baltimore as grand marshal of the Columbus Day parade. He stayed two days, under what could be described as self-duress, to help a friend, Ralph DeChiaro, celebrate a birthday. DiMaggio was paid handsomely for the patronage but complained about how long it was taking for the party to start.

Joe was an impeccable dresser, once voted the eighth-best-dressed man in America. He carried himself with a certain nobility and liked having one or two traveling companions to assure his privacy. Meanwhile, they were caring for whatever his heart desired — be it a limousine, lining up an autograph session where he might make upward of $100,000 or getting him to the airport to catch another plane.

In a 13-season American League career, in which he led the Yankees to 10 World Series, he three times won the Most Valuable Player award, put up a .325 lifetime average and, momentously, had a stretch in 1941 during which he hit successfully in a record 56 straight games.

His approach to baseball, how he chased down line drives, threw to bases with exacting precision and whipped the bat with the speed of a cracking bullwhip, made him one of the sport's all-time accomplished performers.

Band leader Les Brown introduced a hit song, "Joltin' Joe DiMaggio," that the country began to sing in the early 1940s. He was a heavy coffee drinker and smoked a pack of cigarettes a day, Camels (the kind he endorsed), during his playing years.

Sitting around a hotel suite on an afternoon when he had nothing else to do, DiMaggio started to reminisce about San Francisco, where it all started. He played with boyhood friends on what they called Horse Field, which was where a dairy used to stable the horses that pulled milk wagons.

He vividly remembered the moment in Cleveland when his unprecedented batting streak was stopped by two incredible plays by third baseman Ken Keltner and another by shortstop Lou Boudreau. Had he gotten a hit in the game, which would have been 57 in a row, the Heinz food corporation and its 57 varieties was prepared to pay him $10,000 for a commercial.

On the night it all ended, he forgot his wallet in the clubhouse lock box, so he borrowed $18 from teammate Phil Rizzuto and went to a quiet bar for a few peaceful drinks and deep reflection. After the miss, he resumed hitting safely in his next 16 games, which would have given him 73 had he not been so rudely interrupted in Cleveland.

Significantly, as a green, 18-year-old minor-league rookie, he had batted in 61 straight in 1933 with the San Francisco Seals of the Pacific Coast League.

DiMaggio had a distinctive stance, legs wide apart, and generated power from his hips, upper body and wrists. Taking only a short, sliding move with the front foot, he followed breaking balls extremely well, and woe to the pitcher who threw him a changeup, because the minimum foot action allowed him to wait before committing the swing.

He was married to two movie queens, Dorothy Arnold and Marilyn Monroe, but a close Baltimore friend, Frank Cuccia, once said, "Joe wanted them to be glamour girls but also to be able to cook like his mother."

After Monroe's death, columnist Bob Considine said, "He gave her the one thing in death she never had in life — dignity," as Joe kept her funeral from turning into a Hollywood circus.

Joe DiMaggio, an enigma whose awesome ability as a baseball player was wrapped up in an aura of loneliness and aloofness he alone created and peculiarly coveted.

A man who desperately isolated himself, yet played the game in front of multitudes, with an exceptional competence that elevated him to the ultimate standard of baseball excellence.

Long gainer, 'Red' Grange

Jan. 29, 1991

INDIAN LAKE ESTATES, Fla. — From the "Golden Age of Sport," born of the "Roaring '20s," five personalities transcended all others: Babe Ruth in baseball, Jack Dempsey in boxing, Bill Tilden in tennis, Bobby Jones in golf and Red Grange in football. Now the last one has left us.

Harold "Red" Grange, 87, died yesterday of complications from pneumonia. He had been hospitalized since July.

As often happens with undefined mortality, a reporter was to have visited him last Friday at 3 p.m. His wife, Margaret, or, as he called her, "Muggs," suggested, "I don't think it's a good idea. He had a terrible night and is on oxygen." Those wishes, disappointing to hear, were respected.

Grange built such prominence and adulation after a glittering career at the University of Illinois that he signed with the Chicago Bears and gave the then-6-year-old National Football League the credibility it lacked.

Welcomed at the White House by President Calvin Coolidge, along with coach George Halas, he was both pleased and astounded. Coolidge, who didn't know much about football, said, "Glad to meet you young gentlemen. I've always enjoyed animal acts."

They were too polite to correct him and restrained their laughter. Grange often said playing football as a pro was "then about as socially acceptable as going off to join the Al Capone gang."

A member of both the College Football Hall of Fame and the Pro Football Hall of Fame, Grange was projected to the attention of the nation when, within the opening 12 minutes against Michigan, he ran for touchdowns of 95, 65, 54 and 48 yards. Still later in the game, he scored on a 15-yard run and passed for a sixth touchdown.

He was an old-fashioned hero, pleased to be recognized and willing to exchange pleasantries when stopped by strangers in public. There wasn't anything vain about him, yet he was aware of his role and felt obligated to fill a certain personal responsibility.

We once told him that because he was living in a quiet, somewhat remote part of central Florida, it would seem he must have a lot of time for golf. "No," he answered, "hitting a golf ball is as boring as kicking an extra point. I'd like it a lot better if after swinging at a golf ball I had to avoid a tackler."

Grange carried two distinctive nicknames, "The Galloping Ghost" and "The Wheaton Ice Man." He worked as a youngster for the Luke Thompson Ice Co. in his native Wheaton, Ill., where his father was chief of police.

"Carrying ice made me strong and helped my wind," he once told us. "It also enabled me to develop strength for a good stiff arm. My running style, whatever it was, came naturally. You can't create that. It's something you get from God. But no runner can make a go

He was an old-fashioned hero, pleased to be recognized and willing to exchange pleasantries when stopped by strangers in public...

of it without blocking."

At Wheaton High School, he scored 74 touchdowns and 82 extra points in three years. Entering Illinois, where he brought fame to jersey No. 77, Grange set records without benefit of an athletic scholarship. He paid his own tuition with money he earned carrying ice, along with what his father gave toward his education. From a football perspective, he called Bronko Nagurski, a Bears teammate, the "greatest offensive and defensive player I ever watched, and I have seen a lot of them over the years."

For a further insight into Grange, he talked about Claude "Buddy" Young, who followed him, two decades later, to Illinois. There were whispers the university didn't want Young to break Grange's marks because he was black.

But Young, who died in a car crash six years ago, debunked it and said he had ample opportunity but didn't produce. Now to Grange on the issue: "There was never a nicer guy. I adored Buddy. There was a false story that the university didn't want Buddy to break my records. Buddy said it wasn't true. I believe that, too. Illinois never had a better player than Young. I would have loved to have seen him break my records."

Grange, likewise, had deep admiration for John Unitas, the premier pro quarterback. "He could have played any time, any place and for any team. In our day, you had to play both ways, but I believe John could have done that, too." When Red made an appearance in the East to play Pennsylvania, the *New York World* newspaper engaged Laurence Stallings, author of "What Price Glory," to cover the game.

Stallings watched as Grange scored on runs of 65, 45 and 35 yards in rain and mud. In the press box, Stallings closed his typewriter and uttered, "The story's too big for me. I can't write it."

Harold "Red" Grange . . . an American phenomenon, who, it was once said, contributed as much to making football the popular, respected game it is as Charles Lindbergh did for aviation.

Campanella one of best ever

June 30, 1993

There was an artistic elegance to the way Roy Campanella handled a catcher's mitt. As a young boy, the year was 1945, we watched intently from the old wooden grandstand as the Baltimore Elite Giants played at Bugle Field (named for a coat and laundry company). It took only a thimble of awareness to realize he belonged in the major leagues — and would have been except for being born with what was then considered the wrong complexion.

Organized baseball hadn't yet lifted the racial barrier, so Campanella was confined to the Negro National League. The Elite Giants signed him in 1937, when he was only 14 years old, for the grand sum of $60 a month. He had earlier delivered milk from a horse and wagon for the Supplee Dairy in his native Philadelphia.

Campanella went on to easily become the most famous of all Baltimore Elite Giants players, later earning the Most Valuable Player award three times in the National League as a Brooklyn Dodger and the ultimate — enshrinement in the Hall of Fame.

It was all hard work. Then, at age 36, on a January night in 1958, the rented automobile he was driving while his own was being repaired went into a spin on a highway of ice, and the ensuing accident left him a quadriplegic. He would spend the rest of his life, until he died at 71 on Sunday morning, in a wheelchair.

The Dodgers "discovered" Roy when he was with the Elites, and the man who recommended him to general manager Branch Rickey was a perceptive scout, a one-time catcher, Clyde Sukeforth, who was astounded with his ability to catch the ball with natural finesse and to throw with a wrist and forearm snap that was strong and accurate.

Campanella had 2½ years in the Dodgers system, playing at Nashua in the New England League, Montreal in the International and St. Paul in the American Association. When Ty Cobb, always sparing in praising players other than himself, saw Campanella, he insisted he'd be "remembered more than any other player of his time."

From a historical standpoint, Roy was the first black catcher in organized baseball and the first to manage, when Walter Alston was ejected from a game in Nashua in 1946. That initial year in the Dodgers' farm system found him taking an enormous cut in salary. He made $1,017.50, which was the going rate in what was then a Class B league. He left the Elites and a higher contract ($3,000) for the chance to try the promise of a greater opportunity.

"There were times with the Elites when I caught three games in one day and night," he once said. "In fact, I remember catching four games. It was an afternoon double-header in Cincinnati and another double-header in Hamilton, Ohio, that night. But I loved it, including the travel, even if it was by bus, but most of all just playing baseball."

In the files of the Dodgers is a 1948 letter Campanella wrote to Al Campanis, then a Dodgers instructor, about switching to the outfield because the catching position seemed well stocked with Bruce Edwards, Bobby Bragan and Gil Hodges.

The opening sentence to Campanis read: "First of all, I want to thank you again for your help and your friendship. You're one good Greek." Then he went on to ask, "Do you think I'd have a better chance to make the club if I tried out as an outfielder? . . . I've played it a little bit in the colored league. . . . What do you think? Would I just be kidding myself?"

The answer was forthcoming early the next season, when Campanella was recalled by the Dodgers. The first complete game he caught was against the Boston Braves, and his pitcher, Rex Barney, delivered a four-hit victory. It would have been a blunder of momentous proportions if the Dodgers had used him any place but behind the plate.

Although catching is a vulnerable job, there's no telling what he might have put into the record book if he wouldn't have had to endure almost continual injuries to his hands. Yet he never begged off. "If I can walk, I can play," he insisted. In 1956, with a numb left hand and a broken right thumb, he forced himself to stay in the lineup to help the club win the pennant on the final day.

Talking about his average, which dipped to .219 that season, Campanella said, "I still hit 20 home runs that year practically with no hands." Roy Campanella never complained. He rationalized that in everyone's life there were good and bad breaks and what's dealt must be accepted.

The beauty of the man, plus his craftsmanship as a catcher, gave him a special identity.

What about Bednarik?

Sept. 21, 1994

Selection of the National Football League's 75th anniversary team, accompanied by the fanfare of drums rolling and trumpets blaring, was nothing more than ceremonial. It would have to be. There was no Chuck Bednarik.

He personifies, this man of concrete and steel, what the game is all about: a physical specimen strong enough to knock down a building, tougher than pig iron and a gifted athlete endowed with coordination, agility and an ability to make all the plays. A winner.

Name any linebacker in history. We'll take Bednarik. A two-time All-American, the first player picked in the 1949 NFL draft, eight years an All-Pro with the Philadelphia Eagles, member of two world championship teams and the last man to go both ways, the full 60 minutes — linebacker on defense, center on offense — in the 1960 title win over Green Bay when he was 35 years old.

The physical part of Bednarik is so imposing, 6 feet 3, 235 pounds, it's easy to dismiss something more important . . . the man himself and the character within. There's a strong sense of right and wrong, a desire to be counted in all controversy and a desire to defend the weak against the strong. Bullies beware.

Bednarik took a shop course at Liberty High School in Bethlehem, Pa., and admits to being overmatched academically at the University of Pennsylvania. But every night, instead of spending his time socializing in such off-campus beer joints as Smokey Joe's, he craved the assistance he received from a tutor, who patiently reviewed the day's classroom work and prepared him for what was upcoming. He knew football wouldn't earn him a degree from the Wharton School of Business.

Bednarik has always done things the right way. He was 18 when he enlisted in a pilot program during World War II. But the country had an oversupply of candidates, qualifications were tight and Bednarik became a mid-gunner on a B-24.

At age 19, he completed 30 missions over Germany.

How far was a bombing run?

"About nine hours," was his reply. "That's if we went to Hamburg. Four-and-a-half hours to get there because we had a full load of bombs, close to the same time coming back. German planes would be up in the air to greet us on the way over and some of the same ones were meeting us on the way home, shooting holes in the fuselage."

He remembers how the debriefing would go after they got back to England. Once on the ground, the crew would huddle around a table. There was a fifth of whiskey at each end in case the airmen needed something to settle their nerves. The intelligence officers wanted to know where they met resistance, their observations en route, where was the anti-aircraft fire the thickest and if the target they were assigned to hit was taken out.

Was there a low point in the war for Bednarik? "Yes, I won't ever forget Christmas, 1944," he said. "The other crew in our Quonset hut didn't make it back. That meant you had to pack up their belongings and ship them home. Pictures of parents, wives, girlfriends. It tore you up."

He knew firsthand the severe toll war extracted. When they were bound on a mission, the mess hall served fresh eggs, as if it might be their last meal. Otherwise, if they weren't flying, eggs were artificial.

Bednarik, fearless on a football field and deeply religious, is a man who believes in a higher power and admits to praying his way through the war.

"I promised the Blessed Mother if I got home safely, I'd say a rosary every day in thanksgiving," he said. "I don't know if you know anything about Catholics, but a rosary is over 50 prayers. I've never missed. Not a single day in 50 years.

"Sometime, I say eight or 10 rosaries as I drive my car. I might be praying for a friend whose wife is undergoing surgery or a kid who has become a worry to his family. Then I miss a three-foot putt on the golf course and curse in disgust. I look up and say, 'Please, God, forgive me for that kind of language.'"

On Sunday, at church, the Bednarik family is invariably in the first row, front and center. "If you go to a Broadway play, you want to have the best seat, don't you?" he said. "That's how I feel. I'm no religious freak, but my faith is a part of me."

After his football career was over, Bednarik was drawn to golf. He hit

1,000 practice balls a day, picked them all up, and went from a 24-handicap to the club championship at Whitemarsh Country Club in only a year. Does this tell you about incredible determination?

The morning he was married in Bethlehem, Pa., he asked his wife, Emma, if she would mind going to a baseball game after the ceremony. So the new Mrs. Bednarik sat in the stands while Chuck caught a double-header for a town team. Then they headed for their honeymoon.

Pro football has made Bednarik, now 69, a legendary figure, but his persona is distorted. He's enshrined in both the college and pro football halls of fame. The NFL named him to its 75th anniversary two-way unit but not to its all-time team, which is a sacrilege.

There's no reputable way to pick a lineup of the game's elite and not include Charles Philip "Chuck" Bednarik, whose parents emigrated from Slovakia and gave America a football warrior of extraordinary talent, plus a man of sensitivity, whose deeds almost read like fiction — except it's all hard muscle and fact.

--- --- --- --- --- --- --- --- --- --- ---

Tittle rightfully takes his place

March 6, 1989

WASHINGTON — Ever since man took the stuffings out of a football and substituted air, there had been an ongoing quest to throw it with precision, poise and, when necessary, power. Most purists of the pass put forth the Hall of Fame names of Baugh, Unitas, Van Brocklin and Namath as being among the leaders of the class.

There is one more — Y.A. Tittle, who deserves to be voted No. 1 from the aspect of making a bullet spiral appear a thing of exhilarating beauty, delivered with ease and consistent accuracy. This reporter has seen every passer in the so-called modern game, and Tittle's style — not to mention the flight characteristic of a three-quarters motion — gives him an edge over all the others.

Y.A. was so good he's the only man in history to be drafted in the first round three times. This happened when he was drafted No. 1 twice in 1948, by the Cleveland Browns of the All-American Football

Conference and the Detroit Lions of the National Football League. Then, after playing three seasons, he was put back in the draft when the Baltimore Colts franchise was withdrawn. The San Francisco 49ers selected him as their first choice in 1951.

The occasion to dwell upon Tittle's sterling accomplishments came when he stepped forth to be the latest inductee into the National Quarterback Hall of Fame, as selected by the Washington Quarterback Club, in elaborate black-tie ceremonies put on for the benefit of the Cystic Fibrosis Foundation.

Norm Van Brocklin also was added posthumously to a group of enshrinees that includes Sammy Baugh, Sid Luckman, Bobby Layne, Otto Graham, John Unitas and Bart Starr. Contemporary quarterbacks from every NFL team were present, along with leaders of government, including Supreme Court Justice Byron "Whizzer" White, who was once a starting halfback for the Pittsburgh Steelers and Lions.

It remained for Tittle to charm the capacity ballroom crowd with his own brand of down-home humor.

"There are four stages of being a quarterback," he said. "First, when you are young and everyone is behind you. Then in the middle of a career everything that goes wrong, every dropped pass, is automatically your fault. The fans tear you apart. But once you become 30, you are a grand, old veteran and everyone is pulling for you again. The final stage is right now for me. Only the good things are remembered. That's what I like best."

Tittle was with his wife, Minette, the only girlfriend he ever had from the time they went to different grade schools in Marshall, Texas. If it hadn't been for football, what does he think he might be doing? "Probably chopping cotton," he said. But in the world of business, heading a vast insurance business in Palo Alto, Calif., he has been immensely successful.

Coming out of Louisiana State University in 1947, Tittle was so naive about pro football he didn't realize there were two leagues competing for players.

"Down South, the game was practically unknown. So when the Cleveland Browns offered me a $2,000 bonus and a $10,000 contract, I signed. Then two weeks later, the Detroit Lions told me I was their No. 1 selection. They wanted to talk bigger money, but I was committed.

"Then, before I ever reported to camp, Cleveland just gave me to Baltimore to help a weak team. That was a break. I loved the Colts. Besides, if I had stayed with the Browns, I wasn't going to play ahead of Otto Graham."

Tittle praises the current lineup of quarterbacks. "But, you know," he whispered, "I think I could pass with any of them. That's because our quarterbacks are like pitchers in baseball. Either you can throw or you can't."

Asked to select the finest man at the position, he quickly answered, "John Unitas." He went on to relate an amusing story of when the 49ers traded him to the New York Giants in 1961 after coach Red Hickey erroneously decided the "shotgun" was the formation of the future and Tittle lacked the mobility.

"We played the Giants an exhibition game, and I noticed Andy Robustelli, when he came in on me, didn't unload. And then Sam Huff red-dogged up the middle and veered off. I thought this was all so strange. But the Giants told me on the way to the locker room they had a chance to get me in a trade and coach Allie Sherman said if anyone hurts Tittle before the deal could be closed, it was going to cost them $1,000."

Like every player, Tittle remembers facing football fires for the first time. "I was so nervous when I got in the game as a rookie, taking over for Charley O'Rourke, that I almost didn't know where I was. My knees were shaking. I called a pass over the middle to Lamar 'Racehorse' David, and the Los Angeles Dons, the team we were playing, put a hard rush on me.

"I threw it for Davis, but I was way too strong, being all fired up. Then I got hit and was under a pile and the crowd was screaming. I figured I threw an interception. I got up, looked downfield and there was another of our receivers, John North, standing in the end zone with a touchdown. I had overthrown Davis, my target, by at least 20 yards, but North caught the ball in full stride deep downfield. What a beautiful mistake."

From there, he went on to a 17-year career, playing for the Colts, 49ers and Giants. Twice he was the league's Most Valuable Player. And, among the coaches and teams of his era, when the great natural passers are assessed, Tittle is placed in a special category. His arm had the resilience of a rubber band, the accuracy of a sonar scope and the cracking firepower of a bull whip. When he had a pass airborne, it was, indeed, a football picture to behold.

—·—·—·—·—·—·—·—·—·—·—·—·—·—·—

Cheers have turned to honks

Dec. 24, 1995

ST. MICHAELS — Instead of cheers accompanying his name, reverberating about a stadium as booming claps of thunder, there's now a cathedral-like silence to Kyle Rote's surroundings. The nearby waters of the Miles River lap against bulkheads and, overhead, geese honk, emanating a haunting sound more characteristic of barking dogs chasing after a fox than waterfowl.

It's a laid-back scene on the Eastern Shore of Maryland, far removed from the crazed surroundings where Rote, a bona fide football hero, covered himself with glory at Southern Methodist University and then as a New York Giant. The personal quality that set him apart was a genuine humility that attracted friends and, more importantly, kept them.

The box score shows 14 of Rote's former teammates in college and the pros paid him an ultimate testimonial. They named a son after the man they so admired, who was at his best under pressure, carrying himself with a sincerity and self-effacing manner that was deeply respected. Even though the spotlight played on him, he never sought it.

"Gee, it's quiet here," he says. The feeling that's imparted is he's at peace with himself, far removed from the streets of New York, their clutter and clamor. His wife, Nina, a biochemist, and he moved here two years ago to enjoy the serenity that country living provides.

Rote's career was bountiful. He was an All-American at SMU, where his performance against Notre Dame in 1949 was voted the greatest single effort by a Texas athlete in the first half of this century. He then became the first player picked in the 1951 NFL draft, when the Giants won Rote with the bonus choice. Both knees were damaged in his first three years, but he played on, 11 seasons in all.

Jim Lee Howell, late coach of the Giants, said if Rote hadn't been the victim of injuries, he would have been better than Red Grange, who was the dominant figure in the 1920s and remains a standout in perpetuity. Rote was a strong runner who broke tackles with intensity and showed an obvious delight in playing the game.

At one period with the Giants, the team was in the NFL championship game six of eight years, including the historic sudden-death contest with the Baltimore Colts in 1958.

What thoughts come to mind as he reflects on one of the epic events in league history? "Mainly of John Unitas," he answers. "It's probably a bad analogy, but he was like a fine artist putting images on canvas. He was just the best at what he did."

Rote remembers another outstanding quarterback performance, this one in college, when SMU almost upset Notre Dame, but a kid from Baltimore, Bob Williams, brought the Irish back for a 27-20 win to protect the national championship in 1949. Doak Walker was injured for SMU, but Rote put on a show, running for 115 yards, passing for 146, scoring all three of his team's touchdowns and punting for a 45-yard average.

"Notre Dame was a 27½-point favorite," he remembers. "We got a thorough scouting report from Michael Brumbelow, who watched Notre Dame four or five times. He was a friend of our head coach, Matty Bell. He gave us a lot of information. After the game, a newspaper ran a great headline, 'SMU Wins, 20-27.' The oil market was thriving in Texas then. All the oilmen took the points, so, from that standpoint, we won big."

Notre Dame thought so much of Rote's performance that in a subsequent celebration it invited him to its campus to name him an honorary member of the 1949 team. "A great bunch of fellows, like 'Six-Yard' Sitko, Leon Hart, Jim Martin, Jim Mutscheller and Bob Williams, a gentleman I finally met at a College Football Hall of Fame banquet and liked very much."

As a Giant, he enjoyed playing for Howell and, later, Allie Sherman, but remembers that the greatest assistants any coach ever had, Vince Lombardi and Tom Landry, were both in New York under Howell.

"Truthfully, Jim Lee called the team meetings to order but let Vince and Tom do much of the coaching, which I guess just about everyone knows. Both went to the Hall of Fame, Lombardi by way of Green Bay and Landry by way of Dallas."

While in the NFL, Rote was a leader in organizing the players association. He says a meeting in 1956 in New York, before the Giants routed the Chicago Bears for the title, had to do with the kind of double-bar face guard the players were wearing. Paul Brown, coach of the Cleveland Browns, had invented a different type, but Rote and others wanted to be able to use what afforded them the most protection.

"That's exactly how the union started. At the first meeting, some players were so afraid of being disciplined by their team owners they didn't want it known they were even there. Eddie LeBaron told us George Marshall of the Washington Redskins would put him on waivers if he found out about it. So Eddie was invisible; he couldn't even get in the 'team picture.' The same with others, but that was the beginning of the association."

Rote's knee injuries changed him from a runner to a slot back or wide receiver after only three years. He hurt his left knee as a rookie while working out before an exhibition game, and two years later tore up the other knee in an exhibition.

"The second time I got hurt, I was admiring my kickoff, looking up into the sky, when a blocker hit me from the side."

So no longer able to rely on power and speed, he developed moves as a pass receiver and went on to play in four Pro Bowls. Kyle Rote, acclaimed and adulated, personified the best that football offered . . . as a player and man. The genuine goods in ability and character.

Chapter 10

LORDS *of the* RING

Boxing best of all-time

April 13, 1989

Put Sugar Ray Robinson in a telephone booth and throw a handful of rice at point-blank range. Not a kernel would hit him. He was elusive and wise, carrying knockout drops in either hand. The boxing beauty of Sugar Ray Robinson was the way he could dance all night. He might have had a better pair of legs than Betty Grable.

He was clever, deft and so adept. Boxer, gymnast, dancer ... he was all of those. Put taps on his boxing shoes and he would have been the equal of Fred Astaire or the other Robinson of showbiz fame, the man they call Bojangles. Chasing after him in a ring was like trying to corner a cat whose tail had been dipped in kerosene.

The movements were blinding — in and out. Then he would go laterally, come back inside, pull away, feint with a left hand and deliver a right cross. And before the opponent could retaliate, he was putting down a new pattern of dazzling footwork.

How that Sugar Man could move — firing shots from all angles, doing what had to be done. Comparing others to him is an insult to his memory and erroneous, too. Why patronize imposters?

He was indeed the original, no carbon copy or facsimile. He was the genuine article ... Sugar Ray Robinson. He went down for the count at age 67 yesterday after fighting three rivals at one time — diabetes, hypertension and Alzheimer's disease.

The death of Robinson takes away a fighter of multiple skills, combining speed, stamina and style. The sport probably has never had such a gifted boxer-puncher. He was active from 1940 until 1965, and five of his 19 defeats in a quarter-century took place in the last six months of his career, when he had extended himself at 44 to taking

*It was said,
without dispute,
that Robinson was
the most competent fighter,
pound-for-pound,
boxing has
ever known ...
Measure him
against all
the others,
past and present,
and there's no contest.*

bouts so he could make a payday.

Robinson was the middleweight champion five different times. It was as if he would put the title out on loan to Randy Turpin or Gene Fullmer or Carmen Basilio or Carl "Bobo" Olson. He always came back to reclaim it. Watching him box and punch, delivering those jackhammer blows, was an unforgettable experience.

Away from boxing, he carried himself in a flamboyant manner. He lived up to every dollar. He owned a night club, a boutique, a barber shop and a wardrobe with more than 1,000 suits. And when he was making money by the ton, he drove a flamingo pink Cadillac, usually with the top down. He carried a regal-sized entourage with him on the road, including a valet, manicurist, secretary and barber, who also served as his golf pro, and enough hangers-on to fill up ringside.

"I went through $4 million, but I have no regrets," he once said. "Money is for spending and having a good time." Why not?

Robinson had a reputation of driving a tough bargain. Promoters found him difficult to deal with because of the financial terms he imposed. Once he was to box at Memorial Stadium, but was a "no show."

In a tax battle with the Internal Revenue Service, he won a split decision. It was a landmark case that introduced the law that permits income to be deferred over a period of time. But Sugar Ray enjoyed the bright lights and the champagne, the pretty dolls, the music and the sharply tailored clothes. Boxing is a hard business, and he believed in partaking of what it could give him in purchased pleasure, along with the notoriety and the clamor his presence created.

It was said, without dispute, that Robinson was the most competent fighter, pound-for-pound, boxing has ever known. It was repeated with such redundancy it became a cliche. Challenge the statement if you want, but as a fighting machine he had every quality. Measure him against all the others, past and present, and there's no contest.

The excitement he generated didn't come from any contrived jitterbugging, be-bopping or idle jiving. There was a purity to his satin-smooth movements ... the way his fists flashed out so sharply and crisply and those magnificent legs, carrying him so effortlessly, as though he were riding a bicycle. They took him to brilliant performances all over the world.

Sugar Ray Robinson was a virtuoso with eight-ounce gloves. The music he played, with his hands and feet rocked foes to sleep. He was so poised and pleasing to watch that boxing, which goes back to Cain and Abel, never had one to compare.

Old Man River

March 27, 1988

Scoring more knockouts than anyone in the entire evolution of boxing qualified Archie Moore for distinct recognition. He held the light heavyweight championship longer than any other man in history, His true age was never defined except that he might have been a year older than Old Man River.

And here he is back for a nostalgic visit to Baltimore, the scene of some of his greatest triumphs, a place where he pursued a dream that carried him to the highest position of personal respect plus professional accreditation — the Boxing Hall of Fame.

He fought 16 years before gaining a title shot, beating Joey Maxim and then doing it twice more in rematches that went the 15-round limit. Archie retained the crown nine years, but took on heavyweights any time a promoter called, often giving away as much as 30 pounds. The 141 knockouts in a career that stretched from 1936 into 1963 is an all-time record.

He was only stopped seven times in 229 fights — by Jimmy Bivins, Len Morrow, Eddie Booker, Rocky Marciano, Floyd Patterson, Ezzard Charles and Muhammad Ali, when he was still Cassius Clay. The last four were either heavyweight champions of the world or eventually got there.

Baltimore was a second home, a base of fiscal and fistic operations for Moore. He appeared here in main events 22 times, from 1945 when he decisioned Nate Bolden, until 1961, when he stopped Pete Rademacher in six rounds. The only loss in the 22 outings was to Holden Williams, a 10-round decision he reversed a month later with an 11-round knockout.

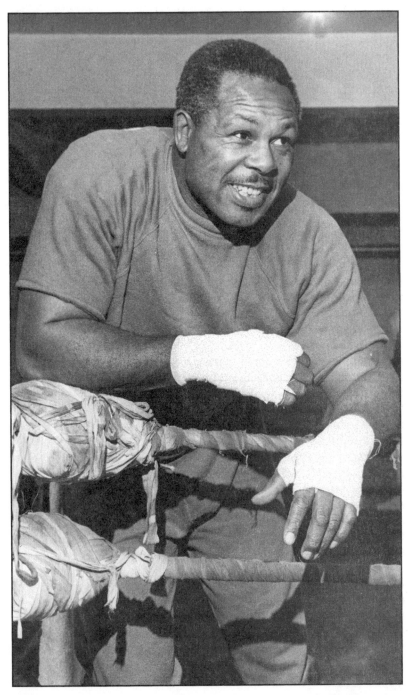

"Holden was slick as grease and hard as lard," recalled Archie in the glib and graphic way he talks. "You couldn't hurt him. He was one of the few guys to ever beat Charles Burley, who a lot of folks insist was the greatest of them all. Holman beat me the first time. I knew it. He'd give you a lot of action and it was confusing. I was always missing over the top on him.

"It was Beau Jack, the lightweight champ, who told me to pound him to the body and then when I had him bending over to jar him in the kidneys. It worked. I trained in Baltimore with Leo Matricciani, who had just gotten out of the Army. He got me in shape. I know Leo died a couple of years ago. Please tell his family hello and let them know how much I thought of him."

Showing consideration to others is characteristic of Moore. He arrived in Baltimore inquiring about Rodger H. Pippen, a sports editor who had been kind to him, and Sylvan Bass, the matchmaker for the old Century A.C., which promoted most of his fights at the Baltimore Coliseum. There isn't much that happened to him, in what he refers to as the "tunnel of time" that he has dared to forget. Ask about the past, and colorful stories flow forth.

Part of his approach to life is found, succinctly, in the last two lines of rhyming homespun philosophy he imparts: "If the labor is great or small, do it well or not at all." That's the way he has always been, be it a boxing match or a business commitment.

Archie came up in an era when blacks, in and out of sports, were treated as third-class citizens, but he doesn't carry a chip. "The three beautiful 'J's' opened things up for us," he says. "You know who I mean ... Jesse Owens, Joe Louis and Jackie Robinson. They, the 'J's,' made things happen and brought attention to our human cause in a grand way."

Moore knew a time in the late 1930s and early 1940s when black fighters had difficulty getting work. But he kept busy for what he called "not much more than walking-around money." The top purse he made was close to $200,000 with Marciano in 1955. And the least? That, as he explains, was $10 in Quincy, Ill., in 1936. He won the fight, but, after the manager and cornerman were paid, he was in arrears $5 for payment of the state boxing license.

Although a rugged campaigner who got punching leverage with either hand from any angle, he knew how to avoid trouble. How else does a man fight his way into four different decades if he can't stay out of heavy fire? There's also an inherent kindness he brings with him, a quality the public has recognized and admired.

Last night, as the weekend guest in Baltimore of two former fighters, Sid Bernstein and Joey Longo, the legendary Moore was at the A-

1 Crab House near Essex and was under pressure from all sides by men and women wanting to shake his hand and extend compliments. His dinner, by actual count, was interrupted 16 times.

What does he think of Mike Tyson, the new champion? "I haven't seen him fight," he answered. "If you understand what I mean, it's that he hasn't really fought, only guys who seemed afraid. Larry Holmes could beat him. Now, there was an underrated fighter. I liked Holmes from the time Earnie Shavers put him down twice but he got up to win. Holmes could beat Tyson. It all depends how hard he wants to get the title back."

He was asked about his own fight with Marciano. He believes he might have been able to beat The Rock, except referee Harry Kessler, an otherwise competent official, gave extended time before starting to count and cleaning Marciano's gloves after a knockdown.

"I wondered if he would have done the same thing for me, had the tables been reversed?" Archie says.

Asked if he was now 70 or 73 years of age, the gentleman smiled and said "neither," so there was no point in trying to ascertain if he was 52 or 49 when he had his last pro fight in 1963.

Archie Moore, born Archibald Lee Wright in either Benoit, Miss., or Collinsville, Ill., depending upon which birth certificate you accept, lives in an expensive house in San Diego, works with boys clubs and by his mere presence, on either side of the ropes, upgrades humanity.

Chapter 11

The
COLTS

Ameche: The humble 'Horse'

Aug. 9, 1988

It was a celebrated moment. A time when Alan "The Horse" Ameche, who came from a humble past and went on to become an All-America and All-Pro football player, plus a multimillionaire in business, was being honored in his hometown of Kenosha, Wis.

The banquet hall was crowded to capacity, but, strangely, the guest of honor was absent. A hurried search found him in a shoemaker shop, playing cards with an old Italian cobbler.

This is the first of a moving montage of recollections that come flashing into focus with the stunning news of Ameche's death at age 55 in a Houston hospital after undergoing heart surgery. Alan Dante Ameche was that rare athlete who was gifted academically, had an affinity for the common man and went on to an immensely successful career off the football field, giving so much to those he touched along the way.

He was a philanthropist. A model husband. A father to six children. Always, when he became financially able, he was interested in doing for others in a non-obtrusive way. Six-feet-1, 217 pounds and with shoulders that seemed a yard wide, he helped the Colts to consecutive world championships over the New York Giants in 1958-1959.

It was Ameche's touchdown that ended the first overtime in football history and gave the Colts a 23-17 victory in 1958. He made his professional debut three years before against the Chicago Bears. The first time he ever touched the ball, he went 79 yards for a touchdown.

Red Saunders, the former coach at UCLA, watched the powerful Ameche play for Wisconsin in the Rose Bowl and said, "He's the strongest runner football has ever known, not excepting Bronko Nagurski."

In 1955, after being the No. 1 draft choice of the Colts, he led the NFL in ground gaining, the first rookie to do so since Bill Paschal with the New York Giants in 1944.

He was a man so carried away with his own importance he kept the Heisman Trophy packed in a box, out of view of his family, because he didn't want his sons growing up looking at it and believing they had to try to do the same.

From afar, Ameche may have looked the part of the typical forceful fullback as he battered would-be tacklers and headed for the goal line in a peculiar kind of duck-like gait. But, no, he was much more than that.

There was strong character and substance, highlighted by a profound understanding of classical music. He became a sponsor of both the Baltimore and Philadelphia symphonies, rather unusual endeavors for an ex-football player.

Bobby Hines, a football player-boxer who went to Wisconsin with Ameche from Kenosha High School, said, "He was a B-plus student. I lived with his family for a year during high school. His mother and father treated me like a son. When we got to Wisconsin together, there was a tough professor who taught music appreciation. It was a study of all the great works back to antiquity, and the teacher was a taskmaster. In 28 years, I heard he only gave two perfect grades ... and Alan got one of them."

When Billy Vessels, another Heisman recipient who played for the Colts, learned of Ameche's death, he commented, "I'm deeply upset. We last saw each other at the White House in April. The president had invited former Heisman winners for a ceremony honoring Pete Dawkins. We had a great visit. I think it's rather odd the way our careers entwined. I saw him play in the Rose Bowl when he had that great game. I went with a teammate from Oklahoma. Eddie Crowder.

"When I came to the Colts, he made me feel at home. I was there in Baltimore, sitting in the stands with the Fort Still army team and saw him run 79 yards on the first play against the Bears. A great football player, but an even greater man."

There was a caring, considerate side to Ameche that set him apart. After becoming a spectacular success in helping build a huge Eastern restaurant chain with former teammate Gino Marchetti (which was later sold to the Marriott Corp.), he made untold contributions to charity — especially in the area of educating children living in the ghettos of Baltimore and Philadelphia.

"One of the worst moments in my life," he once said, "was when the Colts would go south for exhibition games and players such as Lenny Moore, Milt Davis, 'Big Daddy' Lipscomb and the other blacks couldn't stay in the same hotel with the rest of the team. I felt crushed. I regret now, as I'm older and look back, that we even took the field. We should have refused to play."

Football never devoured Ameche. He kept it in ideal balance. On the day of the 1959 world title game, played in Baltimore, he was driven to the stadium by a former teammate and friend, the late Joe Campanella. "I was amazed what the 'Horse' told me as we headed for the park," related Campanella. "He simply said if he wasn't playing, he doubted if he would even be going to the game."

Jim Mutscheller, the end who put the ball in position for Ameche to score in overtime in the 1958 classic against the Giants, calls him "one of the great individuals I've known. He was witty, nice to be around. I remember being involved in a fund-raising effort in the black community. Alan gave an immense check to make the drive a success. His concern for others set him apart. He always wanted to help."

"I feel the same way," said John Unitas, another ex-teammate. "He was at the head of the class, the kind of individual it takes to make a team a winner ... a really wonderful person. When you had Alan blocking, you knew the job was going to be done. He was a winner all the way through life."

In Baltimore, Ameche was to play six years, giving up the game after tearing an Achilles' tendon against the Detroit Lions in 1960. He could have continued, according to the surgeon who performed the operation, but there was an aggravation football presented that he didn't need. So he went on to become a momentous success story by developing an extensive chain of drive-in restaurants.

When he first joined the Colts, as one of the most prominent players in American college football, we asked him to accompany us to Sagamore Farm, then owned by Alfred Gwynne Vanderbilt, to have a publicity photo taken with Native Dancer, the famous thoroughbred. It would be The Horse and "The Horse."

Ameche consented, but complained all the way during the trip from training camp. When he saw what was planned, he changed his mind, exclaiming, "This will be fun. I just hope the horse doesn't kick me." And he didn't.

Another time, a blind child from Reese, Md., came to a practice and said he wanted to meet the "The Horse." After practice, Ameche talked with the boy. "Can I ride you, Mr. Horse?" the child requested as he felt his uniform. With that, "The Horse" Ameche dropped to his hands and knees. He put the lad on his back and rode him about the sidelines. "Can 'The Horse' neigh?" the child next wanted to know. And, with that, Ameche mimicked the whinny of a horse. He had truly made a youngster happy.

For an old sportswriter friend, when it came time to retire, he said, "I want you to have the story, if you think it's worth anything. I'm not even going to call the club. Would it help if I didn't answer the telephone until after 5 o'clock, so the other reporters can't confirm it?" And that's precisely the way it happened.

There was an abundance of talent within Alan Dante Ameche, but this was exceeded by his most profound consideration for those he met along life's highway. Forgive the personal note, but last night there was a bright new star glowing in the heavens.

OT period mystified '58 teams

Dec. 21, 1988

Most of the players didn't know what to do when regulation time expired. They looked at one another, found no answers forthcoming and commenced to walk away. They obviously weren't prepared for sudden-death overtime. It had been talked about as a tiebreaker but put aside as kind of a vague vehicle that would never have to be employed — until the gloom and glory of the gloaming of what became an unforgettable day ... Dec. 28, 1958.

President Dwight D. Eisenhower was watching on television from his farm in Gettysburg, Pa., and it's doubtful if he realized what was coming next. The National Football League had instituted the rule in 1947, specifying that if a championship playoff concluded in a deadlock that an extra period would be played. Some cynics said the NFL, then struggling to gain acceptability, only arranged the overtime rules so it wouldn't be faced with having to pay to send two of its teams to the College All-Star game in Chicago in the event there was a title tie.

But the rule had to be there. Imagine, if you will, the outcry if a championship was all even on the scoreboard and the competing clubs split the money instead of having a divergent share for the winners and the losers. They had to find a way to bring about a result, and sudden death was it.

"I didn't know we were going to be a part of history," says Jim

Parker, the Colts Hall of Fame tackle, who went up against another Hall of Famer, the Giants defensive end Andy Robustelli. "It was a hard day for both teams. We gave it our all. Andy was tough, aggressive and never let up. We tired each other out."

With the clock winding down to the two-minute mark, the Giants were confronted with a third-down-and-4 situation. They either manage to make the first down to maintain possession or punt the ball away. On the critical play, Frank Gifford headed to the right and turned off-tackle. He was met by Gino Marchetti and Art Donovan, plus three other Colts — including 6-foot-6, 282-pound Eugene "Big Daddy" Lipscomb.

Marchetti broke his ankle on the play and, after being lifted to the sidelines, refused to go immediately to the locker room. He was being carried on a stretcher, but asked Bill Neill, Vince DePaula and Bill Naylor to put him down so he could turn to watch what was left of the game. The crowd in Yankee Stadium, alive with emotion, was booming, "Gino... Gino... Gino."

The measurement after the Gifford run was controversial. The Giants insisted they had gotten far enough to record a first down, but referee Rob Gibbs and umpire Charley Berry insisted otherwise. "There was no big protest on the part of the Giants," says Gifford. "That's because the players then were better disciplined. Today, they would be jumping all over the place and carrying on to create a scene."

Gifford holds to the belief, with unwavering resolve, that he got far enough for the first down. The Colts insist he didn't. But on fourth down, with inches to go, coach Jim Lee Howell of the Giants sent in Don Chandler to punt.

"I had gotten in the game to replace the injured Gino," recalls Ordell Braase, who played exceptionally well. "A lot of the Giants players wanted to go for it instead of punting and were screaming in disagreement and slamming their helmets on the ground when Howell told Chandler to kick."

The Giants were noted for their defense and figured if they backed the Colts deep in their own territory it would be difficult for them to move. But John Unitas was never better. Aware that he was in a race with the clock and fighting the Giants, he drove the Colts in a relentless advance down the field.

He utilized Raymond Berry, who was finding the open spaces as a primary pass receiver, and used Alan "The Horse" Ameche, Lenny Moore and L.G. "Long Gone" Dupre as his thrusts on the ground. From the 19-yard line with only nine seconds left, the destiny of the Colts and of professional football was to be decided on the thick right leg of Steve Myhra.

Teammates frequently called him "Blinky" because of the nervous way he blinked his eyes, or "Mumbles" for the manner in which he talked. "But our team had played so hard, I told myself I couldn't let them down," exclaimed Myhra. "And if I had, it would have been a long, cold winter back home in the wheat fields of North Dakota."

That field goal knotted the score, 17-17. The Giants were fortunate enough to receive in the sudden-death period, but again came up inches short on third down during the possession, and had to kick. Once more, Unitas, starting from his own 20, orchestrated a march, spotlighting passes to Berry and runs by Ameche. Finally, on second down at the Giants' 7-yard line, he defied the book and passed to Jim Mutscheller in the flat, who didn't have much running room and fell out of bounds at the 1.

On the next play, the Colt who was a "Horse," Ameche, took it over for the score through a gaping hole at right tackle and Baltimore won, 23-17. The goal posts came down. The band paraded. Pro football was changed from that moment on because of the dramatic impression it made on the press and public.

"It was the day the sport turned the corner," is the way Alex Webster, a Giants halfback, still describes its value as a centerpiece for the NFL.

There can be no quarrel with that. It's a game Baltimore won't let die, because it was the city's first major championship in 62 years and came in New York against the Giants, one of the league's most consistent winners. But, apart from the provincial aspects, it was an event that has lived for three decades and no doubt will prevail, like good wine, for the ages.

Berry flawless in every way

June 25, 1993

This was a homecoming for Raymond Berry, who was such a remarkable young man that some teammates, given to a torrent of profanity, would clean up their language when he approached. That was the ultimate sign of respect.

Berry didn't "wear religion on his sleeve" and wasn't about to force personal beliefs on others. He was, though, an extraordinary man and football player, graduating from SMU before a 13-year career as a pass receiver with the Baltimore Colts earned him enshrinement in the Pro Football Hall of Fame.

"I dream," he said, "of waking up some morning and hearing Baltimore has another football team. Also that Robert Irsay decides to give back the Colt name that rightly belongs to Baltimore. It would be good for him and Indianapolis, too."

Berry has been a stand-up witness for Baltimore. He was coaching the New England Patriots when asked his reaction to the loss of football in the city where he had gained so much distinction. Berry could never be political. He told a wire service it was appalling such a despicable incident could have happened.

By way of contrast, another ex-Colt, Don Shula, coaching the Miami Dolphins and with a forum similar to Berry, merely said, "I heard a lot of bad things happened there."

Shula, for reasons known to himself, didn't take the same stance in 1984 as Berry, who denounced the robbery of the Colts without qualification or deliberation.

Berry and wife Sally decided Baltimore meant so much to them they wanted to come back for a visit.

"We had been here for overnight stays, but nothing lengthy," said Raymond. "I had a hankering to see Western Maryland College, where we trained. It's a beautiful school. It's where it all started for me. I drove through Westminster. The town is pretty, well-kept and has a lot of character. I never saw it much when I was a player. I rarely went into town.

"Just to be back in Baltimore, though, is a high point. My being here is different. So many of the other players stayed. I went into coaching after playing and have moved around. I talked to a lot of people about the Colts, and some became so emotional they had to walk away."

He rejoiced in relating his Baltimore past. "The 1958 championship in New York was my biggest thrill. I was 25 years old at the time. I got to play with John Unitas, and there's not much else you can do in a football way after being with that kind of a talented quarterback."

It was in Baltimore where he admits to finding the spiritual side of life. "I had always gone to church, but a teammate, Don Shinnick, talked to me about the Lord in a special way," he said. "Playing in the '58 championship was a powerful experience. But I wondered what else the future held. I remember being at National Guard camp in 1960 and knowing the Lord and true peace for the first time."

Berry comes from Paris, Texas, and saw how blacks were segregated and put down. But not with Raymond. His treatment of all men, regardless of race or religion, emphasized a compassion that was never a grandstand play.

A sportswriter, observing Berry close up, once wrote he was the "finest man to have walked the earth since Jesus Christ." A powerful statement, not intended to be sacrilegious but an effort to convey the exemplary qualities of an individual.

"Raymond is that one person you meet in your lifetime," offered Lenny Moore, a fellow Hall of Fame member, "who is totally genuine. He is free of the kind of faults so many of us have."

Berry's father, now 89, was a high school coach. He had an ability to extract the maximum in application. How?

"Because he always felt his team was capable of winning and got each boy to believe he could achieve," said Raymond. "As a young coach, my father saved his money and would go to clinics put on by Knute Rockne. He has high respect for Rockne and what he meant to the game."

"We've been deeply touched," said Raymond's wife Sally, a native of Tyler, Texas. "We felt very blessed to be a part of something special, how Baltimore loved the Colts."

The Berrys plan to go to Washington to visit the Holocaust Museum before returning to Denver. Yes, Raymond Berry is a man of depth. He once went to Pearl Harbor, and the reaction to being in such a location was more than he anticipated as he dwelled on the loss of so many young men in a war they didn't start.

Raymond Berry is in a Hall of Fame for football achievement, but more importantly, a Hall of Fame for humanity. He elevates his fellow man.

Ewbank had the winning touch

Sept. 27, 1993

That Wilbur "Weeb" Ewbank coached and won the two most celebrated pro football games of the last 50 years sets him apart. It's a distinction that is his alone to cherish and treasure for perpetuity.

The Baltimore Colts and Ewbank beat the New York Giants, 23-17, in the first overtime the NFL ever knew in winning the 1958 championship. Then, after being fired in Baltimore, he rebounded in New York and took the Jets to a 16-7 victory over a Colts team that was a 16½ -point favorite in the Jan. 12, 1969, Super Bowl.

Both events delivered historical impact. Ewbank was the maestro. He held the baton, planned the strategy and orchestrated the victories. He had two Hall of Fame quarterbacks, John Unitas in Baltimore and Joe Namath in New York, to work with, and for personal reasons will not put himself in a position of naming which was better.

Ewbank, still bouncing about the country at age 86, is visiting Baltimore for today's Pro Football Legends Golf Classic sponsored by Larry Brown and Unitas for the Kidney Fund. It's a time for him to contemplate the pleasures of the past, which Baltimore offered when he finally got his first coaching job with the pros at the rather advanced age of 47.

He realizes Baltimore is in line for an expansion franchise if the NFL approves, and he gives the city a strong endorsement, while also aware of his own connection with two competing cities, St. Louis and Charlotte, N.C.

It was in St. Louis where he coached Washington University, his only college position, before being hired as an assistant with the Cleveland Browns.

As for Charlotte, the prospective owner there is Jerry Richardson, whom Ewbank drafted on the 13th round for the 1959 season.

"Jerry was a high-type boy and a hard worker," he recalled. "I remember he scored a touchdown in the title game when we beat the Giants for our second straight championship, the game we played in Baltimore."

The most impressive aspect of Ewbank's career as a pro head coach, embracing 20 years, was an ability to organize a squad, from training camp through the regular schedule, and, of course, to evaluate talent. He excelled at both, using the skills to lift two poor teams, the Colts and Jets, to championships.

He first looked at Unitas, who had been discarded in Pittsburgh without even getting so much as a chance to play a single down in an exhibition game, and recognized the potential. He liked Unitas, saw something in him when others didn't.

"I can't remember Weeb cutting a player who went somewhere else and made an impact," said Unitas. "That's the way to measure a coach. Does he know a player when he sees one? Some of them

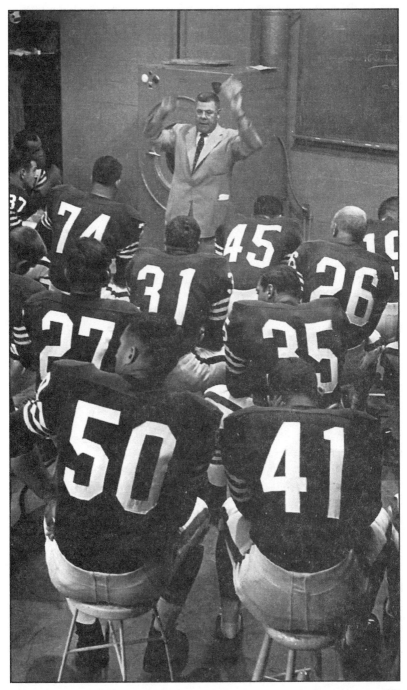

don't; others do. Ewbank was the best at that."

With the Jets, he had an All-America selection, Namath, deposited in his lap. Namath was the antithesis of Unitas, but Ewbank knew what to do with him. He never tried to change Namath's style of passing or his lifestyle, but accepted the ability he brought with him.

The Jets didn't have a license to beat the Colts in Super Bowl III, but Ewbank knew how to lull the opposition into believing his team was a soft touch and then, when they were "all puffed up like a big toad," to use his expression, lowered the boom.

He got the Jets to play the game of their lives. They were ready. The Colts felt totally superior to the Jets. Such an attitude can be fatal — and it was. Jets 16, Colts 7.

From that momentous surprise, go back to 1958, at Yankee Stadium, when the Colts were preparing to meet the Giants. Ewbank's locker-room remarks dealt with how many of his players had been rejected by rival clubs, including Unitas, Art Donovan, Bert Rechichar, Art Spinney, Buzz Nutter, Carl Taseff, Leo Sanford, Ray Krouse, Fred Thurston, Jackie Simpson, Milt Davis and others. He emphasized this was the opportunity to prove how wrongly they had been judged.

It was an inspirational message delivered in the same stadium, the visitors' locker room, where Knute Rockne emoted his famous "Win One For The Gipper" pep talk in 1928 when Notre Dame came from behind to beat Army, 12-6. There was little difference, except the Colts played for money and pride; Notre Dame for the sis-boombah glory that went with winning a college game.

Wilbur "Weeb" Ewbank knew his subject, football, and didn't need a road map to tell him how to reach the goal line. He took the players available and extracted the maximum — which is the most profound compliment that can be paid to any coach, regardless of what sport he's pursuing.

Pellington was rugged warrior

April 27, 1994

If a sculptor wanted to mold the face and physique of a football player, the perfect working model was Bill Pellington, who spent 12 impact years with the Baltimore Colts and distinguished himself with an intensity that earned respect and created intimidation.

Pellington epitomized the individual toughness the game demands — not the cheers, the adulation and the so-called glamour, or taking bows.

The respect he gained came from more than his looks, the deep-set eyes, strongly structured jaw and thick neck fastened to a 6-foot-2, 238-pound frame that made him a force who quickly gained the attention of rival teams.

His death at age 66 came after almost five years of being a victim of Alzheimer's, a disease that had his wife, Mickey, two sons and a daughter caring at all times for his presence and welfare.

Pellington was a defensive captain of the Colts, a true warrior of the team's glorious past. When the ball was snapped, Pellington reacted with demonstrative zeal, either blitzing rival quarterbacks, punishing would-be receivers, filling the hole when the linemen in front of him were blocked or pursuing ball carriers to all sides of the field.

Football represented such a craving he was the only player in the 35-year history of the franchise who hitchhiked to training camp, from his home in Ramsey, N.J., to the Colts' facility at Western Maryland College in 1953. Yes, the game meant that much to him.

"I'll never forget our first training camp," he was to say later. "It was a brutally hot summer. Most of the free agents were assigned rooms on the third floor of the college dormitory. There was no air conditioning. The slate roof overhead held the heat, even at night. All we could do was take cold showers, get in bed and hope sleep would overtake us."

Subsequently, every player on the entire floor was released until only Pellington remained. It was lonesome. Would he be next on the cut list? He had no one to talk to, unless it was the four walls, but they never answered back.

That's when he dropped down a flight and came in close touch with such veterans as Don Shula, Bert Rechichar, Tom Keane, Ray Pelfrey and Carl Taseff.

On a Saturday afternoon, the players got their first furlough from camp. They had two hours of leave time. Pellington was thirsting for a glass of beer. He found a tavern near the railroad tracks, just off Main Street in Westminster.

"I had two or three drafts and when I came out of the place, guess what? As soon as I shut the door and hit the street I ran into two assistant coaches, Nick Wasylik and Ray Richards. They were walking by. I figured they'd go back to camp and put me on waivers."

But no. The coaches, especially Wasylik, recognized the raw talent Pellington represented. Two years later, Elroy "Crazylegs" Hirsch of the Los Angeles Rams came to Baltimore to promote a movie and his conversation focused on Pellington.

"The first time I played against him, I thought he was a 'lamb,'" said Hirsch. "But then last year, he hit me with everything but a baseball bat as I came off the scrimmage line. He became a 'tiger' in one season. How could that have happened?"

After World War II and service in Panama, Pellington returned to civilian life and was waiting to enter Defiance College. His high school basketball coach, who had taken a job at Billings (Mont.) Polytechnic Institute, came east with a team comprised almost entirely of American Indians.

However, several of them were partaking of too much firewater. The coach recruited Pellington, John Ryan and Joseph Mullooly, gave them phony Indian names and let them play against Hofstra.

"Mullooly had too much of an Irish face to be an Indian, but they called him 'Three Irons,' and it was a riot," remembered Bill. "The team had a bear cub mascot that liked to eat basketballs, clawing the leather until the ball exploded. The coach, a great guy named George Fielding, got fired when he got back to Billings. The school president realized he used players who weren't even enrolled."

A void in Pellington's 12 years with the Colts is that he never once made the All-Pro team, even though worthy of the honor. He was, in the main, an outside linebacker, and middle linebackers such as Ray Nitschke, Bill George, Chuck Bednarik, Sam Huff and Joe Schmidt were usually picked — which was grossly unfair.

But Bill Pellington never complained. He was a football player, never interested in personal promotion or self-aggrandizement.

Spinney was block of intensity

June 1, 1994

BOSTON — There was almost a spiritual devotion in the way Art Spinney played football. He had an intensity that set him apart as he blocked with proficiency for Baltimore Colts teams that won successive world championships.

Two former teammates from the Colts and Boston College, Art Donovan and Ed King, were present today for Art Spinney's funeral in the nearby community of Saugus. Spinney, 66, died from a heart attack last week after telling his wife he was having trouble breathing.

Spinney played in two Pro Bowl games as a Colt and was voted All-Pro in 1959 during a nine-year National Football League career. Spinney, like the other highly dependable guard, Alex Sandusky, was a converted defensive end. They became a vital part of the interior line during the Colts' most successful reign. Art was the complete offensive lineman, a solid blocker for the passer who led running plays with equal competence.

Against the New York Giants and opposing defensive tackle Roosevelt Grier, it was no contest. Spinney nullified Grier's size and strength in a way that made it appear the Giants were playing with only 10 men. Coaches and fellow players, in an effort to exhort Grier to greater heights when they got ready to meet the Colts, would accuse him of catching a "case of Spinneyitis."

But Art never gloated. He was too much a professional. After the 1959 title game, the second championship for the Colts, Spinney sought out Grier and told him, "Big fellow, you were tough to handle."

Quarterback John Unitas, whom Spinney always referred to as

"our meal ticket," remembered the domination and related an on-the field anecdote.

"In the 1958 championship," Unitas remembered, "Grier complained of being held. On the next play, Art drove Rosey off the line with a tremendous block, then looked at the official and said, 'How was that, Mr. Official?' The official smiled and answered, 'A great block, son, a great block.'"

Donovan, a teammate of Spinney's in the college and pro ranks, shook his head in obvious respect and exclaimed, "What a tough guy and competitor. He never took a cheap shot. He gave the game everything and never let up. I loved him like a brother."

King, the only NFL player ever to become governor of a state (Massachusetts), also played with Spinney at BC and the Colts of 1950.

"He was the toughest single person I ever encountered," said King. "He handed out punishment with clean, hard hitting, but he'd play himself into total fatigue. As an individual, he was one good, solid American man."

Donovan and King recalled he was the only non-war veteran, just a kid out of high school, who started on a talent-laden BC team comprised of older players returning from World War II. He played four straight varsity seasons, joined the 1950 Colts and then, three years later, returned to Baltimore from the Cleveland Browns in the same trade that brought Don Shula, Carl Taseff and Bert Rechichar.

"He was held in the highest esteem as a player and gentleman," said end Jim Mutscheller, another former Colt who attended the funeral. "A lot of times, players on the line would forget their assignments on a play, but Art would tell them as they headed to the line of scrimmage. He could have played on any team in any era of football."

Spinney was one of the few Episcopalians to play at Boston College, a Jesuit school. That came about after Cornell forgot it sent him to Manlius, a military prep school in Syracuse, N.Y., and he was left "high and dry" after coach Ed McKeever resigned at Cornell. Fortunately, Spinney's high school coach, Dave Lucey, had joined the BC staff and provided entree for him to enroll there.

During the glory times of the Colts, the Bethlehem Steel Co. hired 12 players for an off-season training program that would lead to top management positions.

When it was over, Steve Eusted, a Bethlehem official, said, "All the players performed well. But it's our opinion the standout is Spinney, who has exceptional leadership qualities. I believe he could go to the top in our company if that's what he wants to do."

But Spinney wanted to marry Mary G. Pappas, a girl from his

hometown of Saugus, Mass., and live there. He rejected the Bethlehem proposal and went into coaching with the New England Patriots, later turning down Don Shula when he wanted him to become an assistant with the Miami Dolphins. For the past 15 years he worked for the Massachusetts Port Authority and then the State Department of Transportation in public relations capacities.

Art Spinney was tough, tenacious, talented. He possessed well-developed techniques that made him one of the most skillful guards in an era when salaries were modest and pro football players were a select fraternity — only 12 teams with 34 players on a roster, which tells you much about the quality of the game and the men on the field.

—·—·—·—·—·—·—·—·—·—·—·—·—

Marchetti reflects on earlier era

Oct. 24, 1994

OCEAN CITY — Personally, Gino Marchetti was passive, not at all interested in the spotlight and content to let performance convey his statement.

Professionally, among historians of the game, he is the greatest defensive end the National Football League has ever known.

Election to the all-time team in the NFL's 75th anniversary season was a foregone conclusion. His size (242 pounds, 6 feet 4), his speed (as fast as any halfback for the important first 5 yards) and physical strength earned Marchetti All-Pro status nine times — more than any other Baltimore Colt in history.

Marchetti never went into a victory dance after making a tackle or a sack. Football was a team sport and, in his era, individuality repressed itself. Only the result counted; cheap acts of grandstanding were intolerable and rarely, if ever, occurred.

While attending a weekend reunion of Colts heroes in Ocean City, arranged, oddly enough, by a former Green Bay Packer, Tom Brown, for the benefit of a Salisbury youth fund, Marchetti was asked his views on an assortment of subjects.

Sacking the quarterback: "I wish they didn't count them, because they aren't a true measure of what a defensive player does. I hate to see football become like baseball, a bunch of statistics.

"Suppose one end or a tackle is double- or triple-blocked. That means someone else gets the tackle or a sack. If a quarterback runs from the pocket and you take him down, that's a false sack. The player who pressured him is the one who made the play possible."

So, sacking the passer usually evolves from the collective contributions of teammates. That's Marchetti's reasoning for what generally happens.

The best tackle he ever faced? "That's easy. Forrest Gregg of the Packers. Not too big, but he knew what he was doing. Vince Lombardi said he was the best player he ever coached."

About Baltimore's fanatical love of football, particularly the Colts of the 1950s and 1960s, Marchetti explains how he remembers it: "It was special in our lives. We regularly had 57,000 or more in the stadium, and I think I met them all at one time or another.

"I talked to Willie Lanier, the Kansas City Chiefs linebacker, at the Hall of Fame in Canton, Ohio. He came up and told me he was at Morgan State in Baltimore at the time we were playing and, to this day, he can't get over how the fans expressed themselves for all the Colts back then."

Was there any one player they put on a higher pedestal than the others? "Yes, Bert Rechichar. In those early years, he had the town in the palm of his hand. Raymond Berry, Lenny Moore, John Unitas, Art Donovan, Ordell Braase, Jim Mutscheller, any of them, will tell you the same."

Marchetti was asked to explain his little-known role in Don Shula's becoming coach of the Colts in 1963. Now, for the first time, he filled in the details.

"The year before Shula took over, we got hammered by the Chicago Bears. On Monday, I got a call to meet our owner, Carroll Rosenbloom. I thought maybe he was going to trade me. I felt so bad after the beating the Bears gave us.

"When I walked in the room, Carroll asked me why I was depressed. I told him because we lost. But he was smiling. Then he said, 'Don't worry; now I got my chance to fire Weeb Ewbank.'

"He asked me to recommend a coach. I told him Shula, who had played with us and was then a coaching assistant for the Detroit Lions. We were playing them the next week. A meeting was set up on the Saturday before the game between Rosenbloom and Shula.

"It was supposed to be secret. No one was to know. But Shula said he was working for George Wilson and, as the Lions' head coach, he wanted to tell him or he wouldn't go through with the idea. He informed Wilson. The meeting was then held and Shula, after the season was over, got the job."

What about Ewbank? "I thought he was the greatest judge of talent I ever knew," said Marchetti. "If he had a weakness, it was being too nice."

His vote for the toughest player of them all was a roommate, linebacker Bill Pellington. And the most talented? "Lenny Moore. He could do anything anybody does today and do it better. I used to tell him before games, 'Lenny, if you go, we go.' How true."

The current demand for autographs, for player jerseys and other memorabilia astonishes Gino. "I guess maybe I should have kept every shoelace, old socks and jockstraps if I had known things were going to be like this," he said.

Marchetti, 67, now a retired millionaire from the fast-food business, lives in suburban Philadelphia. But Baltimore, he says, "was the greatest time" of his life.

All because of his association with a certain football team.

_ _ _ _ _ _ _ _ _ _ _ _ _ _ _ _ _ _

Art Donovan, Colts good humor man

June 6, 1994

Family and friends turned out to get sentimental over Arthur Donovan, a walking-around wonder of the world, on his 70th birthday. It was a time for what he does best — reminiscing — only others were doing it. There were cheers and, yes, even a tear or two.

It was a party at the Valley Country Club (where else, since he owns the place?) put on with affection and respect for a perpetual good humor man who brings the priceless quality of laughter to followers who surround him as if he's a modern Pied Piper.

Donovan finally caught up to number 70, the Baltimore Colts jersey he wore with Hall of Fame distinction. His notorious dietary and drinking habits are unconventional. He may order four double cheeseburgers and a six-pack of beer for a before-bed snack, or even more. The nutritionist aren't happy, but have reluctantly come to realize there are exceptions to every rule.

Surrounded by family and friends, including ex-teammates, two of his doctors, a dentist and four priests, Donovan felt so comfortable on his birthday that he became the contented listener. Donovan, premier entertainer, never spoke to the gathering, but his wife, children and others in the ballroom talked about him with profound admiration, citing his consideration and sacrifices as a father and husband.

He mentioned to a guest that 50 years ago to the day, when he turned 20, he was in World War II combat as a Marine for the first time.

"I was on the San Jacinto, what was called a small carrier, near Guam, and shooting a 40-millimeter gun at the Japanese planes that tried to blow us out of the water," he said. "I was so scared I wet my pants."

Two Colts, Jim Mutscheller and Alex Sandusky, thanked him for what he meant to them personally and, on a broader scale, to the city and state. Dr. Edmond McDonnell, the retired surgeon who cared for the injuries of Baltimore sports teams, said, "We've all been blessed to have known such a remarkable individual. God created only one of him."

Elmer Wingate, another former Colt, added, "A once-in-a-lifetime kind of individual. He does what he wants and says what he wants in his own inimitable way."

Larry Beck, known as the "Trophy King" of Baltimore, commented, "A genuine, realistic guy. No phony." Joe Wyatt, a businessman, said, "He's so special he belongs in a hall of fame for humanity." And Fred Kail, a sculptor, remarked, "He's a link to an era I'm afraid the world may not see again."

Donovan came to play for the Colts in 1950 after four years at Boston College, on a team that sent such outstanding players as Ernie Stautner, John Kissel, Art Spinney, Ed "Butch" Songin and Eddie King to the National Football League. "I got paid $4,500 for the season," he remembers. "Sisto Averno just reminded me we also played seven exhibitions and two or three intrasquad games. That was a lot of tough work for so little pay, but I loved it.

"There was a brewery going out of business called Weisner's. We bought cases for 50 cents and stacked them in the hallway of where we stayed, the old St. James Hotel in downtown Baltimore. We had so many beer cases in the place they reached to the ceiling."

But Donovan, with a legendary capacity for being able to consume beer, only liked it out of cans. If it was in bottles, he wasn't interested. His tastes are discerning. But he has never been inebriated and has a tolerance for beer that can be explained by the fact he is 270 pounds. At birth he weighed in at 17 pounds, which is tackle size for a baby.

He was attracted to football while growing up in the Bronx and nearby was the campus of Fordham University and its outstanding teams of the mid- and late-1930s. Athletics come to him quite naturally. His grandfather, Mike Donovan, was the middleweight champion of the world and served as President Theodore Roosevelt's private boxing instructor. His own father, Arthur Sr., was a prominent referee.

All three of the Donovans are in their respective halls of fame, which says much for the kind of genes they shared.

Donovan's humor is never hurtful, and he enjoys the give and take of repartee.

"I made an appearance on the Eastern Shore at an auto repair shop," he was saying, "and, honest to God, a woman asked me to have my picture taken with a dog. Guess what the dog's name was? It was 'Hemorrhoid.' That made the trip worthwhile. If you can't laugh at that, then you just can't laugh."

When Donovan was about to retire, after 12 NFL years, he called to notify a sportswriter. He had to fight for control of his emotions. Yes, that's how much the game meant to him. It wasn't just a job, a chance to make money.

Art Donovan, bottom line, has been much more than a football player with Hall of Fame ability. He has a way of making you smile and laugh. Crowds are drawn to him with a magnetism that continues to endure because humor, you see, is so good for the soul.

— · — · — · — · — · — · — · — · — · — · — · —

The unforgettable Bert Rechichar

Nov. 16, 1997

WEST NEWTON, Pa. — Standing under the motel marquee, obviously waiting for a friend to arrive, was this man in a western hat, green jacket and blue jeans, lighting a cigarette. He looked as if he had hurried in from herding sheep or else stepped off a movie set. But, no, this was a scene from real life and the same character was still playing himself.

It was a chance to again see Bert Rechichar, who always looked and talked tough and, most assuredly, played the same way. He once told Howard "Hopalong" Cassady, a Heisman Trophy winner, after tackling him hard along the sidelines, "Listen, Cassady, this ain't Ohio State. This is the National Football League, and we tear out your eyeballs."

Rechichar, on the field, had a somewhat demonstrative way of expressing himself. It was an attempt to intimidate opposing players, or at least give them something to think about. "You come over here," he'd shout at Harlon Hill or Bob Boyd, "and I'm going to rack you so hard you're going to think you got hit with a pickax."

Ball carriers, when they went down in a pile, rarely knew it was Rechichar on top of them who was twisting their heads the way he might unscrew the cap on a soda bottle. Just providing a physical annoyance, you might say. Pro football, in his era, when there were only 12 teams and roster limits of 33 players, attracted a different breed — and, by necessity, they were required to bring more ability with them.

This visit with an old Baltimore Colts hero led to a table in the motel dining room. There, he turned and hollered to the hostess: "Hey, Sapphire, bring me an ashtray." The woman didn't like the tone of his voice or the name he used to get her attention, but she responded. Bert Rechichar always got results.

He was 6 feet 1, 208 pounds and all-out physical, a safety who also kicked field goals. His first attempt at a field goal, in 1953, was the kind of a scenario that wound up in "Believe It Or Not," the longtime syndicated feature of Robert Ripley. Never before had Rechichar lined up to try a field goal, but he kicked the ball 56 yards, on a line, to erase a record set 19 years before by Glenn Presnell of the Detroit Lions.

It was four seconds until the half, in a game against the Chicago Bears, when Rechichar headed for the locker room as Buck McPhail prepared to try a desperation kick. Quickly, an assistant coach of the Colts, one Otis Douglas, had a second thought and hollered for Rechichar, who turned around to say, "What the hell you want?"

So Rechichar trotted on, not actually knowing how far he would be kicking, and McPhail came off. Bert told holder Tom Keane: "Get that ball down, because I got to go to the bathroom." Then he drove the kick, on his initial try, clear over the back line from 56 yards.

The then-record kick made Rechichar an instant celebrity. And he managed to do it while wearing a regular, soft-toed football shoe, not the box-type of kicking boot he would later use, like on the afternoon in 1957 when he hit four field goals — from 52, 44, 42 and 41 yards — in

Ball carriers, when
they went down
in a pile, rarely knew
it was Rechichar
on top of them
who was twisting
their heads the way
he might unscrew
the cap on
a soda bottle.
Just providing
a physical annoyance,
you might say.

the Pro Bowl and was voted the game's Most Valuable Player.

As a rookie, he was drafted No. 1 by the Cleveland Browns and a year later dealt to the Colts in a 10-for-five trade that also involved Don Shula, Carl Taseff and Art Spinney coming to Baltimore. "Paul Brown was a great coach," Rechichar said.

"He kept his distance from the players. He was stern and demanding. I remember Otto Graham once changed a play Brown sent in the game. At the meeting, as we reviewed the film, Brown told him in front of all of us: 'When this team is run from two sources, that's the time we crumble; you understand that, Otto?'"

Rechichar, of Slovak descent, was the youngest of 10 children in Belle Vernon, Pa., where his father was murdered by a man who took his pay envelope, and a brother, Frank, was killed in the mines. Bert was such an outstanding halfback, even though born without vision in his left eye, that he played both ways during the two-platoon era at a then "football factory" known as the University of Tennessee.

"I lost 27 pounds in the Sugar Bowl against Maryland. I went back to the hotel, fell across the bed and drank almost a case of 7-Up. We were the No. 1 team when Maryland beat us. What happened is, the previous spring, Maryland coach Jim Tatum, who was a good friend of our coach, General Bob Neyland, spent time watching us practice. He knew our system like he knew his own.

"I told the general at halftime against Maryland we ought to set our line unbalanced to the left instead of to the right because we were running into their strength. I guess the general wasn't used to suggestions from enlisted men, because we didn't change a thing. Maryland was good. Jack Scarbath and Bob Ward were something special."

Rechichar spent seven of his 10 pro years in Baltimore and was a part of two championship teams. But he came into disfavor with the head coach, Weeb Ewbank. "Yeah, and I remember one year we were in Santa Barbara, Calif., getting ready to play the Los Angeles Rams, and ol' Weeb begged me to talk to Carroll Rosenbloom, the owner, to keep him from getting fired. Then he paid me back by getting rid of me.

"Weeb and Don Kellett, the general manager, said they were trading me to the Chicago Cardinals because I was associating with undesirables [bookmakers]. I went there, stayed a week and went right to the top. I called commissioner Bert Bell and said I wasn't happy playing for an undesirable owner, Walter Wolfner. So he sent me back to the Colts. In the first practice, the players cheered when

I came down the hill at Westminster.

"On the first play, I got a wink from John Unitas. I knew he was throwing to Raymond Berry. I picked it off and ran through the whole offense. Weeb didn't like any of that, especially when the players applauded again. I liked Unitas. I call him 'Peas.' He was never a prima donna. He was great at checking off. Joe Montana and Terry Bradshaw were no match for him. I told Weeb, after Unitas came to us, he had the best quarterback on the bench and he ought to put him in the game."

Rechichar remembers the 1958 championship and said, "I never saw happier people. Do me a favor. Say hello to Bucky Levin, my main man; Bill Neill; Dr. Ed McDonnell; Doug Eggers; Jim Mutscheller; Lloyd Colteryahn; Lenny Moore; Buzz Nutter; Art Donovan, who I guess is still wearing that same T-shirt he had on in 1953; Andy Nelson and the rest of 'em. I remember ol' Andy when we went to New York and he looked up at all the lights. Just a kid from the country. He said: 'I'd sure hate to pay that electric bill.' "

A playful rogue, even at 67 years old, Rechichar is beloved and unforgettable. He's retired but still works part time for the Donegal Construction Co., out of Latrobe, Pa. He's a throwback who once put his philosophy into words: "The hell with all but six; keep them for pallbearers and walk quietly around the dead."

In a trip through life, you only meet one Bert Rechichar.

-- -- -- -- -- -- -- -- -- -- -- -- --

Milt Davis blends intellect, humanism

Nov. 22, 1998

Being a two-way minority, African-American and American Indian, gave Milt Davis a distinction and perspective on life that lifted him into a dignified and rarefied realm of humanity. He grew up in a Jewish orphan home while practicing the Roman Catholic faith. Such a diverse background has created an extraordinary man gifted with enormous intellect and individuality.

There's respect for what he believes and the way he expresses himself. Educated, with three degrees, he has a certain refinement and gentility. A classic antithesis of the stereotyped put-down known as the athletic mentality.

Milt Davis is special unto himself. His family escaped the Dust Bowl of Oklahoma in a Model T Ford that overheated its way along Route 66, accompanied by all earthly property tied to the roof.

The faraway objective to reach the promised land of California was fulfilled during the Great Depression when his parents and assorted kin made their "Grapes of Wrath" odyssey from Fort Gibson, Okla., to what they hoped would be the better world of Los Angeles.

Father was a Muskogee Creek and black. Mother was from the Kiowa tribe and black. The early 1930s represented a constant struggle for a family that was desperate to escape the dirt-poor poverty of Oklahoma.

"I became a Catholic when St. Odelia's Church at 53d Street and Hooper Avenue in South Central Los Angeles gave children a doughnut if you came to Catechism class," he said. "When problems arose in our family, I lived at a Jewish home facility, Vista del Mar. I was there for 17 years, even after I got married. I didn't play football but loved baseball."

He never thought of football until his college years at UCLA, where his speed in track made him an interesting study for the coaches. He became a defensive All-America halfback in 1952. This led to being drafted by the Detroit Lions, and then, in another strange bounce of the ball, becoming a Baltimore Colt and starting in two championship victories in 1958-1959.

Davis arrived in Baltimore for the 40th reunion of that first title team. It was almost an accident he wound up with the Colts, via a dirty play by management in signing him off the band squad of the Lions by refusing to recognize a gentleman's agreement that free agents in such a role would not be bothered by a rival club.

"The reason I was receptive is after the second game of the 1956 season, the Lions released me and Pete Retzlaff over the public address system at Willow Run Airport. It happened that way. Just imagine. We were coming back from playing the Colts in Baltimore, and coach Buddy Parker had it announced over the PA that the two of us were being placed on waivers."

The next year, Davis was in Baltimore, signed as a free agent after Eugene "Big Daddy" Lipscomb worked out with him at Denker Playground during the off-season and told him he was going to tell the Colts about him. General manager Don Kellett called, and Davis consented.

In the 1958 championship, he was the only player wearing low-cut basketball shoes. It was thought he wanted more traction on the partially frozen Yankee Stadium field. But that wasn't the case. "I broke the metatarsal bone in my right foot against the Los Angeles Rams two weeks before when I accidentally bumped a teammate, Steve Myhra," he said. "I wanted to disguise the injury, and the softer shoes, instead of cleats, were easier to wear. I took a shot of novocain to ease the pain before the game, but the fallout was painful when it wore off in the fourth period. But John Sample took over for me and was outstanding."

After the 1960 season, he left football to get a doctorate in education at UCLA. Then he went to work 12 years as a scout in the NFL, representing the Colts, Dolphins, Browns and Lions. He also was a movie extra and was cast in television commercials for Texaco and Western Airlines.

Davis has been married for 42 years to the same woman, of French and African-American descent, and now makes his home in Elmira, Ore., in the foothills of the Willamette Valley. He calls his 50 acres "Leave It if You Can" in reference to the scenic surroundings.

He has 20 head of sheep, raises and sells lambs, and engages in a select harvest of the Douglas fir trees on the property.

Davis was asked if there were times when he felt out of place in the Baltimore of 40 years ago because of segregation. "Yes. I have to tell you that. One of the most embarrassing moments was when I asked a young white priest from St. John's in Westminster to go to breakfast in Baltimore. When we went to a restaurant, the manager would say, 'You can come in,' meaning the priest, 'but you can't,' meaning me. I didn't want to create a scene, but I asked, 'Is this the land of the free and home of the brave?'

"Once in Westminster, I went to the movies with some of the players. They wouldn't admit me. So Alan Ameche and Raymond Berry said, 'Give us our money back for the tickets, we're leaving with our friend.' And we went on back to training camp and the Western Maryland College dorm. The way to refer to Alan and Raymond is how they put it in Oklahoma. They say high caliber."

The Davises have a daughter teaching Native American studies at the University of Oregon and two sons — all making their way in life in a pleasing way. Milt says part of the reason for the racial divide is "history never seems to be taught correctly, because a lot of the media seem to interpret and dictate false doctrines. People in the movie business don't help. They're pretenders, and I don't like pretenders. But even the great philosophers don't know the answers.

It's not always color that divides us."

Milt Davis says he doesn't go to a formal church any more. He calls himself a "practicing Native American" and is proud of his lineage. His ancestral background brings him to the realization that there is indeed a Great Spirit. And he takes comfort in the thought.

Unitas TD streak stands alone

Dec. 12, 1999

It'll soon be 40 years and John Unitas has hardly been challenged, meaning the unapproached record of throwing a touchdown pass in 47 consecutive games. A mark that seems sacrosanct, almost indelible as his exclusive property. Hundreds of quarterbacks have tried to reach the same, magic number but have yet to generate even an idle threat.

Unitas is alone — 47 straight games putting a passing touchdown on the scoreboard. An individual distinction. He never set out to create such havoc for rival defenses. His inherent, God-given ability allowed him to do what no other quarterback has done in the 80-year history of the National Football League.

The latest to charge Unitas' achievement is Peyton Manning of the Indianapolis Colts, who has accounted for a scoring pass in 25 consecutive games. He'll have to nearly double what he has done so far if he's to pass Unitas.

Does Unitas believe his record will be tied or exceeded? "It wouldn't surprise me," he said. "Peyton Manning is a logical threat. Teams now play four more games in the schedule. Quarterbacks also throw a lot more, like 40 to 50 passes a game."

The celebrated ball that gave him the record in 1958 was taken out of play during the game in Los Angeles and presented to Unitas as a memento. But he has no idea where it is. "I guess some kids got it from me. I always thought a football was to be played with, not looked at."

Before Manning got in the throwing contest with Unitas, others made a brief volley but never got there, specifically Dan Marino, who reached 30 and stopped, and Dave Krieg, with 28 successive games before he slammed into the wall. Others took, in the past four decades, their best shots and failed, such as Chris Chandler, Daryle Lamonica, Frank Ryan, Sonny Jurgensen, Warren Moon, Jeff Blake and Dan Fouts.

Yet they never seriously approached Unitas, who four times led the NFL in passing and became an incredible play-caller, beating the clock in pressurized situations and displaying a physical durability that earned the lasting respect of teammates and rivals. The mark of 47 straight games recording a passing touchdown is the attention-getter and provides enduring credibility to his marksmanship.

Some interesting ironies evolve from a study of Unitas' record, especially what might be called the Los Angeles factor. It was against the Los Angeles Rams at the Memorial Coliseum in 1956 that he started the streak; then two years later he surpassed the previous NFL mark of 23 straight games, held by Cecil Isbell. In 1960, again in Los Angeles, what began four years before came to an end. Strangely enough, all three games were losses for the Colts.

A box score of touchdown receptions during the extended string shows Raymond Berry with 38; Lenny Moore, 27; Jim Mutscheller, 24; Alan "The Horse" Ameche, four; L.G. "Long Gone" Dupre and Alex Hawkins, three; and Jerry Richardson, two. The longest pass play was an 82-yard completion to Moore in San Francisco in 1957, and the shortest, for 1 yard, on two occasions in 1960 went to Hawkins, first in Green Bay and later in Baltimore against the same team.

On the day Unitas moved past the former Packers passer, we interviewed Isbell regarding Unitas by telephone at the Milwaukee Athletic Club. "He's a fine fellow, a real good person and I'm happy for him," Isbell said without any hint of regret. Then he paused and added, "Tell him I hope he leaves that short one for me," meaning a 4-inch toss from Isbell to Don Hutson in 1942 that became the shortest scoring pass in NFL history.

The league later decided to remove the "shortest touchdown pass" category from the listings, so Isbell was deprived by the statisticians. Among the witnesses in the immense crowd of 100,202 in Los Angeles when Unitas passed Isbell was the Hall of Fame leader of the Packers, Earl "Curly" Lambeau, who was Isbell's coach throughout his career in Green Bay.

Asked for a critique of the young Colts quarterback, Lambeau said: "Quite a thing for Unitas in only his third season as a professional quarterback to do something like this. I understand Cecil Isbell said he was happy that as fine a kid as Unitas came along to do the job. I must say I feel the same way."

During the streak, Unitas hit on 713 passes in 1,336 attempts for 10,827 yards, had 103 touchdown tosses, 62 interceptions and a completion average of 53.4 percent. His average yards over the four-season span figured out to 230.3 a game, an average of 8.1 yards a pass. In 1958, after he returned from the casualty list, giving way to backup George Shaw, he was to carry the Colts to their 23-17 championship win over the New York Giants, and Unitas was voted the most valuable player.

The baseball batting record of Joe DiMaggio, who hit safely in 56 straight games for the New York Yankees in 1941, is frequently cited for comparison with Unitas. Or maybe it's vice versa. Yet the differences between the two sports must be considered. Baseball is played every day, but football kicks off once a week during a shorter season. One is a passive sport; the other involves all-out physical contact. Had DiMaggio missed a game because of illness or injury, his streak would have stopped. In football, the rule is different, and rightly so.

A painful injury caused Unitas to miss two games in 1958. The Colts routed the Packers, 56-0, and a defensive back, John Symank, jumped on Unitas after he was on the ground, puncturing a lung and damaging his ribs. Doctors refused to let him play for two weeks. Then, fitted with a protective jacket under his jersey, Unitas returned to beat the Rams, 34-7, while throwing touchdown shots to Moore, for 58 yards, on his first pass attempt and a 12-yarder to Mutscheller.

There were times during the streak when he threw multiple touchdown passes, on seven occasions as many as four in a game. Perhaps the closest he came to having the streak end was in Game 40 at Green Bay, a 35-21 loss to the Packers. He didn't connect until 70 seconds were left, pitching to Hawkins for the final score.

While Unitas was putting up his amazing total of 47 in a row, there was little attention brought to what he was doing. The country had become aware of his rich natural ability, but there was only casual mention of how, game after game, he was firing touchdown passes.

After he kept the skein alive in Green Bay, he was asked how important it was to maintain the TD consistency, adding to the count each Sunday. "Records don't mean a thing to me," Unitas said. "Nothing is as important as winning. You go into a game to win as a team and not set records. I imagine if I was record-hungry, the thing wouldn't have been extended this far. It makes no difference to me when it stops."

Now the question: Will "47" be duplicated or surpassed? It's impossible to say it's never going to happen, because records, regardless of who sets them, have a way of being surpassed. John Unitas' football immortality, in truth, isn't based on numbers, regardless of what happens to "47" and those amazing touchdown totals he put together.

— · — · — · — · — · — · — · — · — · — · — · —

Secret fumble recovery

Feb. 3, 1993

Deep under the stack of sprawling bodies, a man squeezed a football and thought it was going to remain the property of the Dallas Cowboys. Dave Manders, to his everlasting regret, was soon to learn otherwise.

Now, 22 years after the fact, he continues to insist the fumble that granted the Baltimore Colts a goal-line reprieve in Super Bowl V should have been ruled in the possession of the Cowboys.

Manders has no reason to invent a story or perpetuate fabrication. This is what he has been saying since late that afternoon, Jan. 17, 1971, when the Colts, smiled on by fate, won their only Super Bowl as Jim O'Brien kicked a 32-yard field goal with time running out for a 16-13 victory.

The fumble play was pivotal. Instead of the Cowboys' being at the Colts' 2-yard line, first-and-goal, and going in for another touchdown to extend their lead to 20-6, they relinquished the ball. Baltimore, as is said, escaped the bullet.

A score at that point, early in the third period, would have dictated an abrupt change in strategy and attitude. Dallas would have been fired with confidence and able to alter the pace, because the Colts weren't moving.

Duane Thomas, a powerful, straight-up runner, had a standout year for the Cowboys and, if memory serves correctly, made a second effort as he neared the Colts' end zone. It was then that he fumbled it away.

"The ball came right to me," Manders recalled in an interview. "I was all by myself in this little space. Nobody was even around me, so there was no judgment call about whether one player had more of the ball than the other guy.

"Billy Ray Smith [Colts veteran defensive tackle] jumped on my back and started yelling, 'I've got the ball, I've got the ball.' Without hesitation, [official] Jack Fette turned and signaled, 'First down, Baltimore.'

"I handed Fette the ball. Craig Morton and I argued, but he told us, 'One more word and you two are out of the game.'"

Manders, then the Cowboys center, believes a 20-6 lead, since scoring was so limited, would have resulted in a Super Bowl triumph. This observer, a nonpartisan, is in agreement with the theory.

But, in Super Bowl V, some extraordinarily good things were happening to the Colts, almost as if a greater power wanted it to be that way. A John Unitas pass in the second period, before he suffered a rib injury, sailed high to Eddie Hinton.

The ball deflected off Hinton's hands and was literally fingertipped by Cowboys defender Mel Renfro. It then went directly into the arms of a surprised John Mackey.

Mackey stormed the last 45 yards to put Baltimore on the Orange Bowl scoreboard. In the final minute, all tied at 13-13, another high pass, this one from Morton to Dan Reeves (new coach of the New York Giants), bounced off his hands for a Mike Curtis interception.

That put O'Brien in position to win with a pressurized kick from the 32. O'Brien and holder Earl Morrall jumped into the air, and all Baltimore celebrated.

Now, back to the alleged Colts recovery that influenced the outcome and helped make Baltimore the winner and Dallas a loser.

Smith's con job on the official, screaming he had the ball when he didn't, qualifies as one of the most persuasive selling efforts in Super Bowl annals. The Colts, most emphatically, got a gift.

But, in an earlier year, 1965, they were blatantly wronged in a playoff against Green Bay. A Don Chandler field goal, decidedly wide of the right upright, was declared good. That led to Green Bay's going on to win in overtime and then to play for and win the NFL title.

So most things, in a mystical sense, have a way of evening up. Manders doesn't retrace the scenario for the purpose of offering an alibi. He's merely testifying as a witness who was under the pile holding a ball he believes to this minute rightfully belonged to Dallas.

This past summer, when Smith was in Baltimore for a Colts reunion, he was asked his version of the fumble. All of a sudden, he started making funny noises, tried to change the subject and, finally, began to laugh.

Now, 22 years later, Manders and the Cowboys still discuss the controversy. Billy Ray Smith had screamed the loudest and got the only man who was important to listen.

Certainly, it's all in the perspective. A sad and dismal day for Dallas, a glorious, yet tainted, one for Baltimore.

A player convinced an official of something that never happened and it makes for an eventful, intriguing chapter in Super Bowl history.

--- -- -- -- -- -- -- -- -- -- -- -- --

Missed flea flicker still super memory

Jan. 12, 1994

He never was one to offer a cheap alibi or to blame others. Those are qualities that distinguish Earl Morrall as the consummate professional. He has for too long had to live with a play that went wrong and influenced the outcome of the most astonishing of all Super Bowl games — which transpired exactly 25 years ago today.

It was the case of the failing "flea flicker."

Morrall purposely didn't watch the film version until late last summer, because he wasn't interested in reviewing his most disappointing moment in a long, distinguished quarterbacking career.

"I have no excuses," he said. "You can't change the result, so why try to explain it?"

But there's another element to what happened, and his Baltimore Colts teammate, Tom Matte, says it's wrong, even remotely, to blame Morrall in the 16-7 loss to the New York Jets in Super Bowl III, which was the first time the championship was designated by Roman numerals.

"It's a part of football," insisted Matte. "We were all in it together. We just got beat. But when I took the handoff from Earl and ran to the right, stopped and passed the ball back, I threw it in a difficult position for him to catch it. He had to reach for it and, when he turned his body, kind of blocked off some of the left side of the field."

Morrall then wasn't able to locate his primary receiver, Jimmy Orr, who, when realizing he wasn't being recognized, began to frantically wave his hand at the 10-yard line. He resembled a man on a life raft signaling a passing ship in hope of rescue. An almost-certain touchdown awaited if only he got the ball. There wasn't a Jet within 20 yards. But Morrall didn't see Orr. There were only a limited number of seconds for the so-called "moment of decision" when a quarterback has to instinctively implement a judgment and either go for the completion, throw the ball away or resign to being sacked while surrendering a loss of yardage.

Morrall was at ground level, without the elevated advantage of those watching from the stands or press box, and the traffic around him would soon get more congested. The play was known as "439-Flea Flicker." The clock was winding down to close out the first half, and the Colts were at the Jets' 42-yard line. This was an ideal setting for a surprise.

"I took the handoff and ran to the right," was how Matte began to describe it. "Then I pulled up and threw the ball to him in a slightly backward direction. Meanwhile, Orr was kind of finessing his way down the opposite side of the field. My toss, a lateral to Earl, was a little high and off to the right. He caught it and turned to see Jerry Hill open in the middle, and that's where he went."

Meanwhile, Orr was uncovered but had, for some reason, virtually vanished off Morrall's optical screen. Morrall's first look downfield showed fullback Hill in the middle, an easy target, so he went there. The Jets were putting on pressure, and the Colts quarterback's reflexive intuitions told him he better expedite whatever it was he was going to do.

He quickly elected to "feather" the pass to Hill, but Jim Hudson cut in front to make the interception. The Jets thereby escaped a score and held on to a 7-0 halftime lead over the Colts. It was Super Bowl III. Date: Jan. 12, 1969. Place: Miami's Orange Bowl.

Baltimore, before the kickoff, had been described as one of the standout forces in National Football League annals and installed as a plausible 16½-point favorite. But the Colts, this so-called wonder team, came out flat, a condition brought on by massive overconfidence, and were ready to be had.

The end result qualifies as the most momentous upset since the Super Bowl was originated. Baltimore had won 15 of 16 games, including a 34-0 pounding of the Cleveland Browns for the NFL title.

With quarterback Joe Namath boldly predicting a Jets' Super Bowl victory at a Thursday night banquet, it meant he thereby called his shot and helped make it reality with a performance that included 17 completions in 28 attempts for 206 yards.

"It wasn't a fluke the Jets beat us that day," said Matte. "We never got in gear because of careless mistakes. Maybe it was lack of concentration. We had the better personnel, and if we played them 10 additional times we would have won each time. That's not to take anything from the Jets. It's what I like to think is an objective evaluation."

The game, from the perspective of semantics, was the first to be called a Super Bowl. The outcome also enabled the American Football League, which would soon merge with the NFL, to gain respectability.

Earl Morrall was not the victim, merely one of 39 players on the losing side.

Glory of day hasn't dimmed

Nov. 19, 1998

They came from the hardscrabble, shot-and-a-beer steel towns of Pennsylvania, where football was next to religion, from the seemingly endless prairies of the Dakotas, from the black-gold oil fields of Texas, from the congested neighborhoods of New York, Boston, Miami, Philadelphia and Los Angeles.

And diverse points in between, such as Athens, Ala.; Kenosha, Wis.; Greenville, Miss.; Perry, Okla.; and Parma, Ohio. A geographical and cultural mix. The Baltimore Colts, as with other teams, were by the nature of the business a migrant community unto themselves, gathering for a fall ritual known as the National Football League season and then hopeful of finding an off-season job to fill out the other six months of the year, because how else could they survive?

They gave unstintingly in all manner of physical effort and, in turn, their devoted followers in the stadium offered them their hearts and souls.

It became the Colts' destiny to play and win "The Greatest Game Ever Played," a badge of honor they wear for perpetuity. The sterling character of the men set them apart, and a city that fell in love has continued the romance for 40 years, dating to the time when Eisenhower was in the White House and the Kingston Trio was singing "Tom Dooley."

The Colts went out to beat the New York Giants in pro football's grand finale, attended by 64,185 eyewitnesses (7,000 under a sellout) in the canyon-like theater of thrills known as Yankee Stadium.

The Colts came from diverse backgrounds, young men with down-home Southern accents and the crisp, broad A of New England. One player named Milt Davis was part African-American/American Indian, a Roman Catholic raised in a Jewish orphans' home. He knew and practiced ecumenicalism before it was even fully defined.

A slender end, Raymond Berry, with poor vision and one leg shorter than the other, caught passes as if he had a cesta on each hand. Two of the enormously gifted linemen, Art Donovan and Gino Marchetti, had fought, under fire, in the dugouts and foxholes of World War II — Donovan on those pin-point dots of islands in the Pacific and Marchetti in the Battle of the Bulge.

A lithe, Lithuanian quarterback, John Unitas, showed up as a free agent and was happy merely to be getting the chance, plus a flat, $7,000 salary that provided no bonus or guaranteed contract. He became the meal ticket. And a horse-like fullback, Alan Ameche, who was more interested in the compositions of Brahms and Beethoven and a quick card game than he ever was in football, was a massive force for grinding out yardage and protecting the passer.

Then there was the acceleration and smooth, sliding strides of Lenny Moore, who taped his ankles over his high-top shoes and thereby achieved the nickname of "Spats." He produced electrifying moves, and with his speed and finesse, offered a dimension no other runner could match.

But this is only intended as a capsulated recitation of the still glowing past and the team's extraordinary deeds. There was Alex Sandusky, from the smallest of schools, Clarion State Teachers College, and Jim Parker, by way of Macon, Ga., Toledo, Ohio, and Ohio State.

A smart, rugged pulling guard, Art Spinney, showed a feisty half-back, L.G. Dupre, master of the cutback, the lane to the goal line. And, oh yes, L.G. had a colorful nickname, "Long Gone," representative of his initials, which evolved from Louis George. And there were others — such as "Big Daddy," "The Reading Rocket," "Tennessee Stud," "Champ," "Chester," "Goucho," "The Horse" and "Johnny U."

Once, on his first trip to New York, Andy Nelson, raised in the quiet of Athens, Ala., went on a sightseeing tour with Bert Rechichar, who was showing him the bright lights of Broadway and

Times Square. Nelson looked up in awe, turned to his friend and said, "I'd sure hate to pay the electric bill."

A coach, Wilbur Ewbank, called "Weeb" because a little brother had trouble pronouncing his first name, put all the pieces together. He was in a class by himself when it came to evaluating personnel and in teaching the rudimentary elements of a game that is both basic and complex.

It was a team, by its achievements, that the entire country quickly learned to respect and admire by the excitement it created. And in Baltimore it remains, until this day, the subject of a pulsating love affair. The game of Dec. 28, 1958, has even had two books written about it from both the New York and Baltimore perspectives. Yes, whole books pertaining to one game.

America, to a large part, discovered pro football that day. Forty-five million watched on television, a record then for a sports event, as two skilled craftsmen, Chuck Thompson and Chris Schenkel, captioned words to the black and white pictures. It was to become the first game to extend into overtime, as subplots, intrigue and second-guessing were part of the circumstances.

Unitas stirred the imagination of the nation and, with his calculating hand on the switch, paraded the Colts 86 yards, under unrelenting pressure, to tie the score, 17-17, and the next time he got to touch the ball took them 80 yards to win, 23-17.

To show its enthusiasm and gratitude, a crowd of 30,000 stormed the airport, shut down plane service, going and coming, for a chance to welcome the return of the victors. Some parents named their children for their heroes, and one family, the Taylors, named a son born that day for the whole team, which is why 40 years later he answers to the name of Colt.

People in Yankee Stadium told of actually seeing fans from Baltimore on their knees praying in the aisles of the cold end-zone bleachers. They were asking for God's intervention while Giants partisans believed their vaunted defense would assert itself as it always had. Score points for prayer as to overcoming wishful thinking.

It remains, 40 years later, as the Colts huddle tonight for a reunion at Martin's West, as a game for the ages. A keepsake to be revered and cherished, much as if it were a family heirloom.

And, indeed, it is.

A fan like no other

April 24, 1989

Blind adulation and an almost religious devotion toward a football team — while being a sincere friend to every football player who pulled on a jersey — set Hurst Loudenslager apart from all the other happy faces in the crowd. It would be difficult to comprehend any man, woman or child being so deeply in love with the Baltimore Colts. They were, indeed, "his team."

He reveled in the uncontested role as the No. 1 fan, and the coaches and players enjoyed having him on their side. They were stunned here and across the country to learn he died yesterday morning of an apparent heart attack while visiting Ocean City and making plans for the Colt Corrals' annual June convention.

A close friend and Corral Club member, Mike Gregor, put it all so succinctly when he said, "The formal death notice will read April 23, 1989, but he died the night the Colts went to Indianapolis in 1984."

Loudenslager, 74, was known as "Loudy," a derivation of his last name. In demeanor, he was never loud or brash, only consistently enthusiastic. The house where he lived was his own museum to the Colts with extensive memorabilia, including autographed pictures, splinters from goal posts, shoes, helmets and jerseys that the players had presented him. Outside, he raised the team banner on a flag pole.

At last count, he had sent 3,059 birthday cards and 3,797 Christmas greetings to the players. His wife, Florence, baked 726 black walnut cakes for them to celebrate birthdays during football season. The practice started in 1960 with Ordell Braase, a Colts' defensive end, and continued as a tradition.

"I did it because the players were away from their homes, and Flo and I wanted to make sure they weren't forgotten," he said.

Before every road game, Loudenslager was at the airport gate to bid the Colts a fond farewell, and was there, too, when they returned, win or lose, regardless of the hour. He carried a portable record player and welcomed the team with a rendition of the "Colts' Fight Song." The night the Colts were torn away from Baltimore, he broke down and cried.

"Bob Irsay may have owned the franchise with his money, but I owned them with my heart," he said. Not even Irsay could have denied it.

At home games, he waited outside the locker room and greeted coaches and players as they left. He knew their parents, wives and children. Loudenslager was the organizer of Colt Corral #2, formed in 1957, and was president of the Council of Colt Corrals, the group that presides over the rules and regulations of the fan club organization that had 32 different chapters.

Hall of Fame quarterback John Unitas was at a party for Chris Polk, an ill child Loudenslager had asked Unitas to visit, when the news of his friend's death reached him.

"What a shame," said Unitas. "He was so interested in all of us. He never missed welcoming the team home, regardless if it was 3, 4 or 5 o'clock in the morning. I doubt if he ever forgot to send a birthday card to a player. There isn't anything bad anyone could ever say about him."

Jim Parker, another Hall of Fame member, insisted no sport in the country ever had a man so deeply attached: "I played college football at Ohio State, where the fans are unbelievably enthused, but, when I met him, I couldn't believe the love he had for every player — not just the so-called stars, but every Colt who played here."

Burial plans have not been decided, but the Rev. James McNamara, S.J., chaplain for the Colts when they were in Baltimore, and the Rev. Joseph Ehrmann, a minister and former Colts tackle, will participate in the final rites.

Loudenslager, per his request, is to be buried in blue and white, the Colts colors, and will be wearing a team sweater and the gymnasium shorts he frequently wore to training camp after the late general manager, Joe Thomas, appointed him an assistant equipment manager.

"He was some guy," said Art Donovan, also of the Hall of Fame. "There will never be another like him."

Colt Band president John Ziemann said he talked with Loudenslager three weeks ago and felt his spirit was down. "He mentioned to me then he would never live to see a team back here, and I tried to tell him to keep his morale high," said Ziemann. "I realized that he wasn't feeling well."

George Kelch, associated in numerous Colts promotions with

Loudenslager, said, "If you had one friend in life like him, it was all you needed."

Honored by the Colt Corrals and virtually every sports organization in the state, he would continually say, in his acceptance speeches, that "the most important thing for all of us is to be kind to each other." And that, indeed, was his philosophy.

It would be easy to classify Hurst Loudenslager, who fought in World War II and then served as a sergeant with the National Guard, as some kind of extremist. And he was ... about the Baltimore Colts. When he's carried to his grave at Glen Haven Memorial Park, the mourners will be singing, low-key, the appropriate line of the team fight song, and where it says, "Fight on for Baltimore and Maryland," they'll add "and for Hurst Loudenslager, too."

Chapter 12

RETURNING
to the
FIELD

City has gone from martyr to pawn

Nov. 7, 1995

No longer a martyr. Baltimore, once so pure and sanctimonious, has blood on its hands. The aura of pseudo-purity has been stripped away. Regret, shame and embarrassment prevail on an occasion that should be one of explosive elation. Euphoria is conspicuous by its absence. Rightly so.

Under a Colt-blue sky on a glorious November day, the Cleveland Browns became the Baltimore Browns. And quickly, just like that, Baltimore became another stop on the NFL's floating craps game. The man who appeared to be suffering the most during this historic moment was Art Modell, who turned his back on Cleveland, where he lived for 35 years, walked away and took his football team with him to Baltimore.

Never again will he feel welcome enough to go back there and sleep in his own bed. He'll be selling his house and forming new friends. An emotional man, he was a study in dejection as the welcoming news conference droned on and the governor offered self-serving comments before introducing Modell as the newest citizen of Maryland — the reason being that he can't go back to Ohio because of the backlash he created.

Baltimore wanted to regain its stature in the NFL, but not at the expense of the Cleveland Browns. When Bob Irsay deserted Baltimore and went to Indianapolis under the cover of darkness in 1984, he didn't have the vaguest idea what he was doing.

But with Modell, it's different. There's no way to compare him to Irsay in substance and talent. But the deeds of Modell and Irsay, taking away something we used to hear was a public trust, are precisely the same. His friend who welcomed him to the NFL in 1961, the late Art Rooney, the gentleman owner of the Pittsburgh Steelers, would be disappointed, even if Modell is complimenting Baltimore by bringing it a franchise.

We remember so well that afternoon in 1951 while visiting with Rooney at Pimlico and awaiting his answer on how he felt about transferring the Steelers to Baltimore. He admitted considering it for weeks, but finally said, "I can't do that to my town."

When Baltimore was violated by Irsay, Rooney often mentioned, in that wry way of his, "the man isn't wrapped too tight." Modell is the antithesis of Irsay. He's smart, alert, articulate, humorous and knows that 11 players constitute a team on the field. Some of his Cleveland chums will be crossing to the other side of the street if they see him coming. Not good. A deliberate rejection.

Modell was one of the first citizens of Cleveland, involved in worthwhile civic projects, decorated with more awards than he has space to display and a nonstop giver to charitable causes. So it's totally out of character for him to deprive Cleveland of what's so dear to its affections.

Yes, yes, Baltimore wanted to be accommodated in the NFL, but not this way. Cleveland feels abandoned, angered with Modell and down in the psychological dumps that its team of 50 years, the Browns, has taken it on the lam. Baltimore offers empathy to its Ohio neighbors. There's no rejoicing in Maryland . . . certainly not the kind you'd expect to accompany what could have been a momentous moment.

Seated on a platform in the middle of the old railroad property that is Camden Yards, where the new, $200 million, rent-free stadium will be erected for him, he appeared to be the loneliest man in all the world. He signified by his presence that he wanted to be in Baltimore, but it appeared, under the trauma of the moment, it was not exactly a comforting experience.

He had to be recalling all the good times he had known in Cleveland. Modell, though, found it impossible to resist the lure of the Baltimore deal — which is profitable for him, costly to Cleveland and expensive to the Maryland Stadium Authority with its free rent for 30 years, plus the right to charge a permanent seat license (otherwise known as an act of extortion) before a fan is entitled to buy a ticket.

The NFL owners will have to vote on the Cleveland-to-Baltimore move, even though Modell is committed to taking up residence on the crab flats of the Chesapeake. Approval or rejection from his fellow NFL owners won't happen until mid-January, and some of them are not too happy.

There's a feeling the NFL will launch into damage control and try to repair the breach. One way would be to get Modell to go back to Cleveland or take over an expansion club in Los Angeles, and let his friend, Al Lerner, who is a part of the Browns' ownership, own a Baltimore expansion franchise that would be absolutely committed . . . in writing . . . while getting on with construction of the new football facility.

Advisers to commissioner Paul Tagliabue on the expansion effort in 1993 obviously gave him bad advice that is now traumatizing the NFL. Instead of first putting expansion teams in Baltimore and St. Louis, two cities that had lost their clubs and deserved to be cared for, the recommendations were ill-conceived.

Charlotte and Jacksonville could have waited and been flattered to be so considered. But by skipping over St. Louis and Baltimore, it presented the opportunity for the Rams to leave Los Angeles and the Browns to check out of Cleveland. That's why so much chaos is present and Tagliabue is trying to curtail the domino reaction.

Baltimore in its best football day never compared to Cleveland, and this isn't demeaning the place where the Colts used to play. Modell was against teams being allowed to cut and run, and at all times was a strong voice for keeping order within the ranks.

Weeks and months from now, the impact of the Browns' moving will fade away and spectators will be going to the games in Baltimore with little regard to what happened and how the team got here. The passage of time has a way of diminishing the shock and the hurt . . . even for Cleveland.

Modell once was regarded as the epitome of respectability among owners, but the harm he has done to himself and Cleveland seems almost irreparable. It's as if they're saying, "Et tu, Brute."

— · — · — · — · — · — · — · — · — · — · —

NFL needs a close look at itself

Sept. 2, 1996

It was a game, yes, but a resounding statement that had as much to do about the past as the present. Baltimore belongs.

Only the ineptness of the National Football League and a woeful lack of even elementary understanding kept a deserving but abused city from enjoying a continuation of its own heritage.

And the message for the NFL is that when you forget where you came from, the roots of your franchise success, there's reason to be ashamed and, yes, maybe even doomed at some future date to self-destruction. Commissioner Paul Tagliabue needs to take an introspective look at himself to see how he and his advisers could have been so wrong.

How could anyone within listening range of Memorial Stadium dismiss the thunder-charged sounds that emanated from within as a throng numbering 64,124 helped rally the home team to a victorious 19-14 return to pro football over the Oakland Raiders? A continuous roar, with all the intensity of a million Niagaras, lifted a newly named entity called the Ravens, once removed from Cleveland, to a successful opening page in the football history book.

Thus this became a fulfilling day of retribution. Baltimore, even when it had no such motive, embarrassed the NFL for the blundering ways of its club owners and the staff of commissioner Tagliabue that refused it admittance. The league allowed the Colts to run away under the cover of darkness 12 years ago and then twice slammed the door in the face of the city when it came begging, with helmet in hand, for an expansion franchise.

Even Art Modell, who was to cash in on the deal, voted against awarding a franchise to Baltimore — but now he has a team known as the Ravens in a city he rejected in the expansion process.

It may be a bit premature to arrange Super Bowl excursions, but coach Ted Marchibroda is more of a firebrand, a stronger leader, than he was when he served a previous term as coach of the Colts.

Christmas Eve of 1977 brought the same two cities together, Baltimore vs. Oakland, but Marchibroda played it too close for comfort and took his lumps. The conservative Colts were beaten in the second overtime period, 37-31, and that was the beginning of the downward spiral of Baltimore football. The Colts had been in three straight playoff games and were 0-for-3, the proverbial collar.

It's now almost 20 years later, and Marchibroda is still the same astute tactician, but he's more assertive — a gambler — and a strong-willed leader who has a way of getting players to give their maximum.

Before the game even started, John Unitas, as Baltimore's celebrated Hall of Fame quarterback, delivered the ceremonial opening football to the officials. As he headed to the sidelines, Marchibroda charged out to meet him.

What a story line! It was Marchibroda who made Unitas a Colt, because in 1955 the Pittsburgh Steelers decided to keep Marchibroda, Jim Finks and Vic Eaton as their quarterbacks and put Unitas on waivers — a judgment that had a pronounced influence on football history. A year later, the Colts recovered the Steelers' most embarrassing blunder and watched Unitas achieve the status of an icon.

But there they were in Baltimore, the year of 1996, clasping each other in friendly jubilation — Unitas as a guest, Marchibroda the head coach. A tableau worthy of remembrance.

The sun-kissed gathering of 64,124, jubilant to the point of exhaustion in the 84-degree temperature, provided the largest attendance for professional football in the state of Maryland, surpassing the best of what the Colts were able to do during 35 years of earlier residency.

As a point of historical reference, the highest crowd count for a football game, per se, came in 1924, on the same site but in a sprawling wooden structure known as Municipal Stadium. On that occasion, Army and Navy played to a massive turnout of 80,150.

Yesterday's presentation was an excellent mix of days gone by, with 40 former Colts present and the marching band offering all the nostalgia needed, plus the presence of a new team.

A rebirth provides happiness and hope. Baltimore has become born again in its own distinctive football way.

Chapter 13

The ORIOLES

Vi Ripken should have a Hall of Fame

Jan. 31, 1989

ABERDEEN — Rare is the sports banquet worth the exercise expended in walking across the street, much less going off to another county. If you've been to one — be it Bangor, Baltimore, Butte or Biloxi — you've seen them all, unless it's the annual gathering of friendly, over-the-back-fence kind of home folks who gather annually to honor the Ripkens — Cal Sr., Cal Jr., Bill and now dear Violet.

The Ripkens are extraordinary. This time the tributes were being heaped upon the feminine head of the family, who is wife to Cal Sr., and mother of Cal Jr. and Bill, the brothers who play alongside each other in the Orioles' infield.

"Blame Vi," said a jocular coach Jimmy Williams, a retired coach. "After all, think how many more pennants the Orioles would have won if she had five or six more kids."

Rex Barney, the former Brooklyn Dodgers pitcher, said he thought everyone in the room was named Ripken, adding, "There's not a family like this in Harford County or anywhere else."

He's right. Never in baseball history, going back more than a century, has any woman had a husband who managed a major-league team with two sons also playing for dear, old dad. As with every manager, Cal Sr. was fired last season, but couldn't be blamed for the infamous start in which the Orioles put together a 21-game losing streak.

Among the speakers at the Ripken assemblage was Roland Hemond, who was the general manager when Poppa Cal was terminated. But the character of Hemond and his inherent decency came to the fore when he went to the microphone, before Cal's family and friends, and offered a stand-up-and-be-counted kind of commentary.

Almost an apology.

Most men in the situation would have had themselves invited to some imaginary function in Williamsport or else forgotten to show up. Not Hemond.

"It was a tough year for the Orioles, a tough year for me and tough year for the Ripken family," he said. "There was a lot of trauma, and I respected them for the way they handled it. I will never forget it."

Hemond proved himself a man of strength and sensitivity. He drew the loudest applause of the evening as a succession of speakers followed, including sports announcers Jack Dawson, Tom Davis, Jon Miller, Joe Angel, trainer Richard Bancells, traveling secretary Phil Itzoe and publicity director Bob Brown. They all had kind and justifiable things to say. But what else can be said about Violet Ripken, the First Lady of Baseball?

Cal Sr. talked about all the places where he played and managed, where Vi put the children in the car and pulled a trailer that had the dishes, pots, pans, mops, broom, bedding and all the other essentials needed to set up housekeeping — in such diverse points of employment as Appleton, Wis.; Pensacola, Fla.; Leesburg, Fla.; Little Rock, Ark.; Elmira, N.Y.; Miami; Kennewick, Wash.; Wilson, N.C.; Amarillo, Texas; Ashville, N.C.; Dallas-Fort Worth; and in two Aberdeens, the one in Maryland, where Cal was born and lived, and the one in South Dakota, where he played and managed.

"I think of the times when we were separated and how she handled so many problems and was both a mother and father to our four children when I was away on the road, before school let out, and she could come join me," said Cal Sr., the husband, father, manager and now a coach. "She is a dear, deserving person. I wouldn't trade any of those experiences we had together."

Cal Jr. had his turn. He related how he played with matches as a child, not that he was a would-be arsonist or anything. Mother always dealt the discipline, sometimes using a bread-cutting board to demonstrate a point or two with love taps across the part one uses to sit down.

"Then one day, she broke the cutting board," he recalled. "Guess what? Then she had two weapons to get our attention. As a baseball person, Mom knew more about how the game should be played than all the Little League managers combined. I only hope I can be half as good a parent as Mom has been."

Bill, the younger of the Ripken brothers, followed by relating how his mother was always around to offer encouragement. "I remember when I was pitching for Aberdeen High against Fallston High," he said.

"The temperature was about 30 degrees. The wind was blowing. And she was the only parent in the stands on either side of the field. She thought enough of me to come there.

"Then in 1982, when Cal was opening the season for the Orioles, she went to see him play, as she should have. But then she apologized to me because she didn't see my game that same afternoon. She's a great mom. I couldn't blame Mother for the stats I had in 1988 [a batting average of .207]. She's much too good a mom for that."

For gifts, the master of ceremonies, Jim McMahan, general manager/vice president of radio station WAMD in Aberdeen, presented Vi with flowers, a clock-radio to listen to Orioles games and an Alan Anderson portrait of herself, plus an Orioles shirt that had the number 7-A on it to differentiate from her husband Cal, who wears 7, and the boys, Cal Jr., with 8, and Bill, with 3.

What did Mother Ripken think of all of this? With a whimsical approach, she set the record straight: "The day I married and signed my first contract, it meant bad pay, hard work but great benefits."

If there could be a Baseball Hall of Fame for women, Violet Ripken would enter via acclamation as a charter member.

Palmer hasn't forgotten

Aug. 3, 1990

COOPERSTOWN, N.Y. — Acceptance into the Baseball Hall of Fame is the ultimate in recognition; the epitome of accomplishment. It's also an occasion for Jim Palmer to soberly reflect on a time when he knew rock-bottom anguish and uncertainty.

The early part of his career, upon signing with the Baltimore Orioles in 1963, was as he had hoped. Promising and productive. He won 11 games, lost only three at Aberdeen in the Northern League in 1964. Then 5-4 with the Orioles and, a year later, was 15-10, followed by a World Series shutout against Sandy Koufax and the Los Angeles Dodgers.

Yes, the credits are imposing. But now it's two days before fulfillment of his own Hall of Fame fantasy. He pauses in a pensive way to examine the past. There was a man who owned a Greek restaurant in Elmira, N.Y., who befriended Palmer and the rest of the players on the Orioles' farm club that was based there in the Eastern League.

Palmer has since attained the pinnacle, the Hall of Fame, but, back then, he was suddenly and without warning at the crossroads in a still young but threatened career. It was possible he might never throw another baseball because his arm wasn't fit enough to let him.

"This Greek man, who had an eating place, was exceedingly kind," he said. "He operated what you'd call a 'Coney Island hot dog' spot. He cooked meals for the players, steaks and all, and charged us like 85 cents. When I hurt my arm and was finished in Elmira, he worried about me. He even wanted to drive me to Baltimore, but I told him I'd be able to make it on my own."

But what about the origination of the arm problems? The Orioles had sent him to the minors in 1967, after he opened the season by winning three of his first four games. "I developed a lot of arm and shoulder pain. Doctors couldn't find out what was wrong. The next year, 1968, I didn't win a single game anywhere. They had me in Elmira, Rochester and Miami."

Yes, but was there one pitch you still remember? "Most emphatically. I threw an 0-2 fastball to Billy Conigliaro, who was playing for the Boston Red Sox farm team in Pittsfield. I heard something 'pop' in my shoulder. I didn't know it then, but I tore the rotator cuff."

For the entire season, assigned to three different teams in as many classifications, he pitched in a grand total of only 10 games, a mere 37 innings. So in 1968, only two years after his spectacular World Series, he was struggling to survive. He hadn't been able to win a game anywhere. Not in Elmira, Rochester or Miami.

This was the same Jim Palmer, who, ultimately, concluded with 268 American League victories and 3,948 innings pitched. But in 1968, he wondered if he had a baseball future. "I remember playing catch with Billy Hunter, who was coaching the Orioles. I couldn't even lob the ball back to him." Moments like that never fade away ... the trauma, the pain.

Right there, Palmer wondered if he ought to return home to Scottsdale, Ariz., and enroll in college. He didn't know what to do or where to turn. Harry Dalton, then the Orioles' director of player personnel, now general manager of the Milwaukee Brewers, decided Palmer should go to the Puerto Rican Winter League, where the heat of day might assist the healing process.

But the Santurce club, managed by Frank Robinson, couldn't afford to pay a lame-arm pitcher who was convalescing in the sun. Dalton, however, promised Santurce if it took Palmer the Orioles would be

responsible for his entire salary.

"Here they wanted me to go to Puerto Rico, to face a lot of big-league players," he said. "I had just come out of the International League and couldn't even get out rookie kids. They hit shots off me. My arm was in bad shape."

Before he left for Puerto Rico, there were two extraordinary developments. He visited the Sinai Hospital rehabilitation clinic for an appointment with Dr. Stanley Cohen, who is now the president of Sinai. An electro-myography machine was used to test the various muscles in the arm, shoulder and back in an attempt to ascertain the damage.

"Everything was normal until the needle reached the infra spinatus muscle," Palmer said. "There was no nerve response. Right then, they knew what was wrong. It was important, too, since it confirmed that what I had been complaining about wasn't in my mind. They were wondering if what I had been saying was more mental than physical. Then we all knew for sure."

Before treatment could be prescribed, Palmer went to see the Baltimore Bullets play in the Civic Center with a friend, Marvin Foxman, a pharmaceutical salesman. "I told Marvin what I learned at the hospital. While watching the game, he said maybe I should try a medication called Indocin. I took it that night, flew to Puerto Rico, ran the day after and then warmed up. I threw without pain. My velocity suddenly went from around 80 to about 95 miles an hour."

So here's Palmer, preparing to enter the Hall of Fame, mentioning the owner of a hot dog stand in Elmira, the names of Conigliaro, Hunter, Cohen and Foxman. And, of course, Indocin. Getting medication from a drug salesman at a basketball game is out of the norm, but, of course, the patient wasn't a conventional kind of pitcher either.

— — — — — — — — — — — — — — — — — —

O'Dell original bonus boy

April 5, 1993

Time expires with the blink of an eye, but pleasant experiences along the way count for something on the scoreboard of life. Such relates to enjoying the Opening Day homecoming for Billy O'Dell, who was the Baltimore Orioles' first "bonus baby" when the team was refranchised in the American League 40 years ago.

O'Dell was pursued by every team in the majors in 1954 while a standout at Clemson. The school's athletic director, Frank Howard, and coach Bob Smith didn't want to see the young left-handed pitcher leave while a junior, but told him if the financial proposal was attractive, it was in his best interests to sign.

A conservative general manager named Arthur Ehlers, who didn't believe in being careless with the Orioles' money, was impressed enough to sign him for $12,500, on the recommendations of scouts Red Norris and Fritz Maisel. The late Ehlers' granddaughter, Evelyn, works in the Orioles' executive offices, which gives O'Dell a continuing relationship to his Baltimore past.

He's here as the guest of the Babe Ruth Museum and plans to return in July, when he'll be an important part of the All-Star Game ceremonies. In 1958, the only previous occasion the event was held here, O'Dell retired nine batters in a row and earned the first most valuable player award conferred in the history of the All-Star Game. O'Dell, who lives in Newberry, S.C., is now 60, which is evidence that even baseball bonus babies grow older. He retired as a personnel director in a cotton mill and spends his time fishing and hunting, usually with bow and arrow.

"When the call came to the bullpen in the 1958 game," he recalls, "I was surprised. I thought manager Casey Stengel would bring in Billy Pierce. Everything went well. After the game, I never got to talk to Stengel."

But Stengel, anytime O'Dell was pitching against the New York Yankees, would holler from the dugout, "I'm going to get you."

O'Dell took it as some kind of a threat. Then Bobby Richardson, a friend who played second base for the Yankees, explained the reason. Stengel, according to Richardson, was impressed with O'Dell and wanted to get him in a trade.

"Finally, in 1962, when I was with the San Francisco Giants, I was warming up in foul territory, adjacent to home plate, before a game with the New York Mets," said O'Dell. "Finally, Stengel, then managing the Mets, walked over.

"I had never seen anything like that before. Casey looked at me and said, 'Mr. O'Dell, I didn't have a chance to thank you for the wonderful job you gave me in that All-Star Game in Baltimore. I want you to know I appreciated it.' I just never forgot that."

O'Dell recalled some early Orioles teammates, names such as Willie Miranda, Gus Triandos, Skinny Brown, Bob Nieman, Lou Sleater and

Clint Courtney. O'Dell pitched 13 years in the majors, spending additional time with the San Francisco Giants, Pittsburgh Pirates and Milwaukee/Atlanta Braves.

The toughest hitter he faced? "Without a doubt, Frank Robinson. I'd like to know his average off me. It got so I knocked him down a lot. But he never complained. He'd just get up and drive my pitches harder and farther. What a hitter."

Late in his career, Billy became suspect for throwing a spitball.

"I tried to give the impression that's what I was doing," he said. "Truthfully, it was to give the hitters something else to think about. I'd pretend to go to my mouth. To throw a spitter, you have to work developing it, and I never did. I tried it, but I was mainly a 'fastball away' and a 'slider in' type pitcher."

When it came to looking for an edge, O'Dell admits he would occasionally shorten the distance to home plate by standing in front of the slab to gain a few inches. Did he get away with it?

"Once, I had two strikes on Wes Covington," he said. "When Tom Haller, the catcher, gave me the sign, I threw from a foot in front of the rubber and got Wes for strike three. Covington mentioned, 'You sure got a lot on that last pitch.' I just smiled."

It's called gamesmanship, and O'Dell enjoyed it all. He says he was told by some clubs that at a mere 152 pounds he was too small but the Orioles promised him the opportunity and the $12,500 bonus would mean, under rules then in vogue, he would stay for two years in the majors. As it evolved, he never had to spend even a day in the minor leagues.

—————————————————

Don Larsen and the good times

July 27, 1994

When the telephone rings and the voice says, "Let the good times roll, baby doll," it's the distinctive calling card of Don Larsen, an uncomplicated, gentle man who has never made the mistake of being impressed with himself or the notoriety he achieved.

The first and only perfect game in the history of the World Series, truly an epic baseball achievement, is the sole property of this refreshingly honest-to-a-fault individual who never let a team curfew stand in the way of a good time.

Larsen is visiting in Baltimore with one of his best friends, Frank Ferrari, a man he got to know when he was pitching for the Baltimore Orioles after the city rejoined the American League in 1954.

Actually, they met, as Larsen, an inveterate pinball player, toyed with the machine in an establishment, no longer in existence, known as the Bandbox.

Two years later, Larsen authored his impeccable performance for the New York Yankees when he put away 27 straight Brooklyn Dodgers, striking out Dale Mitchell for the final out. Umpire Babe Pinelli made the call as Mitchell tried to check his swing and 64,519 witnesses in Yankee Stadium couldn't believe the reality of what had unfolded in front of them.

On his return to Baltimore, Larsen, Ferrari and another compadre, Joe Wells, once a quality pitching prospect from Georgetown who signed with the Detroit Tigers, unlimbered their elbows and reveled in a round of story-telling at a leisurely spot called Woody's Inn.

In 1956, the Yankees were paying Larsen a salary of $12,000 as he helped pitch them to the pennant by delivering three straight four-hitters and a three-hitter. He was strong, athletic, a fast runner and respected batter who frequently would get the call to pinch-hit.

While an Oriole, with a record of 3-21 for a team that lost 100 games, he twice beat the Yankees, which is why they were receptive to trading for him in a deal involving a record 15 players. Larsen habitually stayed out late, and the Orioles, for what is believed to be the only time in the 40 years of the franchise, assigned a detective to trail a player. But the report was rather innocuous.

General manager Arthur Ehlers learned Don's routine was to visit a piano bar, listen to the music, refresh himself and then battle the nearest pinball machine.

"I could have saved the Orioles' money," said Larsen. "They only had to ask. I'd have told them what I was doing. I couldn't sit in a room. I had to be out in the city with the bright lights."

You know, "Let the good times roll, baby doll."

The night before his World Series masterpiece, he went to dinner in New York at Billy Taylor's restaurant with sports writer Art Richman, now a Yankees official, and was in bed before midnight. He also gave Richman, while sharing a taxi, a donation for his synagogue.

Larsen, in facing the Dodgers, utilized an unconventional no-

*The first and only
perfect game in
the history of
the World Series...
is the sole property
of this refreshingly
honest-to-a-fault
individual who never
let a team curfew
stand in the way
of a good time.*

windup delivery he had first used in a late-season game against the Boston Red Sox.

"I remember Yogi Berra was hardly in a crouch before the ball was there," Larsen recalled. "It even surprised the umpire. The only one who knew about it was coach Jim Turner. He told me to do what made me comfortable."

The World Series performance created such excitement that Larsen was in demand for public appearances. His top payday was $7,500 for being in a skit on the "Bob Hope Show." Larsen, though, quickly tired of the demands on his time and went home to San Diego.

He now lives amid what is generally agreed to be one of the most scenic panoramas in all of America, the town of Coeur d'Alene, Idaho. "We moved there because my wife liked the name," he jokes. "Our place overlooks Hayden Lake. If you like natural beauty, this is it."

Returning to baseball conversation, the game's tradition dictates that after a no-hitter the club awards the pitcher a $1,000 bonus.

"The Yankees said they'd 'take care of me later,' but never did," he recalls. "I guess they felt the World Series share was enough. The 1957 contract they sent had a $1,500 raise, but I finally got them to up the salary to $16,000."

Larsen decided he wanted to do something to mark the "perfect occasion" and, with Richman preparing a fitting inscription, went to the personal expense of having silver-plated plaques made for teammates, manager, coaches, trainers, equipment handlers, front office officials, umpires, league presidents and the commissioner to commemorate the deed.

As for occasionally coming home when the "birds were singing," he says experience taught him the second day, rather than the day after, is when the result of overindulgence may exact a toll.

While in Baltimore, Larsen asked about such ex-teammates with the Orioles and St. Louis Browns such as Billy Hunter, Dick Hall, Lou Sleater, Pete Taylor and general manager Hank Peters.

There was never anything petty or malicious to Don Larsen, which made him easy to like and admire. For right now, it's a glass of buttermilk for the road and, of course, "Let the good times roll, baby doll."

Larsen doesn't put it into words, but realizes Dame Fortune inexplicably put her fickle arms around him for an embrace that translated into illustrious immortality.

Burkart ended the fight

Feb. 8, 1995

Only when Elmer Burkart threw a baseball was he difficult. The Baltimore Orioles once brought him in for a relief effort during a ninth-inning rally — two on, no outs — and in 10 pitches he struck out the side. Everything was a strike, including a foul ball, in this dream-like performance that unfolded more than 50 years ago.

Burkart, nicknamed "Moose" and built like one, was a superb pitcher in the International League. He died at age 78 and will be buried on Friday.

The hard-throwing Burkart was with the Orioles in parts of seven seasons from 1938 to 1944 and was briefly with the Philadelphia Phillies, the team that originally signed him. Burkart enjoyed telling the story of how he was watching from the grandstand in Philadelphia in 1933, when Hack Wilson, recovering from a hard night, fell asleep in right field while visiting Philadelphia with the Brooklyn Dodgers.

What evolved remains one of the most amusing incidents to ever transpire in a major-league game. The Dodgers were pitching Walter "Boom Boom" Beck, so named because of his propensity for giving up line-drive hits. Beck was taking a pounding when the manager went out to make a change. Meanwhile, Wilson closed his eyes and dozed briefly under the hot afternoon sun while the mound conference continued.

Beck, infuriated he was being removed, vented his anger and instead of handing over the ball, fired it against the right-field wall in old Baker Bowl. The familiar sound of ball meeting fence startled Wilson from his slumber. He quickly reacted, almost on cue, by fielding the ricochet and making a perfect throw to second base . . . except there was no play to be made since the game hadn't resumed.

"What a lot of people missed," recalled Burkart, "is Beck was so annoyed that as he came across the foul line, walking toward the dugout, he threw his glove up in the grandstand. I spent a lot of years around baseball, in the minors and majors, and never saw anything like that ever happen again, a pitcher throwing both the ball and his glove away."

The memorable game when Burkart fanned three straight hitters on 10 pitches was in 1942, the Orioles facing the Rochester Red Wings at Oriole Park.

Burkart, besides continually offering the Orioles quality pitching, was involved in one of the most raucous and regrettable incidents in the history of the Baltimore franchise. It was the year before, 1941, after a bad Orioles team had put together an earlier losing streak of 13 in a row, that a fight broke out.

The club was in Toronto, and, after suffering another loss, outfielders Murray "Red" Howell and Roy Johnson battled in a hotel room that resulted in both being suspended. Johnson was sent to Wellesley Hospital for a five-day period with both eyes blackened, facial lacerations and serious body bruises.

Both had been drinking and were discussing the merits of each other's abilities. It led to a heated argument that became physical. Howell, who had led the league in batting the year before with an average of .359, beat Johnson so severely that newspapers described him as "almost unrecognizable."

Howell was attempting to drop Johnson out of the hotel window when Burkart came from down the hall and intervened. He had to punch Howell, opening a gash over his left eye that required stitching. It was generally believed by the Orioles that because Burkart stepped in to take control that he was responsible for saving Johnson's life.

Actually, Johnson's brother, known as "Indian Bob" Johnson of the Philadelphia A's, was reported coming to Baltimore to meet Howell and "square the account," but cooler heads intervened. Neither Howell nor Johnson ever played for the Orioles again.

"It was agreed that Elmer saved Johnson's life," said Russ Niller, another Orioles pitcher at the time. "It's funny how at a time like this certain memories come back to you. Elmer had everyone's respect. He had a gruff exterior, but was as soft-hearted as they come. A great competitor."

After his pitching career was over, Burkart remained in Baltimore but worked as a general manager of minor-league clubs in the A's system. When the Orioles re-entered the American League in 1954, Elmer was appointed ticket manager and remained in the position until 1963, when he became a real estate salesman in the Towson/Lutherville area.

Elmer Burkart survived baseball's combat when players were hard-bitten, rough around the edges and their rewards only modest. He was much a part of Baltimore's grand baseball history.

—··—··—··—··—··—··—··—··—··—··—

Gentile was best bargain

July 21, 1995

What Jim Gentile represents, among other things, is (1) the finest buy the Baltimore Orioles ever picked up at the baseball bargain counter and (2) one of the most colorful personalities in the history of a franchise that has been in business for 41 seasons.

Gentile qualifies as a top contender in any contest that attempts to define what an unforgettable character is supposed to represent. Often his own worst enemy, he had a temper that would self-destruct, exploding him into temporary orbit. There were arguments with umpires, confrontations with the front office and, yes, even a dugout fight with his manager.

The Los Angeles Dodgers had exhausted their patience . . . and contract options. He was hitting home runs by the bushel in their farm system and after eight years decided they owed him a major-league chance, but with another organization. So the Dodgers, not wanting to give him the opportunity to retaliate against them in the National League, told the Orioles they could have him for a 30-day free look.

It was a deal general manager Lee MacPhail couldn't turn down. The Orioles would take Gentile to spring training in 1960 and, if retained, the cost of his contract would be $25,000. Manager Paul Richards was initially opposed to having him around, but MacPhail, on the week camp opened, asked coach Eddie Robinson "to see if you can get Paul to like Gentile a little bit."

But Gentile produced a dreadful exhibition showing. He batted .216, had only four RBIs and zero home runs. It was Gentile's feeling he wouldn't be coming to Baltimore. "As a matter of fact," he said today, while in in the city for a weekend Oriole Advocates card show, "I remember running into Sparky Anderson, when he was managing Toronto in the International League. He mentioned 'a big first baseman is going to be available, and I'm wondering if that big first baseman would play for me?' I told him if you mean me then, of course, I'd play for you."

Gentile did not expect Baltimore to be his next travel destination coming away from camp. He was stunned, but pleased, when Richards decided to keep him another 30 days because the Orioles got an extension on the deadline for paying the $25,000 to the Dodgers. Richards promised Jim he'd get at least 150 at-bats and then make a final decision. When Gentile heard that, he replied, "Well, that's all I can ask."

The opportunity of a challenge brought out the best. If he was going down, it wouldn't be without swinging. And how Gentile could do that. His stroke was so full and the follow-through so complete that he pounded his own back with the whiplash. The Dodgers feared the constant bruising he gave his own shoulder area might lead to a cancerous condition.

As a first baseman, he could handle the mitt with finesse, had excellent footwork around the bag, especially adept on low throws and, being a converted pitcher, had an exceptional arm. So, objectively, he could do everything but run.

That wasn't necessary, because Gentile drove the ball for distance. His home run power had been proven in every classification but the majors. And he was to do it there, too. In four years as an Oriole, he had seasons of 21, 46, 33 and 24 home runs. It was in 1961 that he drove in 141 runs, still a club record, and finished one RBI behind Roger Maris of the New York Yankees.

But Ron Rakowski, a statistician in suburban Chicago, researched every box score in 1961, and his findings prove Maris was credited with an RBI that erroneously gave him the crown. Actually, according to Rakowski, Gentile and Maris should share the title with 141 and Rocky Colavito in second place with 140.

It's remembered that Gentile was tagged, by those sitting in judgment, as a "bad actor and a playboy."

"Look, I never got in fights, except when I played for St. Paul and my manager, Max Macon, and I had a battle. Max said I didn't have my head in the game; that I was looking up in the stands. But there's another story to that. It was silly.

"But the Dodgers didn't want to hear my side of why it happened. The only version that counted was what Macon told them. That was wrong. When I didn't play well or booted a ball, it ate away at me. It tore me up inside. I never bothered anyone else. Ask Russ Snyder or Rocky Johnson. They used to dress alongside of me in the clubhouse. Now about the playboy stuff, I don't know how that started."

Gentile had to be spoofing. Then he smiled and explained, "Yeah, I liked to go out once in a while. I had a few friends down on The Block in Baltimore and would meet them for a couple of drinks now and then. I always wanted to dress nice. I still do. That's when they started calling me 'Diamond Jim.'"

Some of Gentile's fits of anger were stupendous. Once, he was struck out by Early Wynn on a high fastball that seemed questionable. Returning to the bench, he emptied the rack, spraying bats all over Comiskey Park in Chicago. Finally, Richards came up behind Gentile to get him out of his blind rage.

"What are you doing, boy?" asked Richards, who grabbed Gentile by the back of his belt and told him to go to the dressing room, but first insisted he quietly get himself together. Another time, after going 0-for-4 in Cleveland, a distraught Gentile opened a beer, unusual for him, and slumped in front of his locker.

He was lost in a trauma of torment. "I hardly ever drank beer, but this time I had one. I was sulking, whatever you want to call it. I finally got up to take a shower. Richards dressed across from me and came over and said, 'Son, don't worry. You had a bad game, but it'll be a good one tomorrow; don't get so upset.' Then I looked down and realized some of the guys placed 10 empty beer bottles near where I had been sitting. I guess Richards thought I was turning into a drunk or something."

Gentile, now 61 and married, lives in Edmond, Okla., and insists his all-time hero is Gus Triandos, the former Orioles catcher who will be with him as another card show signee. Jim Gentile admits he may have been late maturing, but he learned to laugh at himself, which is a quality, discovered belatedly or not, that makes everything about life more tolerable.

Appreciate the night, and the man

Sept. 6, 1995

Magic was in the air. And more than a touch of sentiment. This was a night to be preserved as a special memory, to be put away and cherished as a personal keepsake.

Fittingly enough, a marshmallow Maryland moon lit up the sky, accompanied by a canopy of twinkling stars, but the one that shone the brightest was the man wearing a baseball uniform with Orioles scripted across the front and a block No. 8 on his back.

The name is Ripken, Calvin Edwin, to be specific. His identity has become synonymous with the Baltimore Orioles, one of the game's pioneering teams. Mention Orioles and the immediate association is to Ripken, endowed with physical grace, fielding the shortstop position with style, competency and precision. With a bat in his hands, he drives the ball with authority to all fields and plays with natural instincts that make it all look so easy.

Now, he has joined Lou Gehrig by displaying a kind of endurance that tests the powers of comprehension, locked in the same number — 2,130 consecutive games — but that's only temporary.

He'll go past Gehrig tonight in what promises to be the most significant occasion in the sports history of Baltimore, going all the way back to the legendary "Old Orioles" with a cast that numbered such Hall of Fame performers as John McGraw, Wee Willie Keeler, Wilbert Robinson and the first Iron Man, otherwise known known as Iron Man Joe McGinity.

The game last night, an Orioles victory over the California Angels, even offered an appropriate total of runs that coincided with the number Ripken wears on his uniform. The scoreboard showed it was an 8-0 victory, with the guest of honor hitting a home run and gathering two other hits in five trips to the plate.

Ripken, more importantly, had fun. The pressure was gone. The moment had arrived when catching Gehrig was at hand. He enjoyed himself as he caught up to the immortal New York Yankee, holder of a longevity record that for five decades was believed to be beyond the reach of any challenger. Then Ripken, a native son raised in Aberdeen, grew up to play for the Orioles, after working his way through the farm system, and literally wore down the ghost of Gehrig.

It was a momentous event at the ballpark as the Orioles wrapped pre- and post-game ceremonies around Ripken, and this, too, was carried out with imaginative planning. For the way he carries himself and the content of his comments, America has come to admire the maturity and credibility of the man.

He's the best thing baseball has going for it. It would be an exaggeration to suggest he is going to save the game the way Babe Ruth's presence and popularity removed the stain of the Black

Sox Scandal and lifted the sport out of the gutter in 1920. But Ripken is more than doing his part. He's a baseball treasure, admired as much for his gentlemanly ways as how he acquits himself on the field.

"I never thought anything about the immensity of the streak," he said. "I tried to keep it out of my mind. I didn't want to become preoccupied. There are plenty of people who work harder at jobs that are far more important than what I do. Mine is recreation. What they do, in many cases, is essential to living."

And what did he plan to do on the morning of the same day he is in line to play one more game and move past Gehrig? Why, he was going to get up early, like so many other parents, and take his daughter to school for the first time. It's recognizing this kind of a private priority that sets him apart.

The Ripken-Gehrig comparison, meanwhile, continues nonstop. Gehrig wasn't able to get beyond 2,130 because, at 35, the same age as Ripken, he was tragically struck down with an incurable spinal disease.

And, to reflect on a financial aspect of "then" and "now," Ripken's annual contract of $6,871,671, when prorated, comes to $47,719.94. That's for each game he plays. Gehrig, in his best salaried season, earned $39,000 for all of 1938.

In 1939, when he was stricken, the Yankees slashed Gehrig's pay by $5,000, but at the time didn't realize, nor did anyone else, they had a seriously ill first baseman.

The record of Ripken cannot be faulted. He played a more difficult position than Gehrig yet accounted for a higher total of innings on the field.

In the so-called modern era, the records of Babe Ruth, Ty Cobb and now Lou Gehrig have been under attack and rewritten. But only Ripken's achievement carries pure credibility.

Stop to consider that when Henry Aaron topped Ruth, he had 2,896 more at-bat opportunities. Pete Rose came to the plate 2,238 times more than Cobb. And in 1961, the year Roger Maris eclipsed Ruth's mark of 61 home runs in a season, he was in 10 more games and had 50 more at-bats.

The Ripken achievement comes with no such numerical advantage, so what he has accomplished offers absolute legitimacy, and this is expressed with all due professional respect to Aaron, Rose and Maris.

Cal Ripken is about to break a record that was thought to be beyond reach. It encompasses an incredible demonstration of perseverance and durability. His skills at playing the game can't be minimized. If he didn't have ability, he wouldn't be in the lineup, so there's ample talent he brings with him.

What he stands for is a testimonial to himself, a walking-around monument that will someday be put in bronze and acclaimed for perpetuity.

Epitome of grace on and off field

April 16, 2000

Decency, refinement, consideration and an old-world word — dignity — on behalf of others sets Brooks Robinson apart from the rest of the parade. Athletes or what have you. A gentleman in the total context, never given to the human weaknesses of envy or selfishness.

If a disgruntled teammate, acting more as an adolescent than an adult, argued about an official scorer's ruling, in or out of the clubhouse, whether it was a dropped ball or an errant throw, he would defuse the controversy by saying, "Look, just give me the error," even if he didn't have it coming.

Once, while leaving a restaurant in Waverly, umpire Ed Hurley turned to offer the most praiseworthy of all evaluations regarding Robinson: "He plays third base like he came down from a higher league." What a tribute. Say it again, "He plays third base like he came down from a higher league."

He hasn't been in a game since 1977, when he took off the Orioles uniform after his career spanned 23 years with the same team, yet the mere mention of his name or a guest appearance on the field brings a resounding ovation.

Why? The public is smart and observant. It isn't duped or dumb; it realizes the special qualities of an extraordinary individual, a man of good taste and purpose. Worthy of emulation. If his patience is being tested by public demand, he doesn't respond with an equal display of rudeness.

Flash now to 1983. Location: Cooperstown, N.Y., the lobby of the Otesaga Hotel. Hall of Fame induction day. A sportswriter introduced himself to Brooks' mother and said it was regrettable Mr.

Robinson hadn't lived to experience the honors coming to their son. "I have great faith," she answered. "I believe his dad is in heaven and knows about this." Then from the sportswriter came a direct compliment to Mrs. Robinson, "Well, you and his father made him the kind of man he is by the direction you provided as he grew up." "No," she answered, dodging the flattery. "We can't take credit. Where we lived in Little Rock [Ark.] was a block from the School for the Blind and a block from the School for the Deaf. Brooks grew up playing and having fun with those children, and I believe the experience gave him his deep sensitivity for others. He even learned sign language."

His personality is such that he transmits confidence and exudes friendship. Sunshine where there's darkness, a smile when there's sorrow. That's just the way he is; nothing contrived, staged or artificial.

Looking to do for others, for example a lonely soldier in a fire station in Vietnam, where he once waited seven hours to meet a youngster out on a mission, just so he could come back to notify a mother in Parkville, Md., that he had met her son. He carried a message home from the jungle, one of love and Christmas wishes.

That same mother called a newspaper office to say for all the rest of her life she would be on her knees nightly, before going to bed, and in her prayers ask for blessings on behalf of Brooks for what he had done.

And then the call to a talk show, where another story was shared. A small child had a colostomy, rare for one so young. Brooks called Johns Hopkins Hospital to visit, even left a personal check. Then, when the time came for the boy to return home, he found their house in Ferndale, Md., and was waiting to lift him out of the car and carry him into the house.

Once, at a fund-raising banquet for Mary Dobkin, who managed Baltimore sandlot teams made up of kids filled with grime and victims of hard knocks, he flew on a Thanksgiving weekend from Little Rock, where he was enjoying the holiday, to Baltimore, and then back to Little Rock to pick up his wife and children at his own expense. Far beyond the call of duty.

Yes, an exemplary human being. Measure him any way you want. The result is always the same: goodness. After he was extolled during a sports banquet at Towson University, and only by chance, we left the building with Cal Ripken Jr. The walk was across a dark and slippery parking lot on a January night. "Those things about Brooks were beautiful," Cal said. "Stop to think how much time and effort it takes to do all that. It just doesn't happen. Brooks had to want to do it."

Most athletes are not averse to works of mercy. But rarely do they fulfill such good intentions. Some never do. Not even once, or even by accident. Brooks Robinson has — a multitude of times as a player and continuing in baseball retirement.

When he played and after he left the game, he was the signature Oriole; the one player synonymous with the franchise. You connected him in thought the same as John Unitas of the Baltimore Colts or Stan Musial of the St. Louis Cardinals or Bill Russell of the Boston Celtics. The identity was there, player with team and team with player.

Yet Ripken came along to gather more laurels, to compile astonishing records. And Brooks, much to his credit, again demonstrating the kind of humility associated with the type of man he is, said over the public address system at the ballpark, while at a ceremony spotlighting Ripken, that the franchise was now his to hold and to cherish from that point on when it came to individual ties to the Orioles.

It was no longer Robinson; it was Ripken. And he withdrew, quietly getting out of the way so you, the public, would understand. Giving the full spotlight to Cal. It was a realization that might find others of less character reluctant to give up the role.

The achievements of Ripken have earned total respect from Robinson. "It's unbelievable Cal has played as long as he has," says Brooks. "But his attitude was perfect. If there was a game, he wanted to be in it. That's what being a baseball player is all about."

Three thousand hits or 400 home runs by Ripken? What's the most impressive? "I'd take either one," Brooks answers. "But I guess 3,000 hits, probably so. I think of Cal's father a lot. He'd do anything for you. I think if you asked him to hit ground balls to you at midnight, he'd get out of bed and do it. No doubt in my mind."

Along with wife Constance (they've been married 39 years), Brooks spends days and weeks on the road, either traveling for the Major League Players' Alumni Association as its president or representing Crown Petroleum, with which he has an office in Baltimore.

The genuine characteristics of Brooks Robinson qualify him for more than the Baseball Hall of Fame. His inherent decency is not by design. It was God-given. And he has never spoiled the essence of such an elegant birthright.

Chapter 14

CALLING
the ACTION

Thompson makes the call

Aug. 2, 1993

COOPERSTOWN, N.Y. — Performance, longevity and a voice smoother than the consistency of maple syrup, dripping with the rich resonance that has always been his, has brought Chuck Thompson to a cherished and satisfying career achievement — enshrinement in the broadcasting wing of the Baseball Hall of Fame.

In 7½ minutes of acknowledgment, Thompson tried the impossible. It was an effort to compact and convey the pleasurable sentiments of how it felt to be the play-by-play announcer of the Baltimore Orioles, both in their waning minor-league era and then during their celebrated ascendancy to major-league status.

It's a relationship that has endured for 44 years and counting. Trillions of listeners have been in his audience in all that time, and his popularity has been earned by an extraordinary skill in communication.

The Hall of Fame is a coveted honor that is most meaningful in the professional context and important, too, in a personal way for the selected recipients.

As he addressed the gathering of an estimated 8,000 sun-kissed fans before him on an athletic field in this village where the sport of baseball was conceived 154 years ago, Thompson called the occasion a "once-in-a-lifetime experience."

He said he naturally felt comfortable with the microphone and the crowd. Then he proceeded to offer a presentation that he termed "a baseball talk without statistics."

Chuck referred to the start of his career as one of "hit or miss," explaining how a classmate dared him to take a radio audition in

Reading, Pa. The acceptance was so immediately successful he never went back to singing with a dance band.

Thompson, after service in World War II and action in the Battle of the Bulge, went on to become a Baltimore staple, offering a crisp, fresh delivery that contained jackhammer rapidity, clarity and a homey, friendly demeanor. He didn't know it at the time, but he broadcast a Navy-Missouri football game at then-Baltimore Municipal Stadium in 1948 that led to his hiring by the Gunther Brewing Co., and, in turn, an opportunity to cover the Orioles as one of the most-listened-to announcers the city ever heard.

In the crowd applauding Thompson yesterday in Cooperstown was Jerry Hoffberger, former owner of National Brewing Co. Hoffberger was wise enough to minimize Chuck's association with a rival product, and made a handshake with him that lasted for 23 years.

The Hall of Fame ceremony opened with awards to sportswriters Leonard Koppett of the *New York Times* and the late Bus Saidt of the *Trenton Times*. Then Thompson was introduced by a Hall of Fame baseball player, Ralph Kiner, an announcer for the New York Mets.

In his remarks, Chuck emphasized how important his children had been to him, despite the fact he was often on the road in his special line of work. He praised his wife, Betty, and what she has meant to him in their marriage that took place five years ago, after the death of his first wife.

Then he directed his comments to the crowd. "Without you, this wouldn't have happened," he remarked. "I accept it for you and my on-the-air partners." A sizable segment of followers from Baltimore, some wearing T-shirts with his picture on the front, cheered his appreciative message.

He also mentioned associates such as Bill O'Donnell, Herb Carneal, Frank Messer, Jon Miller, Joe Angel and his latest associate in the booth, Fred Manfra. After Thompson's remarks came the main focus of the program — the installation of Reggie Jackson into the Hall of Fame — and the partisan New York gathering was getting restless, even though it offered respect to Thompson while he talked.

There were other things the Baltimore announcer intended to say, but his sense of timing told him to cut it short, and he did. Asked later if he was satisfied with the Cooperstown experience, he answered, "Gosh, yes, in every sense."

The Orioles' organization, headed by general manager Roland Hemond and vice presidents Bob Aylward and Frank Robinson, plus other staff members, were hosts to a party for Thompson and guests from Baltimore when the ceremony concluded.

While much has been offered about Thompson's in-depth vocalizing and the vivid picture he paints, don't overlook his high degree of accuracy. He rarely, if ever, makes a mistake, regardless of the pressure of the moment, and to his credit and the appreciation of the audience, he habitually gets it right the first time.

Chuck Thompson is the 17th play-by-play announcer since 1978, when Mel Allen and Red Barber were so named, to win the award. Succinctly put, it's all because he talks a great game.

_ _ . _ . _ . _ . _ . _ . _ . _ . _ . _ . _ . _ . _ _

Sam Lacy beat back prejudice

Oct. 20, 1993

These 90 years of Sam Lacy, perhaps the oldest practicing sportswriter in the world, have been filled with love of wife and family, unrelenting crusades to knock down the walls of prejudice and a newspaperman's professional satisfaction that comes with finding the appropriate word for the right situation.

He often felt the racial hurt of being turned away at hotels, restaurants and other places that should have offered equal accommodations, including press boxes. It was because of the color of his skin and these personal indignities that caused him and other black Americans to feel the deep pain of segregation and rejection.

His persistence to take on this vast social injustice never waned, because Sam Lacy refused to turn the other cheek.

Lacy's longevity is astonishing. So are his intelligence, perception of history and desire to deal with the problems at hand. Through 60 years of covering sports in Washington, Chicago and Baltimore, he has continually produced quality work — columns that were hard-hitting when need be, distinctive phrasing, insightful opinions and — bottom line — an inherent desire to make things better for his fellow man.

At the same time, there was his willingness to tell any man, black or white, when he thought an attitude or actions were wrong.

Lacy is a walking time machine, ready to recall the past in vivid detail. His well-dressed appearance is conservative, but that, to his everlasting credit, is not necessarily the way he thinks.

Lacy, at a 90th birthday party held at the offices of the *Baltimore Afro-American*, reviewed six decades of reporting sports.

"I believe Joe Louis and Jackie Robinson made the greatest impact of any black athletes in my lifetime," he said. "They are an important part of any history devoted to this country."

What about Baltimore? Was there any individual above all the rest in the sports arena who contributed in a similar way?

"Yes, by all means," he said. "It was Buddy Young. His personality and decency added much to the ongoing quest for racial equality."

After numerous rebuffs to bring Negro baseball to the attention of the then-commissioner of baseball, Judge Kenesaw Mountain Landis, Lacy was appointed to a three-man committee to study the issue of allowing blacks to bring their gloves and bats to the major leagues.

The first proposal in 1945 was to combine the Negro National and American leagues and place the teams at a level similar to the International, American Association and Pacific Coast leagues.

"Mr. Carl Murphy, publisher and owner of the *Afro-American*, hired me from the *Chicago Defender*," Lacy recalled, "and told me to get involved in the effort to have baseball accept black players.

"I went to two meetings with Branch Rickey to talk about it, but Larry MacPhail, the other man on the committee, never showed up. I believe Rickey just decided if it was going to happen, he had to go his own way and sign Jackie."

Was Jackie the best of the black prospects?

"No," answered Sam. "He was the most suitable, not the most talented. He had played with white athletes at UCLA, was articulate and knew what had to be done. I'd like to say Al Campanis, who got involved in a controversy about blacks not having the capabilities to manage, was extremely helpful to Jackie.

"When they were together at Montreal in 1946, Jackie didn't have the arm to play shortstop. That's when Campanis moved him from shortstop to second base and taught Jackie the fine points of the pivot and other things about the position. That certainly wasn't racist."

If Robinson didn't qualify as the finest black player Lacy ever saw, then who are his choices?

"Back then, I'd say infielders Dick Lundy of the Bacharach Giants and Ray Dandridge of the Newark Eagles and pitcher Joe "Cyclone" Williams of the Lincoln Giants and Homestead Grays," said Lacy.

At the Lacy celebration, Clint Coleman, representing Mayor Kurt Schmoke, remarked, "Sam has done more than make a living. He was a path-maker. He made it easy for others to come after him."

Publisher John "Jake" Oliver, in an assessment of Lacy, added, "His opinions are solid. You can't fool him. In evaluating people, his record for accuracy is incredible."

In conversation, Sam has often said, as he looks back through the telescope of life, "Success to me has been happiness on the job, a good wife [Barbara, who died in 1969] and a smile from God."

That's a philosophy that can't be found in a book but only from Sam Lacy, who has lived it.

Chapter 15

The
BABE

A close-up look at a legend

Feb. 5, 1995

More books have been written, movies made and words spoken to describe Babe Ruth than any other sports figure in American history. But, after all that, perhaps the most eloquent and vivid picture of the man and athlete is painted by a former player, Joe Cascarella, who provides a narration that is both profound and personal.

Mr. Cascarella, who is now 87 and has lived in Baltimore for more than 50 years, pitched against Ruth and is the only surviving member of the 1934 major-league all-star team that toured the Far East with him and such other magic names as Jimmie Foxx, Charley Gehringer, Lefty Gomez, Lou Gehrig and Connie Mack — all Hall of Fame members-to-be.

As a rookie with the Philadelphia A's, Cascarella won 12 games in 1934 with a bad team, but Ruth saw enough of him to say, "Why, that little Italian can bend a curve around a lamppost."

Listening to Mr. Cascarella, a literate individual of depth, culture and sophistication, is a captivating experience, maybe the next best thing to seeing the Babe swing a bat.

In his assessment of Ruth, he began by issuing a disclaimer. "He's as close to a fairy tale as any human being who ever lived. In talking about him, you're frustrated because it's difficult to offer a portrayal befitting the immensity of the man."

But then Mr. Cascarella, this gentleman of background and refinement, the antithesis of Ruth, begins his report. It's doubtful if what he has to say has ever been expressed with more elegance and accuracy. The attention given to Ruth's 100th birthday tomorrow in his hometown of Baltimore and around the country does not surprise Mr. Cascarella. You ask, why?

"Well, there will never be a man to fascinate the American public like Babe Ruth," he answers. "The Babe mesmerized me. If people knew he was in a restaurant or a hotel lobby, they would come in off the street to see him. On the trip to Japan, over a million spectators were waiting when we got off the ship to welcome us, but it was because of Ruth. He was astonishing."

Mr. Cascarella puts Ruth ahead of any athlete you can name, including Jim Thorpe, Muhammad Ali, John Unitas, Michael Jordan, Bobby Jones, Joe DiMaggio or Jackie Robinson, when it comes to popularity and recognition. He adds: "The Babe was oblivious to the fact he was grotesque in build. And he was too adolescent to understand his own importance. This was the charm of the fellow. When he walked to the plate, the pitcher was nothing more than a puppet to him. The suspense in the ballpark was like the last act in a great mystery play.

"When the Babe had a bat in his hands, the pitcher was never a challenge. It was as if he could hit any time he wanted. In other phases of the game, running, fielding and throwing, he could perform with the finesse of a ballet dancer. To see him slide into a base was a thing of beauty."

On the postseason trip to Japan and China in 1934, which was Ruth's last year with the New York Yankees, Mr. Cascarella sat at the Ruth table with the Babe, his wife and daughter in the dining room aboard ship. "Babe liked to hear me order from the menu and do a little routine with the waiter that was double-talk," he remembers. "When I'd do it, he'd roar. He was always very nice to me."

What about his intellect? "Well, he couldn't be described as a scholar, and neither could he be called dumb or stupid. And I don't think you'd ask him to go to a tea party at Buckingham Palace. He just never outgrew being a boy."

Ruth appeared to have a hitch in his batting stroke as he began the swing, but Mr. Cascarella disagrees. "That's just the way he started the bat. As an athlete, he had grace. His vision was terrific. I don't care how hard the pitcher threw, the Babe got the bat out in front. He always seemed to be moving into the ball and was never defensive."

In the one year that Cascarella faced Ruth's Yankees, he won two games in relief and remembered getting Ruth out on an overhand curve that he popped high into the air on opening day in Philadelphia. "As you know, you never give a left-handed hitter a curve ball from the side. You better get on top."

In the Orient, where the U.S. team won virtually all the games,

Cascarella went out to pitch and thought the stands were cheering for him. "Then I turned to the outfield, and it was the Babe the Japanese were saluting. They were screaming like banshees in the wilderness. I'm not sure, but I believe that happened in Kobe, where they had the earthquake last month."

Mr. Cascarella's conversation turns to the way Ruth could run as well as hit. "If you ever saw him steal a base, you'd know what I mean. There was this sense of grace. He could have stolen a lot with his speed, but the Yankees didn't want him to because of a risk he could get hurt."

No doubt, Ruth was the complete player, having won 94 games as a pitcher before becoming an outfielder and creating a .342 lifetime average and powering 714 home runs in 22 seasons. As a personality and performer, he had no baseball equal. His deeds live in perpetuity.

— · — · — · — · — · — · — · — · — · — · — · —

Baltimore boy endures as original

Feb. 3, 1995

Even the most imaginative of storytellers couldn't have created Babe Ruth. He was too real for fiction. The personification of the American Dream. Uneducated, unsophisticated, uninhibited yet unsurpassed. An original. There has indeed been only one.

The most meaningful inspiration he provided was demonstrating that regardless of how humble a background, including lack of social standing or academic advantages, the genius of excellence is somehow always recognized and rewarded.

Babe Ruth became America's gift to sports, an icon. Yet had it not been for the Baltimore Orioles, there's likelihood he never would have been discovered and probably would have continued his apprenticeship as a shirtmaker. There's belief among some historians that the Orioles never actually watched him play, but visited St. Mary's Industrial School for Boys in early 1914, where they " scouted" him sliding on a patch of ice.

Reports on George Ruth had been so persistent in Baltimore that Jack Dunn, owner/manager of the Orioles, became his ward in signing him out of the school and sent him to training camp in Fayetteville, N.C., for a contract of $600 for the season. Young George had never ridden a train, slept in a hotel, seen an elevator or watched a professional game. In his pocket, he carried 11 cents.

As Ruth's career is analyzed from his obscure beginning to the pinnacle of achievement, the more mythical it seems to be. But, he was, in truth, vibrant, fun-loving, boisterous and always approachable. No man was ever so earthy or human, possessing frailties and strengths in near equal abundance.

A distinguished jury of educators, commissioned by *Life* magazine, evaluated the passing scene for the century that's winding down. Their conclusion was to list Ruth among the "100 most important Americans of the 20th century" — the only Baltimorean or Marylander so honored.

His performances and personality ultimately allowed him to be the only sports figure to influence the language. Anything " Ruthian," a word in modern dictionaries, refers to massive or majestic accomplishment. Not bad for a kid who came from a home for orphans, delinquents and runaways and had only a rudimentary education.

What he was able to do as the hitter of a baseball is almost beyond compare. He delivered a home run 8.5 percent of the time, far and away the best in history. Statisticians may note that Roger Maris broke his home run record for a season, 60, and Henry Aaron over a career, 714, but numbers don't tell the full story.

For Maris to reach 61, he had to play 10 more games. And Aaron had the advantage of 3,965 additional chances at bat than Ruth to achieve 755 home runs. How many might the Babe have accounted for had he been given the same numerical opportunities?

Students of research have examined him from every perspective. They have, in a sense, stripped him of his clothes to find the truth about a colorful figure of down-to-earth simplicity who was never spoiled with even a tinge of pomposity. He had an astonishing capacity for enjoying the pleasures of life — wine, women and song. This isn't hard to document, because he was always out in the open and never hid in the protective shadows of duplicity.

Ruth's love of children was genuine. It wasn't orchestrated. He remembered his underprivileged past and visited orphanages and hospitals wherever he went. It was as if he were on call. Once at a Cleveland boys' home, as he prepared to demonstrate hitting, a disabled child watched from the sidelines.

The Babe asked the youngster if he ever played. " Yes, I'm a pitcher," the lad explained. Then go out there, he instructed. Three pitches from the boy and Ruth missed all three. It gave a child, too often neglected and with little in life, a boasting right none of the others had. He struck out Babe Ruth.

His popularity never waned. American soldiers in World War II often used his name as an identifying password near enemy lines. When Japanese forces charged U.S. Marines at Guadalcanal, they figured the most penetrating denunciation would be to scream, "The hell with Babe Ruth."

In 1934, when Ruth and a touring team of major-leaguers visited Japan, more than a million citizens showed up. They descended on the motorcade in Tokyo for the chance to touch Ruth or merely to see him. The sheer bulk of the masses and the fanaticism brought the welcome parade to a standstill.

Everything about Ruth was colossal. He powered home runs with frequency and for longer distances than any other man the game has known.

Incredible as it seems, two years he hit more home runs than the entire totals of the seven other American League clubs. He was the first to reach 30 homers, the first to hit 40, 50 and then 60. It almost had to be that way.

At his initial training camp in the Orioles' opening intrasquad game, this green kid from an orphanage struck the longest home run that had ever been hit in the Fayetteville area. A historical sign marks the spot, erected by the state of North Carolina.

His prodigious feats with the bat produced high drama. He accounted for the first home run the day Yankee Stadium opened, was the first to hit three home runs in a World Series game, the first to deliver a home run when the All-Star Game began in 1933.

And don't overlook his Baltimore homecoming with the Boston Red Sox in 1919. It was a two-day exhibition series with the Orioles. In the opening game, he went 4-for-4 — four home runs. The next day, his first two trips to the plate, he delivered home runs. That made it 6-for-6 in home runs. He left at that point, because he had pitched five innings and the Red Sox wanted to rest him for the start of the regular season.

But 6-for-6, all home runs, defies belief. The best of all fungo hitters, tossing a ball out of his hand, would have trouble clearing the fence six straight times.

It's obvious Ruth was born with immense God-given ability. Fortunately, he wasn't spoiled by a coach insisting on specific swing mechanics. It's believed the only model he used for hitting came from watching Brother Matthias, a Xaverian, who taught him at St. Mary's. But the brother never took a bow, because he knew the Babe was a

*Everything about
Ruth was colossal.
He powered home runs
with frequency and
for longer distances
than any other
man the game
has known.*

rare, self-taught talent.

Ruth regarded Brother Matthias with affection and respect. He said he was as proud to be from St. Mary's as any Harvard graduate might feel about his alma mater. After becoming a big-league player, Ruth gave Brother Matthias a new Packard automobile. In two weeks, the car was demolished at a railroad crossing. Ruth bought him another.

Frank Crosetti, who came to the New York Yankees three years before Ruth left, says the ritual of retiring uniforms should be terminated. Crosetti insists all the numbers should be " unretired" because only one, Ruth's No. 3, deserves such distinction. He might well be right.

The school at St. Mary's, which provided Ruth his only education, didn't produce a rock head. Tests at Columbia University in 1921 by psychologists revealed amazing results. In mental aptitude, he rated 10 percent above the average of the country. In vision, hearing and reflexes, he was way above the norm. His overall efficiency grade was put at 90 percent compared with a national average of 60 percent.

Waite Hoyt, a Hall of Fame member and a teammate with both the Red Sox and Yankees, said, "Oh, how we all loved that big bastard." It was a term of affection. When Ruth entered the batting cage, other players crowded around. It's custom for the visiting team, after the workout, to quickly retire to the dressing room to change from a damp sweat shirt into a dry one to ward off colds and muscle cramps. But when Ruth was on the scene, they deferred until seeing him swing.

In retirement, after playing 22 years, he wasn't forgotten. Death came from cancer in 1948 when he was 53. His body was in state for 48 hours in the rotunda at Yankee Stadium, where an estimated 82,000 mourners passed the bier. The funeral at St. Patrick's Cathedral had a stand-up crowd of 6,600 inside and 75,000, according to police estimates, waiting in the rain on nearby streets.

The Sporting News, in an unprecedented move, produced a complete tabloid edition with stories, pictures and tributes. But of more significance is what Connie Mack, the "Grand Old Man of Baseball," told a group of seminarians in the vestibule of the cathedral. "If all of us tried for the next 100 years, we could not adequately thank him for what he has done for our game."

Ruth came to baseball at the right time and emerged, larger than life, to counteract the tainted World Series of 1919 that was fixed by hoodlums. Ruth was the catalyst and also the catharsis that cleaned up the ignominy of the past and quickly brought attention and integrity to the sport when it was in desperate need of regaining credibility. A poor kid from Baltimore made it happen.

In following his own stairway to the stars, the Babe surpassed every Baltimorean in achievement and acclaim, including iconoclastic H.L. Mencken, musician Chick Webb and noted churchman Cardinal James Gibbons, who confirmed Ruth and his schoolmates after Babe converted to Catholicism while at St. Mary's.

To this day, in the 100th year of his birth, the legend of Babe Ruth continues.

As long as baseball lives, he will, too.

—·—·—·—·—·—·—·—·—·—·—·—

A nation says farewell

Aug. 16, 1998

Almost make-believe, except he was authentic, magnetic, entertaining, exploding with vitality and colorfully animated without knowing it. Yes, and susceptible to all the weaknesses of humankind while endowed with overpowering skills that set him apart as baseball's most accomplished player of all time.

His presence had an almost mythical yet mystical impact on America that no other athlete, before or since, has been able to command. A combination of ability, personality and boisterous charm that drew crowds until his dying day and, yes, even beyond, because 6,600 mourners attended his funeral and another 75,000 were standing in the streets under an oppressive summer sky that was dripping rain, while paying silent tribute as the cortege made its way from New York's St. Patrick's Cathedral.

Babe Ruth died 50 years ago today, at 8:01 p.m., age 53, after a consoling visit from a priest and making peace with his maker. He had been a convert to Catholicism while attending Baltimore's St. Mary's Industrial School. The cause of his death was cancer, but, only weeks before, he looked up at a visitor, the esteemed Connie Mack, and said, "Mr. Mack, I think the termites got me."

A child of God. Playful. Laughing. Clowning. Uninhibited. Unsophisticated. Riding a merry-go-round through a life that seemed almost a nonstop trip to fantasy land. He was Babe Ruth. No rags-toriches story born of fiction or fact ever compared to his. Though lacking formal education, he had an intellect that caused psychologists at Columbia University to say his IQ, although not as high as his batting average, put him in the top 10 percent of Americans. His aptitude was exceptional and the way he signed his name carried a grace within the simplicity of his penmanship.

More books, movies and documentaries have been produced about his life than about any other athlete in history. The Baltimore Orioles of the International League signed him without ever seeing him play, basing their interest and trust on merely what they had heard.

"He's the big kid sliding on the ice," the Orioles were told when they visited St. Mary's in early February 1914. They signed him to a contract for $600 for the season and sent him off to spring training in Fayetteville, N.C. In his pocket was the princely sum of 11 cents. He had never been on a train, visited a restaurant, stayed in a hotel or ridden an elevator.

He was George Herman Ruth, German on both sides of his family. For the better part of his life, he thought he was a year older than he was, having been born in 1895.

Had the Orioles not found Ruth at St. Mary's, where his parents took him at age 7 to be placed in the care of the Xaverian Brothers, it's likely he would have been lost to professional baseball, because scouting was not the sophisticated business it became.

The trade he learned in school was that of a shirtmaker, but because he could throw a ball with power and precision, the Orioles decided to give him a pitching trial.

He was naive, unexposed to the wonders of the world that awaited as he left the protection and discipline of St. Mary's and stepped into a baseball environment.

Veteran players in his first training camp wondered who he was, and the answer they got was he's one of "Dunnie's babes," meaning a protege of team owner-manager-general manager Jack Dunn. Forever after he was Babe Ruth.

We've conjectured that the reason he had trouble remembering proper names was because in an orphanage with 800 other boys, nicknames were the true term of recognition. Like Reds, Fats, Rubber Belly, Funny Ears, Stinky, Big Nose, Mickey, Harp, Scotty and Heinie.

Ruth was popular with teammates, rival players, sportswriters and even people who didn't know a baseball from a cantaloupe. They found him to be a study, something astonishing. A type they had never seen before. Also accommodating and effusive.

The Babe was so spontaneous there was no way to even guess what he might do next — be it with bat in hand or expressing himself in conversation.

He once attended a dinner at the Waldorf Astoria to help a charitable undertaking, and a record amount of money was raised, mainly because Ruth was there.

When it was over, Mrs. John Jacob Astor, the sponsor, thanked him profusely. Ruth was uncomfortable with this shower of gratitude. Finally, he said, "Oh, s——, lady, I'd do it for anybody."

In Baltimore, where the saga of Ruth began, he was exclusively a pitcher, and Dunn reluctantly had to sell Ruth to the Boston Red Sox halfway through his rookie season of 1914 because of competition put upon him in Baltimore by the rival Federal League.

The next year, his second season in baseball, as a rookie with Boston, he went 18-8 as a pitcher. When he came home to Baltimore that fall, he played in a game for a community team in Irvington against Catonsville. Consider the chance he was taking. A possible injury in what was almost a pickup game and he might never have played again.

But the Babe was there to enjoy himself. He struck out seven of nine batters in the first three innings. Then the catcher broke his hand. So Ruth put on the chest protector, shin guards and mask, pulled a right-handed catcher's mitt on his opposite hand and caught the rest of the way.

Ruth was the complete player, a better than average outfielder with a strong arm, a good base runner and a picture to behold when he slid into a base.

In the 50 years since his death, there hasn't been any performer or personality to replace him. An original. Unequaled. Unmatched. Unsurpassed.

Chapter 16

REMEMBERING

Old Oriole Park fire burns imprint

July 1, 1994

It was a fire that singularly and dramatically revolutionized the future of Baltimore sports and opened the door of opportunity for coveted major-league identity.

Fifty years ago, the heavens were illuminated in a blaze so intense there was temporary fear German airplanes, this being the height of World War II, had somehow penetrated coastal defenses and dropped incendiary bombs.

The flames on July 4, 1944, which totally destroyed the wooden bandbox known as Oriole Park, became the catalyst that burned Baltimore out of its minor-league confinement and ignited a desire for major-league franchises in both baseball and football.

It meant, because of the emergency, Baltimore was going to be forced to utilize what was then known as Municipal Stadium, which accommodated huge crowds and helped create an enthusiasm that notified the nation spectacular change was under way.

Oriole Park, located at 29th Street and Greenmount Avenue, was made entirely of wood. After every game, the two-man grounds crew of Mike Schofield and Howard "Doc" Seiss would wet down the stands with hoses to make sure all burning cigarette/cigar butts had been extinguished.

They did that night, too, but approximately 4:20 a.m. on the Fourth of July a fire started near the third base grandstand. For 40 years, the wooden structure had been regularly coated with creosote to hold off decay brought on by exposure to weather.

An Oriole Park historian, Frank Lynch, now a Sunpapers editor, said what amounted to a ball of fire rolled around the roof and, almost within the blink of an eye, the facility was totally engulfed.

"Schofield, who slept in an office at the park," according to Lynch, "described the reaction as a 'sheet of fire' that spread faster than anything he had ever seen."

The fire department had no chance at saving the place. Its intent, after the fact, was to make sure falling embers didn't touch off other fires in the Waverly rowhouse neighborhood.

It was certain the Orioles had been burned out of their ballpark. They lost all their home uniforms and equipment — including every ball, bat, glove and spiked shoe. With World War II in its midst, sporting goods companies had turned to producing gun stocks instead of bats and leather boots rather than gloves.

So replacements were difficult to find. The Orioles, with no place to play, became an instant road team and didn't return home until 12 days later to play in cavernous Municipal Stadium (present site of Memorial Stadium). Team business manager Herb Armstrong made all the decisions and arrangements to prepare the stadium for baseball.

It was an unusual setting. A short left field, estimated to be from 260 to 290 feet and over 500 feet to right-center field, gave the game a new dimension of excitement.

With the war on and the area crowded with servicemen and women, plus defense workers with money in their pockets and few venues of entertainment, watching the Orioles became almost a daily ritual.

The opening homestand touched off enormous enthusiasm, fed by the Orioles playing the Montreal Royals, a Brooklyn Dodgers affiliate, in four straight doubleheaders and winning every game.

Meanwhile, crowds were coming to the stadium in sizable numbers, in excess of 20,000, 30,000 and 40,000. Baltimore was attracting attention as attendance figures soared. A then-record minor-league crowd of 52,833 poured into the place to see a Little World Series game against the Louisville Colonels.

The Orioles had won the International League pennant on the last day of the season when the Newark Bears (a New York Yankees farm club) lost a doubleheader to the Syracuse Chiefs and the Orioles split with the Jersey City Giants. Baltimore won by the barest of margins — .0007 in the final percentages.

Oriole Park had been built in 1914 to accommodate the city's Federal League team, which only lasted two years. The Orioles' Jack Dunn, owner/general manager/manager, turned what was called

Terrapin Park into Oriole Park.

The Orioles of 1944, managed by hometown son Tommy Thomas, created a special identity. They had two future major-league standouts in Sherman Lollar and Howard "Red" Embree, fielding phenoms at shortstop and first base in 17-year-old Kenny "Kid" Braun and Bob Latshaw and a free-swinging home run hitter named "Howitzer Howie" Moss.

After the fire, the most prophetic observations came from Rodger H. Pippen, sports editor of the then *Baltimore News-Post* and *Sunday American*, when he wrote:

"At the moment, what appears to be a baseball tragedy, may turn out to be a blessing in disguise. Baltimore rose from the ashes of its great fire in 1904 to be a bigger and better city. Our Orioles will come through just as soon as war conditions permit, with a bigger and better place for their games.

"The new park will be built so in case the opportunity should arise, this city will return to the big leagues. The park which is today in ruins was not suitable for big-league competition. You can't finance a major outfit with a seating capacity of 11,000."

From that point, Pippen led the crusade to return Baltimore to the American League, even overcoming the negative stand by the editors of the Sunpapers, who scoffed at the idea. *The Sun*, more than 40 years later, was to declare Pippen one of Baltimore's most influential sports leaders of the last century.

The fire that leveled Oriole Park literally burned Baltimore back into the major leagues after a wait of 52 years. That pre-dawn fireworks show of the Fourth of July, 1944 was the spark that, in a strange sort of way,sent Baltimore into a renaissance of monumental proportion.

Over, under, around was just the ticket

Dec. 14, 1997

Nothing quite like a privileged childhood, or, put another way, to grow up within walking distance of Municipal/Memorial Stadium. Most of the neighborhood boys didn't have the price of admission, but it didn't always prevent them from attending the games. It was called "hooking in," which by the language of the times meant finding a way to gain admittance without paying for a seat.

It was either go over the fence, tunnel under it or take your chances of encountering a friendly ticket taker who looked the other way, which was a direct signal that he was welcoming you to come in on a complementary pass. If he turned his back, it was an immediate sign that he was extending an invitation so long as his bosses weren't aware of what was happening.

The game plan was to walk the perimeter of the stadium, looking for soft spots that might be exploited in the security coverage. It could get monotonous. And it took staying power. The more guards stationed at their posts, the longer it took to find a way to break inside. Tom Gorman, who was older, sophisticated and from another part of the city, would often mention his gate-crashing credo. "Don't panic until you hear the national anthem," he'd say.

Selling newspapers was an optional way to gain entrance. Distributors from the *News-Post, The Evening Sun* and *The Sun* would arrive on 33rd Street in advance of the kickoff and unload papers. Kids would surround them, begging for a chance to be hired, because if you were hawking a bundle of papers, you could get inside to sell and, of course, see the game.

The old Municipal Stadium, except for the administration building, was made entirely of wood. The planked seats were exposed to the weather the entire year. Bobby Brown, later to be a top hearing judge for the Social Security Administration, would holler, "Seats are damp and dirty. You need a newspaper."

And his friend from school would chime in, "The seats are nothing but splinters." So the latest editions were not always sold for the published lineups of the teams on the field, usually carried on Page 1, but more for protection of posteriors and to keep the women and their escorts from having their clothes soiled by the poor condition of the seats.

At the north end of the stadium was a tall row of trees, lombardy poplars, easy to climb, which afforded a free look inside while the game was in progress. As a small boy, maybe 10 or 11, we remember watching from this bird's-eye view, but weren't able to discern the difference between City College and McDonogh. Both had the same uniform colors, orange and black, so, from afar, it was difficult to determine which team was which.

During weekdays, Jim Gentry, whose house faced the stadium, enjoyed going over the fence with his friend and boldly venturing upon the stadium field for the purpose of kicking extra points. Vicariously, they were both trying to be "Automatic Jack" Manders. Municipal Stadium had a reputation for having the finest cover of grass of any stadium anywhere, which, to this day, we both know to be true — a situation brought on by so few games being played there.

First, Gentry would hold for placements, with his young pal kicking. Then the roles would be reversed. Two kids in front of the goal posts, with a huge stadium of 65,000 or more empty seats, enjoying themselves to the ultimate. You might kick for 20 minutes until the stout stadium manager would venture out of his administration office and scream, "You boys, get out of here." But we'd continue to kick until he was made to walk half the length of the field.

Then it was a race up through the stands, out the exit and a climb over the fence again — only this time we were on the way out. Kids often played their own version of football outside the stadium on a patch of grass that covered part of the dirt parking lot. One or two might have helmets but, for the most part, it was playing bareheaded, minus shoulder pads, in nothing but old clothes and thinking you were John Kimbrough, Nile Kinnick or Brud Holland.

From Waverly and the nearby area surrounding No. 51 school came a more experienced array of stadium frequenters. It was their home grounds.

Included were Jack Blair, who became a member of the Alameda Light Opera Co.; Nelson Filbert; Carvel "Loodie" Howard; Jim "Babs" Rigley; Don Shipley; Bob "Rainbow" Bull; Bob Benson, and a man with a troika of nicknames, plain Jim Smith, otherwise known as "Limo," "Cinder Lip" or "Sweet Words."

They perfected a way to vault the fence by diligent off-season practice. They'd take a run at the fence, where the barbed wire had been pulled away, hit it in a jumping position, grasp the top pipe and throw themselves, in the fashion of a gymnast, completely over the fence. The idea then was to keep running, find a seat and sit down as though you belonged.

Once, during those early teen-age years, Ray "Little Benny" Bengermino was near the Navy bench as time was ticking away on a Saturday afternoon. He tried on a gold helmet and liked it so much that he sprinted out of the stadium wearing it, with Naval Academy equipment managers and Pinkerton guards in rapid pursuit. They never caught him, and on Sunday afternoon, there was "Little Benny" playing in Clifton Park with one of those expensive, shell-type helmets and other kids crowding around to ask if they could wear it when they carried the ball.

Oh, the fun of growing up. Teams visiting Baltimore to play Navy would usually arrive the day before, on Friday, and take a light, hour workout at the stadium. The public was invited to watch. When practice was over, there'd be a rush for autographs. We once ran onto the field to meet the Dartmouth players.

A man in a long overcoat and wearing a dress hat was behind the team. He didn't chase us away, but seemed kind and gentle. We asked questions as he walked off the field, and then he put his arm over our shoulders, making us feel we were somebody instead of nobody. Next, he signed our autograph book. He wrote Earl H. Blaik, and under it added Dartmouth College.

It was all part of growing up within proximity of the stadium and also Oriole Park, located at 29th Street and Greenmount Avenue. That was our retreat during baseball season, or until the Orioles were burned out of their park on the Fourth of July, 1944. Once, walking home from school in the spring of 1945 with George Bauman, later to be a huge success as a television personality, we left him to climb the fence to watch the Orioles' pre-game practice.

An unusual scene awaited. On the mound at the north end of the stadium was Ralph "Red" Kress, a coach, throwing batting practice. Nothing surprising, except all he had on was a pair of baseball shoes and an athletic supporter. No cap, uniform or those white sanitary socks players wear. Obviously, he was soaking up the late afternoon sun.

A sure entree to the stadium during football season was to sell programs. Bill Stetka obviously had the right connections. The money was good, and you were able to watch the game as you walked the aisles. Such jobs were in high demand, and we never qualified.

Shutting down the stadium today brings forth a flood of memories. We just might go out and try to "hook in" for old times' sake.

A kid's dream hadn't yet cooled

May 17, 1998

SALISBURY, N.C. — Stepping down off the train at the darkest of hours, close to 4 a.m., befogged by a lack of sleep, entering a near-deserted station with suitcase in hand, carrying a favorite Stan Musial-model baseball bat and a head full of dreams meant a kid was about to attempt to fulfill the most important ambition of his then-young life. Yes, a long time ago.

The Pittsburgh Pirates had signed him to a contract with their York, Pa., farm club of the Interstate League and, in turn, optioned him to Salisbury of the North Carolina State League. This was the beginning. Everybody has to start someplace.

Salisbury, in the heartland of North Carolina, seemed far from home. The kid was the latest stranger in town as he left the railroad waiting room and took a left on Depot Street, deserted as might be expected, considering the hour. The wall of heat was oppressive. A blast furnace.

Up Council Street, past the Yadkin Hotel, and then a left on Main, across the intersection at Innes, the center of town, while looking for a place to stay. The Empire Hotel had a rate of $4 a night, which meant the price was right. A kid away from home, on his own for the first time, unsure of himself, a role played out since time began.

He wondered if Rollie Hemsley and Del Rice had started this way. A scout named John "Poke" Whalen, a catcher in his playing days, had signed him at age 17 after a game in Baltimore's Carroll Park. The enticement for Whalen was the pursuit of Lou Sleater and Tommy Lind, but he learned, belatedly, that a rival team had beaten him to both prospects.

"Ever think of playing professional ball?" the scout in the Panama hat said to the kid. "You do a lot of things right, but you need to be stronger. That'll come as you get older."

His mother was reluctant to sign the contract he carried home. Her signature was needed. The money didn't matter, $175 a month, which was more than most other untried players were getting at the time. She worried he might be tempted to become a drinker, and that wasn't acceptable.

Eventually, realizing what it meant to her oldest son, she agreed to let him leave. But before that happened, he played in high school the next year, 1945, and then, with only close friends aware of what he was doing, spent weekends in camp with York under manager John "Bunny" Griffith.

But here was a whole new world. Salisbury of the North Carolina State League. Farm director Bob Rice, who learned the baseball business from Branch Rickey, said: "The man who signed you believes you can be a right-handed-hitting Bill Dickey. I like your chances."

A false prophecy. Rich praise, but dead wrong. High expectations, poor performance. After games, the kid would sit on a store step in the middle of a Salisbury night and commiserate with outfielder Bart Pavuk, from Jessup, Pa., who said, "I think I'll see your name in a big-league box score."

Again, it never happened. Not even close. Many are called, but so few chosen. A disappointment to himself and others, too. The only player to make it out of the North Carolina State League that year who climbed to the majors was Tom Lasorda, who was 3-11 at Concord. He was just a kid, too.

The uniform issued in Salisbury, recycled from the major-league Pirates and handed down through the organization, had a red name scripted inside. It read: P. Waner.

Waner had been only the seventh player in major-league history to collect 3,000 hits, and here was a raw rookie, who didn't have even one hit, about to put on the shirt and pants Paul Waner had once worn.

Salisbury, clean and impressive, the home of Catawba College, was replete with beautiful residences and gardens. Historical information related that Andrew Jackson, on his way to becoming the seventh president of the United States, studied law here, drank liquor, chased women and went to cockfights.

Salisbury was home for only a month, rooming with a pitcher from Wilkes-Barre, Pa., named Walter Allabaugh. Then York, in an emergency situation, called, and the kid moved on, only to find himself deeper in debt when it came to ability. There had been an earlier night in Hickory, N.C., when the batboy ran to the bullpen with a message in the ninth inning and said, "You're pinch-hitting for the pitcher." Bad news.

Duke Makowsky, just back from the Army, since the war in Europe had ended and players were starting to return to the game, was pitching and had struck out 14. No. 15 was a foregone conclusion. Makowsky was to change his name to Markell and make it to the majors briefly. He was regarded as one of the hardest throwers in the minors, which, upon reflection, was merely belated solace.

Sunday afternoons in Salisbury meant an open date. Blue laws took precedence, so the team usually went to High Rock Lake to swim. During the week, time was heavy until reporting to Newman Field to get ready to play.

You might talk to the pretty girl selling tickets at the Moroney movie box office or walk through the upscale Oestreicher department store to cool off. It might have been the only place in town with air conditioning.

Players bragged about their hometowns. George Heller, a left-handed pitcher who got to the International League, talked of Honesdale, Pa., as if were an earthly paradise.

Don Spencer, a late arrival from Hiram College, was the team's best prospect and made it to the American Association and then to a most successful business career in York.

A letter from home was balm for an 0-for-4 effort, such as the one any mother might send a son. It went like this: "Just got your latest letter. I am sorry if you were disappointed or hurt because your disappointments are mine. Your brother Tom says you will do okay and come through with a bang.

"Throw it off and don't let it get you down. That would never do. Stick it out as long as you care. But remember I don't want you unhappy. If you would rather come home, send word and I will wire you railroad fare. Say what you will need.

"If you leave, I know it will be in an honorable way. Your late father would want you to be fair and honest with the men in charge of the team. Be sure to get enough to eat because a full stomach is good for low spirits.

"Henry Hoeckel is expected home from Europe before going to the Pacific. The Sweigers heard from Bill and Tom is going in the Navy. Bill Stetka called to see how you were doing. Comp McLernon and Tex Warfield stopped by. Tex says he wishes he could be down there playing with you. Frank Wheltle called up to ask about you and so did Al Cesky.

"Sorry to tell you the paper had a story that Harry Imhoff was killed in action in the Marines. Your brother says he was a fine catcher. Did you know him well? George Eikenberg is playing at Hartford. Tom says Lou Sleater and Tom Lind were on the same team last year.

"Please do not worry yourself. Try to throw it off and hope for better results next game. You have nothing to lose. You are young and perhaps a better field lies ahead if you don't make good in baseball. Perhaps you could take a night course in college or find work on a newspaper.

"Take care of yourself. Be a good boy and say your prayers. Don't put too much trust in strangers. Good night, son. I am going to bed now and will pray for you. God bless you. Love from Tom, Betty and Mother."

Ultimate failure in baseball opened other doors, like friend Frank Cashen interceding to get a job for the kid on a newspaper. Salisbury welcomed him back the other night at an awards ceremony for sportswriters and sportscasters.

It brought forth a flood of memories sitting there in the same railroad station, now gloriously rehabilitated, where he got off a train and frankly felt the pain as a dream fell apart.

Acknowledgements

To all the readers, possessed with more tolerance and patience than could ever be imagined. In a word: indebted. Without you, there would be no stories inside these pages. Thanks for being the best kind of friend, because you let us know you were out there, even when you disagreed with the perspective or weren't terribly interested in the subject matter.

To editors Dave Smith, Chris Zang and Larry Harris, all alert and highly professional copy editors, who cleaned and refined our too often inadequate sentence structures into something more resembling clarity for use in *The Evening Sun* and *The Sun*.

To Ray Frager, the commander-in-chief of this undertaking, who made it happen. An immense effort of culling and then reviewing for publication. His comments and counsel have earned respect and gratitude.

To Jennifer Halbert, creative services coordinator, and Laura Gamble, sales and marketing manager. They made it possible. It was all their idea.

About the author

John Steadman was once a minor-league baseball player. In over his head, he says. He then became a sportswriter and subsequently, at the age of 30, a sports editor for the *Baltimore News-Post* (later the *News American*). At that time, he was the youngest to hold that position at a major newspaper.

For three years, he was assistant general manager/publicity director for the Baltimore Colts, when the franchise was being built into a two-time world champion. Then came his decision to return to the newspaper game. He then spent 27 years as sports editor/columnist at the *News American* before joining the staff of *The Evening Sun* in 1986 and then the Sunday *Sun*.

In 1959, a story he wrote was chosen as "The Best Sports Story of the Year," the only Maryland writer to ever receive the award. And in 1999, he was selected to the National Sportswriters & Sportscasters Hall of Fame in Salisbury, N.C. The man presenting him was Frank Cashen, former general manager of the Baltimore Orioles and New York Mets, who had provided entree to Steadman's first job on a newspaper, paying $14 a week in late 1945.

The Maryland House of Delegates invited him to appear in its chambers on February 14, 2000 for deliverance of a proclamation that cited his contributions to sports, the only time a newspaperman in Maryland has received such a distinction.

Steadman is a graduate of Baltimore City College. *The Sun* has named an internship in his honor that will go annually to a graduate, preferably, of a Baltimore public school.